PRAYING THE PSALMS
A Commentary

By the same author

Les tendances nouvelles de l'ecclésiologie

The Relevance of Physics

Brain, Mind and Computers
(Lecomte du Nouy Prize, 1970)

The Paradox of Olbers' Paradox

The Milky Way: An Elusive Road for Science

*Science and Creation: From Eternal Cycles
to an Oscillating Universe*

*Planets and Planetarians: A History of Theories
of the Origin of Planetary Systems*

The Road of Science and the Ways to God
(Gifford Lectures: University of Edinburgh, 1975 and 1976)

The Origin of Science and the Science of its Origin
(Fremantle Lectures, Oxford, 1977)

*And on This Rock: The Witness of One Land
and Two Covenants*

Cosmos and Creator

Angels, Apes and Men

Uneasy Genius: The Life and Work of Pierre Duhem

Chesterton: A Seer of Science

The Keys of the Kingdom: A Tool's Witness to Truth

Lord Gifford and His Lectures: A Centenary Retrospect

Chance or Reality and Other Essays

The Physicist as Artist: The Landscapes of Pierre Duhem

The Absolute beneath the Relative and Other Essays

The Savior of Science
(Wethersfield Institute Lectures, 1987)

(continued on p. [248])

PRAYING THE PSALMS

A Commentary

Stanley L. Jaki

WILLIAM B. EERDMANS PUBLISHING COMPANY
GRAND RAPIDS, MICHIGAN / CAMBRIDGE, U.K.

Published 2001 by Wm. B. Eerdmans Publishing Company

255 Jefferson Ave. S.E., Grand Rapids, Michigan 49503 /
P.O. Box 163, Cambridge CB3 9PU U.K.

Printed in the United States of America

05 04 03 02 01   5 4 3 2 1

Library of Congress Cataloging-in-Publication Data

Jaki, Stanley L.
Praying the Psalms: a commentary / Stanley L. Jaki.
p.   cm.
ISBN 0-8028-4771-4 (pbk.: alk. paper)
1. Bible. O.T. Psalms — Commentaries.   I. Title.
BS1430.3 .J35   2001
223'.207 — dc21

00-045294

www.eerdmans.com

Contents

Introduction   1

The Psalms in General   9

The Psalms One by One   29

    Book   I, Psalms 1-41   31

    Book   II, Psalms 42-72   95

    Book III, Psalms 73-89   141

    Book   IV, Psalms 90-106   167

    Book   V, Psalms 107-150   189

Introduction

Another book on the psalms? Do not books on the psalms fill shelves upon shelves in theological libraries? Yet new books on the psalms keep coming off the press and will not fail to be written. There must be something unusually attractive about the psalms.

Although the psalms are much more than poems, they are poetry at its best. For that reason alone the psalms will forever fascinate man whose very nature is to act, to make. The very fact that the words "poetry" and "poems" come from the Greek *poiein*, which means "to make," reveals something of the deeper meaning of man's definition as *homo faber*, that is, a being whose nature is to make, to fabricate, to construct.

The proofs of that definition are as old as the oldest of man's prehistoric vestiges. They survived in small stones that man chipped into primitive tools. They all were man's ways of responding to the challenges of objects, so many parts of nature, of an objective natural world.

Much less is known about the origin of the construct, language, whereby man responds to other human beings, the very objects that most intrigue him in his surroundings and on whom he most depends. The enormous variety of languages is a proof that in verbalizing one's response to the objective world man constructs and does so with a creative freedom. Otherwise man's verbalized responses to trees, water, stones, and the sky would be remarkably similar in all languages. But languages number thousands and show startling varieties. At times, groups of people separated from one another by narrow though high mountains are found to speak languages that cannot be related to one another.

The most creative form of that verbal response is poetry, which, more than any other form of human discourse, reveals the intoxicatingly creative and suggestive power of words. The briefest reflection on this should conjure up an immensely vast and instructive subject with obviously many aspects to it. Of those aspects a commentator on the psalms must broach at the outset one aspect which relates to the problem of translation.

Translators can rightly speak of their travails, but nothing gives such a headache to a translator as the task of transposing poems from one language to another. The difficulty should appear gigantic when the poem to be translated is believed to be the carrier of divine truth. Faithfulness to truth is a great challenge by itself but especially so when the truth involves God's own utterances.

Of course, God never spoke Hebrew, but He spoke, above all, to Hebrews. Therefore divine truth, to recall Saint Jerome's famous phrase, is *hebraica veritas* in a far from trivial sense. One major challenge to one's resolve to make the psalms one's own prayer consists therefore in facing that most frustrating of all barriers which is known as the language barrier.

Few have the will (or opportunity) to learn Hebrew in order to read or recite the psalms in the tongue in which they were composed. Such resolute souls will find, though, notable examples in the Christian past. Some devout women of late-fourth-century Rome come to mind. They formed an informal group under the leadership of Paula, a descendant of the Scipios though better remembered as a Saint. Eventually she took herself and some of that group to Bethlehem. There they must have heard Jerome, the greatest of all biblical scholars, recall his own struggle with the Hebrew tongue.

Still they persisted with whatever primitive learning aids at their disposal. Dictionaries and grammar were still very imperfect and exceedingly hard to come by. Texts of the psalms themselves were not much easier to have. While the psalms, so Jerome assures us, were so widely known that even the farmers sang them as they worked in the fields, they certainly did not sing them in the Hebrew. By then, we are around 400 A. D., Hebrew had for at least six centuries ceased to be a spoken idiom. Did those farmers sing the psalms in Aramaic, or in Syriac, or in the *koine*, that universally spoken vernacular Greek?

By Jerome's time the Greek of the Septuagint, hardly the Greek of Pindar or Plato, had long ceased to be a spoken language. Therefore even to those whose mother tongue was the *koine* at that time, the Greek of the Septuagint was accessible only through translation, in part at least. It was true of those farmers, too, if they sang the psalms from that translation, what is true of anyone facing an original not written in his mother tongue: Unless the original is mastered so well that one really thinks in its terms as if it were his second mother tongue, the reading or reciting of any text in the original becomes an instantaneous translation into one's own mother tongue. For the meaning of words will forever be anchored in the tongue one has first learned as a child. The story of the tower of Babel should remind one at least of the need for having translators.

Translations from the Hebrew cannot, of course, make the ambiguities that occur again and again in the Hebrew text of the psalms any clearer in spite of centuries' of work spent in the critical correlation of the best manuscripts. The oldest of those manuscripts, found in the caves of Qumran half a century ago, certainly proved that the work of copying was remarkably reliable in the centuries that preceded by a millennium and a half the invention of printing. Many of the ambiguities, too, were faithfully copied.

Very little in the way of a judicious correlation of the best manuscripts could be done in Jerome's time, which hardly helped his work as a translator. Augustine already complained of the "infinite variety" of older Latin translations. Variants and obscurities abounded in the three Latin translations of the psalms made by Jerome himself. They in turn became known as the *Psalterium romanum* (a revision of the *Vetus itala*), the *Psalterium gallicanum* (a revision of the *romanum* on the basis of the Greek in Origen's *Hexapla*), and finally a translation made from the Hebrew, known as the *Psalterium juxta Hebraeos*. Of these the second enjoyed such popularity as to form later part of the

Vulgate, mainly because of its widespread use in the Divine
Office. Whatever the enormous merits of the Vulgate as a
translation and of the *Psalterium gallicanum* in it, the latter did not
lack those spots that readily derail one's attention from the flow
of the meaning. An all too common experience to the now older
generation of the clergy that began to recite the psalms in Latin as
part of the Breviary.

One can only wistfully think of the kind of commentary
which Augustine, whose prose was so excellent as to read again
and again as exquisite poetry, would have produced if he had at
his disposal something better than the *Vetus itala*. As it turned
out, his *Enarrationes in psalmos* became time and again a string of
incidental, though at times theologically most valuable utterances
on words or phrases that are not necessarily connected with the
plain sense and message of this or that psalm.

Augustine put aside a short hour of his busy day each and
every day for over several decades in order to put in writing his
reflections on the psalms. He did this methodically, taking psalm
after psalm, verse after verse, though at times he gave a special
public discourse on this or that psalm which he then inserted in
his *Enarrationes*. All too often he was more interested in mining
the meaning of a particular verse than in presenting a systematic
exposition of the psalm itself. But he would not have gone on
with that lifelong work had he, weak in Greek and ignorant of
Hebrew, found an insuperable problem of grasping the thrust of
each and every psalm on the basis of the *Vetus itala*.

Augustine's chief interest in the psalms related to their being
prayers and the most excellent ones at that. In ch. 4 of Book X of
his *Confessions* Augustine spoke of the immense delight he
derived from having heard the psalms sung in Milan, often
under the inspired leadership of Ambrose. But eventually he
realized the danger of melodies attached to the psalms. In ch. 33
of Book X of the *Confessions* he branded those melodies as "traps"
for the mind intent on the meaning of the phrases one was
singing. It is not difficult to guess what Augustine would say
today of those who think that they pray simply because they take
immense delight in listening on CDs to the chant of the monks of
Silos though unable to grasp the words they sing. Augustine

would say that aesthetics may be a great help in prayer but it is not yet prayer. Prayer must contain the lifting of the mind to God, an act rooted in conceptualization before it can blossom into the unutterable promptings of the Spirit that in turn are immensely more than mere aesthetics.

It is well to recall that Augustine took Athanasius, one of the greatest minds ever in the Church, for his guide in the matter of praying the psalms. Athanasius, so wrote Augustine in that chapter 33, "used to oblige the lectors to recite the psalms with such slight modulation of the voice that they seem to be speaking rather than chanting." Such problems do not, of course, arise in private recitation of the psalms.

As a wise pastor of souls, Augustine did not urge the abolition of melodies attached to the psalms. "I am inclined," he wrote, "to approve of the custom of singing in church, in order that by indulging the ears weaker spirits may be inspired with feelings of devotion." Yet whenever he found "the singing itself more moving than the truth which it conveys," he took this for a "grievous sin" and at those times he "preferred not to hear the singer." Such was the dilemma of the one appreciative of music and yet even more sensitive to what prayer had to be, an "elevatio *mentis* ad Deum," the lifting of the *mind* to God.

It is not the purpose of this book to resolve this dilemma, which forever will defy a solution satisfactory to all and to all conceivable viewpoints. The purpose is merely to help the reader grasp the basic meaning and thrust of each and every psalm so that the act of praying them might truly become an elevation of the mind to God. Hence the need of ascertaining the original cultural and theological setting (as something more than a mere "Sitz im Leben") of each psalm if the usefulness of praying the psalms may fully emerge.

In view of what has already been said about the need to rely on translations which make it possible for most to use the psalms as prayers, no special pleading is made here on behalf of a choice basic to this book. The choice assumes that a good modern translation of the psalms is sufficient to convey the meaning of the psalms to the mind that wants to raise itself to God in a spirit proper to them. Such a translation is the Grail Psalms that, from the moment of its publication in 1962, took the Christian world by storm. The eminent Hebraist and Old Testament scholar Harold H. Rowley spoke of it as a "very impressive rendering" that deserves "nothing but praise."

A chief reason for that praise relates to the essence of a good translation: it renders faithfully the meaning of the original instead of mirroring its verbal flow. A mirror image would inevitably turn into jarring distortions because no two languages, however closely related, are isomorphic. Further, a poem (the psalms are poems) is a literary form that especially aims at conveying beauty. It is about the translation of poems that one should ponder the facetious remark: Translations are like women; if beautiful not faithful, if faithful not beautiful . . . . Clearly, a balance is to be struck and this is eminently well done in the Grail Psalms.

Once grasped in their truthfulness and beauty, both of which are a mark of the Grail Psalms, the meaning and themes of the psalms will not fail to invite ever new efforts to mine their riches. Most of these efforts never appear in print, but a relatively few do. The present effort is from one who after having used the Vulgate's rendering of the psalms for three decades, switched to the Grail Psalms and began to jot down some reflections. In both phases his praying the psalms has been part of saying the Breviary, an obligation common to every Catholic priest. Therefore these reflections have on occasion some personal characteristics. This will surprise only those unmindful of the astute observation, "all books are autobiographical," in Samuel Butler's *The Way of All Flesh*. It is enough to recall the verse, "To you all flesh will come with its burden of sin," from Psalm 65 to see the relevance of this to reflections on psalms as prayers. In fact even strictly textual interpretations of the psalms may reveal something about their authors. Still, it is hoped that those non-Catholics, who put greater premium on their being Christians rather than Protestants (a name of their own make), will find helpful pointers here for turning the recitation of the psalms into living prayers worthy of Christ's followers.

Personal parameters have no bearing on the fact that since the same thought often recurs in the psalms, reflections on them will inevitably contain some repetitions. In fact few human acts are as repetitive as prayers are. In order to rearticulate the themes of the psalms as prayers, exegesis will be resorted to, though sparingly. It is certainly not the intention of this book to lead its readers into textual technicalities, all too often arcane matters even for exegetes. Since the reflections offered in this book are closely tied to the text of the Grail Psalms, having a copy of it at hand will prove helpful as one uses this book.

The author's main intention is to help the readers of this book to grasp the great themes of the psalms in their robustness and perplexities, as well as in their relevance to anyone praying them today, in the case of some psalms some three thousand years after their original composition. All this should seem crucial if one is to live up to the instruction which the visitor of the choir in San Damiano, Saint Claire's cloister in Assisi, finds written there on the primitive planks, so different from the ornately chiseled stalls of Renaissance and Baroque churches:

Non clamor sed amor,	Not sounds but love,
Non cordula sed cor	Not strings but the heart
psallit in aure Dei.	sings in God's hearing.
Vox concordet menti	Let words agree with the mind,
et mens concordet Deo.	And the mind unite with God.

There is, of course, much more to the task of turning the psalms into a prayer, here and now, than to see the thrust of each of them through a good translation. As to that additional task, a glimpse of it can be caught through the consideration that the psalms are not mere poems but prayers, which ought to be Christian prayers on the lips of Christians. Originally prayers on the lips of Jews, the psalms began to be uttered by Christian lips as *the* prayers of Christians. This shift leads to questions that have to be taken up as part of general reflections, the first section of this book on praying the psalms.

SLJ

The Psalms in General

The psalms as Jewish prayers

Captions are the product of constraint as they must be brief. Therefore, if captions are not to be misleading, they should call for some explanation. The psalms were born on Hebrew lips that not mere genetics but a higher genesis turned into praying lips in the manner in which Jews were meant to pray. That something else was, according to their own awareness, a set of revelations given from above to their principal leaders. Apart from that revelation Jewish lips would not have sounded markedly different from what one finds in the religious lore of great and small nations around them. The psalms of the Jews greatly differ from the "psalms" of ancient Egypt and Babylon whatever similarities they may reveal. If the Jews learned many "songs" from the Ugarites, as lately has become a fashion to claim, they certainly grafted many original traits on them.

Some psalms indicate that the Jews composed songs that served as the nuclei of future psalms. Psalms 124 and 129 begin with a phrase, which they immediately characterize as "Israel's song." The factor that drove and governed the transformation of a mere song, however spirited, into an inspired psalm, was the reverberation of the words of that revelation on the lips of the Hebrews. In the process they turned from Hebrews into Jews and produced religious poems, some of which became gradually recognized as genuinely expressive of that revelation.

About the steps of that gradual development not much is known. The actual set of 150 psalms arose as a compilation in

post-exilic times from several earlier collections. Almost half of
the psalms are assigned to David, although this does not assure
the Davidic origin of each of them. There is no indication that
David himself had collected the psalms composed by him. Much
shorter collections of psalms were made by various groups of
Temple musicians, such as the Sons of Korah and the Sons of
Asaph. Each of these groups seemed to be more intent on
guarding their own compilations than on sharing them with
other groups. This prevented the formation of a streamlined
edition. Hence a few glaring repetitions in the psalms. That
exactly 150 psalms make up the Book of Psalms may reveal a
touch of number mysticism. Their distribution into five parts
(books) by an early Rabbinical tradition was obviously motivated
by the desire to make the Book of Psalms appear similar to the
Pentateuch, taken for five books written by Moses. Part of that
procedure was the fixing of a doxology at the end of each unit
(book). For the fifth book, Psalm 150 forms that doxology.

Far more important than such details, to be found in most
exegetical introductions to the psalms, is to note the role which
the recitation of the psalms played in the formation of the Jewish
religious mind, which, as any other religious mind, had to feed
on prayers. The recitation of the psalms kept fueling the visceral
conviction of the Jews that they were chosen to be the special
people of a God who indeed was very special. He was the most
jealous of all gods, indeed the only truly jealous God. The gods in
the pantheons of other peoples could tolerate other gods and
indeed accept them. Thus the Greco-Roman pantheon has grown
by steady accretion as the Greeks and then the Romans extended
their reach over the Mediterranean and beyond. Restrictions to
further additions to that pantheon were minor. Anyone ready to
sacrifice to the deities already in that pantheon could safely
continue worshiping the gods of his own provenance.

From the very moment when Moses insisted before the
Pharaoh that the Jews had to sacrifice in the desert to their own
God, the Jews were ever more explicitly given the duty to
sacrifice only to One God, their God, who tolerated no other
gods. Inasmuch as the Jews accepted the voice of that intolerant
God, they had to be specially intolerant. This became intolerable

to peoples surrounding them in the measure in which they reflected on the situation. No wonder that things came to a head again and again after the pantheistic Greek mind began to be carried abroad by a vast political institution propelled by the campaigns of Alexander the Great and his successors. But this is not the place to review the assaults of the Seleucids of Antioch on Jewish cult. They proved intolerable to those Jews who stuck by their Yahwist heritage, which they traced to God's choice concerning them. Belief in that choice turned the Hebrews into Jews, determined their historic identity, and was the source of their incredible drama. This word was chosen advisedly. A drama is much more than mere history. No student of the history of ancient Babylon or Egypt would have ever thought of speaking of the drama of Egypt or of Babylon. A historian of Babylon can at most speak of the "Wonder that was Babylon." Historians of the Jews are confronted with a drama.

The drama they confront would burst the framework of dramas that ancient Greek playwrights offered in the first place. Ever since the Greeks, dramas have been conceived by playwrights as having their origin in man's imperfection. A chink in a great man's moral armor or character proves invariably to be his undoing on the stage. In the case of the Jews, the chink relating to their drama is all too clearly spelled out in some of the psalms, to say nothing of the rest of the Old Testament.

Ever since Moses told God on Mount Sinai that his own people are "a stiff-necked" race, their Judges and Prophets have not ceased reproaching them for the same. The psalms abound in verses that call the Jews' attention to the fact that they can only blame themselves.

In return the Jews could blame God for having chosen them for something that was not clear to them. Choices are for a purpose. Was the purpose God's glory? Possibly, but not convincingly as far is this could be judged in that long view that justifies all sound judgments. On the short run there were indications of a purpose. The wandering in the desert came to an end within a few decades. Joshua achieved some spectacular victories. Later there arose Judges who now and then turned dismal situations into triumphs. Then there came David who

conquered everything from the Great River (Euphrates) to the Sea
(the Mediterranean). The glories of Solomon's reign, centered on
a freshly built and truly splendid Temple, could readily appear as
the onset of a final triumph.

But shortly after Solomon's death the Kingdom suffered a
setback in the form of an internal division, which in the long run
proved to be far more serious than external attacks. The ten
northern tribes formed their own Kingdom, only to cease to exist
in less than three hundred years. The Kingdom shrank to Judah,
the main southern tribe. Worse, the conviction about a special
election from above weakened at times almost to the vanishing
point, such as during the half-a-century-long reign of Manasseh
(687 - 642 B. C.). The spiritual restoration initiated by Josiah (640 -
609 B. C.), largely under the inspiration of Jeremiah, was short
lived, because Josiah failed, in spite of Jeremiah's urging, to
distinguish religious revival from nationalistic frenzy. Its
advocates pushed the king into a military confrontation with
Pharaoh Necho, and Josiah himself died in the battle of Megiddo.
Jeremiah also pleaded in vain for an accommodation with the
Babylonians. In 586 B. C. Jerusalem fell to Nabuchadnessar who
destroyed the Temple and carried the leading classes to captivity.

The return from the Exile exhilarated the Remnant, although
some of them soon entertained wishes similar to their forebears
who looked back to the fleshpots of Egypt. From that point on
there were increasingly many more Jews in the Diaspora than in
the Promised Land. Still those in the Diaspora kept sending the
annual tax to the Temple which became so rich as to prompt
Strabo's biting remarks, cited by Josephus, about Jewish wealth.

Yet whatever the coffers of the Temple filled with gold, they
had to appear puny in comparison with the fabulous riches of a
future Kingdom promised to the Jews. Was not Abraham told
that his descendants would be as numerous as the sand on the
seashore? Psalm 72 conjured up a future where corn would pile
up to the top of the mountains and people would be thriving as
grass on the fields. This was long before widespread concern
about the population bomb.

The idea of a Messianic kingdom, heavily political and
economic in its details, failed to materialize. Its onset kept being

postponed as one setback followed another. Who was responsible for this? The answer, and this is a chief theme of some psalms, laid the blame at the door of the Jews themselves. They were far from perfect beings as far as the standards set by Yahweh were concerned. All too often the Jews acted like the other nations. It did not occur to the Jews to see something radically wrong with their own very self. Rabbinical tradition would never take verse 7 in Psalm 51, "in sin was I conceived," for a proof of an original sin in man. At an international conference, I myself heard a prominent Jewish rabbi from the Netherlands excoriate the Christian dogma about original sin as a factor that foments resignation into the status quo. A mere generation after the Holocaust he was firmly convinced that everything could be straightened out, provided man had taken an optimistic, progressive attitude. Whatever the "pessimism" of the dogma of original sin, the optimism in question makes little sense unless tempered by a wisdom steeped in realism. Of all Christian dogmas none is more realistically "empirical" than that of original sin.

There is much more to realism than its being neither optimism nor pessimism. That very important surplus is evoked, and with particular forcefulness, in the dramatic exclamation, "Delicta quis intelligit?" ("Who understands sin?"), the Vulgate's rendering of verse 13 of Psalm 19. My first truly reflective encounter with the psalms is tied to that verse. I was seventeen when a Benedictine teacher of mine in the Gymnasium of my town of birth quoted that verse as he tried to explain to me the suicide of Count Pál Teleki, prime minister of Hungary, who in early April 1941 fired a bullet in his head. He seemed to think that it would have been futile to oppose Hitler's plan to invade Hungary so that the Nazi armies might crush Yugoslavia, prior to their invading the Soviet Union.

Those who think that the Count should have formally rejected Hitler's ultimatum and let himself be captured and tortured, should pause. No such counsel was offered by *The New York Times* as it reported on January 19, 1999, the death of Hanna F. Sulner, because she was the widow of Laszlo Sulner, a prominent Hungarian handwriting analyst, whom the Communists forced to forge false documents from Cardinal Mindszenty's notes. The paper excused the expert, a Jew, on the ground that otherwise he would have been tortured and possibly executed. It would, of course, be vain to expect from a secularist Jewish newspaper that promotes Jewish religion insofar as other Jews practice it, to ponder the question, "Delicta quis intelligit?" except perhaps in terms of Freudian psychoanalysis in which there is no room for sin as an offense committed against God. Analysts shall never fathom why man commits crimes even when he does not do so out of fear of bodily harm.

Much less would analysts cope with the problem, a hard nut to crack even for theologians, of why God's Covenant with the Jewish people did not include a convincing explanation of suffering. The view, so often repeated in the psalms, that all suffering is due to one's own sins, simply did not wash with all facts. Too many patently innocent Jews suffered even then. The Old Covenant did not contain an explanation of that mysterious passage in Isaiah about the suffering Servant of Yahweh. Was that servant the people itself or was he an individual eminently dedicated to serving Yahweh? In that latter case the question, — why should the virtuous suffer?—became even more pressing and further amplified the Jewish drama.

The Jewish drama came about not only because the Jews like all other people had a chink in their moral armor, but also because the drama—as one finds it written down in the Law, the Psalms, and the Prophets—unfolded in terms of a very incomplete libretto. This is the most important thing to keep in mind if one is to understand the psalms as prayers, that is, man's dramatic reaching out to God in response to what God has told him about Himself.

Of course, the God of the Old Covenant revealed about Himself truths incomparably higher than anything available in the religious literature of other ancient peoples. God is strictly one; He is pure spirit; He is not part of this world; He is absolutely holy, eternal, unchangeable, faithful, merciful, and, yes, loving. Man not only has to love such a loving God, but to love God is man's chief duty and most exalted activity. Man has to love that loving God with all his heart, with all his mind, with all his soul, with all his strength. All these propositions and precepts are of Old Testament provenance. At most some vague intimations of them can be found in other ancient peoples' religious literature. Their tightly interlocking unity as they are found in the Old Testament turn its sacred books into a document that stands apart in a class of its own. It is equally a distinctive feature of the Old Testament that it imposes on man the duty to love his neighbor as himself. This duty is not about kindness and good manners and the like, but about love and in that visceral degree evident in a self-love properly understood.

Moreover the Old Testament's God not only loves but loves in that pre-eminent sense which is to care. The history of the Jewish people showed more than one astounding evidence of that care. All this finds a vibrant echo in the psalms that form an unparalleled collection of religious poetry. The psalms are deeply human but superhuman poems as well. "Digitus Dei est hic"—is the only sensible reaction to all this.

But then why is it that the psalms played a relatively minor part in Jewish prayer life, communal and individual? This, of course, is said in comparison with the role the psalms play in Christian context. Both among Jews and Christians prayers are either communal (liturgical) or private (devotional). As to Jewish liturgy, its Pentateuchal legislation, as relating to the Tent of the Ark of the Covenant, contains no formal prayers, let alone psalms. Few of the psalms could be composed before the time of David, who laid down the plans for replacing the Tent with a Temple. None of the psalms that were composed during the First Temple period have explicit reference to their liturgical use. "The origins of the Israelite psalmody," so is stated in the *Jewish Encyclopedia*, "must lie in an independent creation of the religious spirit outside priestly circles."

Those origins mainly lie in the interiorized religiosity which the exilic and post-exilic prophets emphasized. An indirect support of this view is on hand in the self-defeating speculations of exegetes who sought a close correlation of some psalms with the Jewish liturgical year, or at least with its great feasts. Yet the evidence of such a correlation is meager, although much fancy superstructure has been built on it. Exegetical schools arose whose progatonists conjured up a biblical equivalent to the

Babylonian Akitu (New Year) Festival. Evidence was sought in the psalms on behalf of a rite in which the king of Judah re-enacted the birth, the struggles, and the well-nigh extinction of the people so as to assure the onset of a New Year as the pledge of a more propitious future. Some exegetes of the psalms even imagined that not only the King but Yahweh himself had performed a mystical copulation with a female force during that festival. Of such speculations it is better to keep silent. Psalms in which God, the King of Israel, is acclaimed have been used to support the idea that they were generated by an annual feast called the enthronement of Yahweh. Of the existence of such a feast the Old Testament is silent. Silence about it in the Rabbini-cal literature speaks louder than words.

Only a few psalms, such as the great Hallels (Psalms 135 and 136) can be safely attached to the Passover celebration. It is a matter of guesswork whether Psalm 81 was recited in connec-tion with the Feast of Tabernacles. The recitation of no specific psalm seems to have been part of the keeping of Yom Kippur. One can only guess that the so-called pilgrimage psalms (120-134) were sung during the yearly gatherings to the Passover. Not much is gained by taking Psalm 24 for a ritual whereby the priests exhorted those ready to enter the Temple precincts. Beyond this the psalms' relation to official Jewish liturgy prior to the destruction of the Temple remains very conjectural.

In whatever way was the Book of Psalms put together, it contains no indications as to the use of individual psalms either in the Temple liturgy or in private devotion. It is, however, certain that the psalms were diligently used. Thus the Qumran scrolls contain more often the text of the psalms than the text of any other book of the Old Testament.

When after the destruction of the Temple in 70 A. D., the synagogues became the sole religious centers of Jewish religiosi-ty, increasingly more references were made to the psalms in connection with prayer services. The psalms received a running commentary in *Midrash Tehillim* (*Midrash Psalms*). There is hardly a verse of the psalms that had not been expounded in the Talmud and Midrash. The number of psalms included in the statutory prayers gradually increased. At least one psalm became included in various non-statutory prayers, such as prayers recited after meals, before going to sleep, in case of drought, for the sick and by the sick, in memory of the dead, for the blessing of a house or a tombstone. Although "societies of reciters of psalms" (*hevrot tehillim*) were eventually formed, a periodical recitation of all the psalms has not become a custom within Judaism.

Does this mean that the Jews developed a subconscious uneasiness about the psalms? Being capsule formulas for that Jewish drama which has its clue not only in the incompleteness of man but also in an incomplete revelation about God and His intentions, the psalms could not encourage Jews to face up to their often excruciating predicament. It is not easy to feast on dramas that connote tragedies for which there seems to be no answer, for which no better times have an explanation, partly because better times have a way of receding beyond the horizon. The psalms are prayers of deeply religious men who are also profoundly puzzled, because the final explanation seems to slip through their fingers. And when instead of a final explanation a "final solution" loomed large, perplexity knew no bounds. The number of Jews, who survived the concentration camps without their faith in God having survived it, is still to be explored, though not with an oversight of the large number of those who already had no faith when they began to be dragged to those camps and their gas chambers.

The number of Christians who already during the second half of the third century apostatized under the threat of execution should also come to mind. But here the topic is the relatively much heavier use of the psalms within the Church. The frequency with which the psalms and all the psalms began to be prayed within the Church dwarfs anything which Jewish liturgy and devotion can show at any time in their now four-thousand-year-long history. For that reason alone the psalms may be viewed very much as Christian prayers, but they are such for other and much deeper reasons as well.

The Psalms as Christian prayers

About the name "Christian" no comment should seem to be more trivial and yet more crucial than that the name is inconceivable and incomprehensible without Christ. The comment is certainly appropriate in reference to the psalms as Christian prayers. In these times when it becomes a fad among Christian artists to represent Christ with a yarmulke on His head, it may be more important to note that He made much of the psalms, especially during His final confrontation with His own people. For that reason too, He was rejected by His own people, who soon began to spread awful stories about Christ's provenance and resent Christians much more than the pagans. Before long the synagogues resounded with curses against the "minims," curses still recited in some ultra-orthodox Jewish gatherings.

It remains forever a matter of conjecture whether, when as a lad of twelve, Jesus first encountered the learned among His people, He quoted a verse or two from the psalms as He astonished them with His answers. Perhaps one or another of those verses came from the pilgrimage psalms which He himself must have sung as He made His first journey to Jerusalem.

As His last journey to Jerusalem came to a head, He used verses from the psalms to challenge the leaders of His people to recognize His true identity. He characterized His triumphal entry to Jerusalem by quoting verse 26 of Psalm 118, "blessed is he who comes in the name of the Lord." He used Psalm 110 to describe himself as David's Master, that is, the Messiah, in spite of being his son or descendant. From Psalm 118 He took the verse about the cornerstone which, though the builders rejected it, remained "marvelous" nevertheless. During the Last Supper he quoted verse 10 from Psalm 41 to identify Judas as his traitor. The remark, "after reciting a hymn, they went out to the Mount of Olives" almost identically given in Matthew (26:30) and Mark (14:26), conjures Him up as praying with the Eleven Psalms 135 and 136, the great Hallels. Of His seven utterances on the cross two were verses from the psalms. One was the cry, "My God, my God, why have you abandoned me?" (Ps 22:2), the other the trustful resignation, "Into your hands I commend my spirit" (Ps 31:6). When after His resurrection He joined two of the disciples on the road to Emmaus, He used also some psalms to explain to them why the Messiah had to suffer. He summed up to the apostles the years He had spent with them in the following words: "This is what I told you while I walked in your company; how all that was written of me in the law of Moses, and in the prophets, and in the psalms, must be fulfilled" (Lk 24:44).

Since no book of the Bible was so familiar to ordinary Jews as the Psalms, quite a few of which they must have known by heart, it was the psalms that the apostles canvassed for passages as they had to account before the leaders of the people for their startling claims and stance. This set the pattern for the use of the Old Testament throughout the New Testament. Of its 360 or so quotations from the Old Testament, no less than one third are from the psalms.

The reason for this lies in the familiarity with the psalms of those Jews, priests and levites, whose very existence was tied to religion. Moreover, being prayers, the psalms are often directly focused on God, on His great acts, on man's attitudes toward Him. The psalms therefore contain a plethora of references to the One, the Anointed, the Messiah, in whom God's plans are to be brought to fulfillment. While modern Christians are to be reminded of the fact that Christ is a variant of Chrestos, or the one who is called such because his head was anointed with the sacred chrism or oil, for those from the Synagogue this connection seemed very natural. And so was certainly the case with the High Priest who adjured Jesus to answer the question: "Art thou the Christ, the Son of the Blessed One?" (Mk 14:61).

In the memory of the early Christians the passages which in the psalms referred to the Messiah King still could naturally mean Jesus. The various references in the psalms to God's son could but evoke for them Jesus' assertions about His special relation to the Father. Therefore whenever David referred to himself in the psalms as God's servant, Christians could not help but think of Jesus who in His suffering proved Himself to be God's servant in an eminent sense.

Authors of various parts of the New Testament gladly seized on these and other details in the psalms to show that Jesus was indeed the One to come, that is, the Messiah. Therefore, whereas for Jews the recitation of some psalms could be a source of perplexity, the same psalms appeared from the start to Christians as triumphal songs. This is one of the reasons why the psalms quickly turned into the prayer of Christians in a way that by far surpassed their use in the Old Covenant.

An already long established custom is on hand in Saint Cyprian's report, in his Book on the Lord's Prayer, about the daily hours when Christians gather to pray. A hundred years later Saint Basil and Saint Ambrose gave even more specifics about that custom. Of course, as was the case with the Jews, the gatherings mainly consisted of those Christians who were specifically dedicated to religious duties. It was not to the faithful at large but to those embracing the evangelical counsels that Saint Benedict wrote his Rule, a good part of which is taken up by legislation about the Divine Office with the recitation of the psalms forming its backbone. According to the Rule (ch. 13 and 18) the monks were to recite all the psalms within one week and do in some particulars according to the custom of the Church in Rome ("sicut psallit Ecclesia Romana").

That Church and the whole Church with it sang the psalms in the conviction which Saint Augustine put best when he noted that "it hardly ever happens that one would not find in the psalms the voice of Christ and of the Church, either of the voice of Christ alone or the voice of the Church alone, because in part we form the same body" (*Enarrationes in Ps 59*). So much in a nutshell about the Christian use of the psalms, a fact towering and ubiquitous wherever the Church was planted.

This use of the psalms by the Church was a signal evidence of the Church's awareness that if the New Covenant was the fulfillment of the Old, this had to be especially true when it came to prayer, the essential exercise and manifestation of religion. Such is the reason why even now, two thousand years after the beginning of the New Covenant, the psalms are still *the* prayer of Christians, a point reaffirmed in the New Catechism. Christians have, of course, many other prayers as well. The religious vitality of the Church has a telling manifestation in the enormous variety and vast volume of prayers and hymns it has produced as century followed century. But even when those non-liturgical prayers seemed to become a flood, the Church kept insisting on the centrality of the psalms in her prayers.

One such time was the period immediately preceding the rise of Luther who certainly had a flair for presenting matters in a lopsided way. He inweighed against devotional prayers as feeble food for the soul, while holding high the robustness of the psalms, implying thereby that the people were deprived of solid spiritual food. Yet by then scores of printings of various translations of the psalms into German had been available in proof of a popular demand for them as well as of their popular use. In England the psalms as given in the Vulgate were so much part of the Christian frame of mind that the Anglican Book of Common Prayer contains the psalms as translated from the Vulgate and not as they appeared in new translations made from the Greek or from the Hebrew.

On the Continent Erasmus and others took delight in pouring scorn on the Vulgate and on its rendering of the psalms. Soon there followed a new wave of translations into the vernacular that gained further respectability when printed together with the New Testament. This distinctly Protestant procedure was not without its pitfalls. Whereas the accuracy of the New Testament translations was under close scrutiny, this was not so with the rendering of the psalms, so many poems. Being unannotated editions, these New Testament *cum* Psalms printings could not help encouraging their users to seize on this or that verse of this or that psalm and find in it a scripturally emotive support to one's presumed orthodoxy and spiritual disposition. All this greatly reinforced the subjectivism which the Reformation stood for from its start. The psalms' contribution to this could be all the more powerful because possibly no other book of the Bible stands more in need of explanatory and cautelary notes than does the Book of Psalms. This will sound unreasonable only to those who are unaware of the warning which Peter gave in his Second Letter about some difficult passages in the Letters of his dear brother Paul which the unwary twist to their own destruction (2 Pet 3:15-16).

Still in saying all this of the Protestants' use of the psalms I cannot help recalling the backtracking of Ronald Knox, a convert from a sector of Anglicanism hardly prone to effervescence. In fact, Knox began to write *Enthusiasm*, a history of

Protestant revivalism in England, in order to discredit a high-temperature practice of Christian faith. But as he worked himself through his story, he warmed up more and more to its chief actors who found for their fervor a powerful fuel in the psalms.

Compared with the use of psalms among Protestants, the popularity of the psalms among Catholics was distinctly reserved. Of course, long before Tridentine times the Church enjoined the recitation of the psalms on those, priests and religious, who in the Church have for their lot (this is why they are called the clergy) a life exclusively dedicated to religion. Until recently it was their grave obligation to recite within one week all the psalms which form an integral part of the Breviary in addition to readings from the Scriptures and the Fathers. Even today, it remains a grave obligation for the clergy and religious to recite at least two Hours, the Lauds and the Vespers, on days when circumstances make it very difficult to recite all the Hours.

Now that the recitation is in the vernacular, psalms can all the more readily become the kind of prayer which is the elevation of the mind to God. But if that mind is to be a Christian's mind, the psalms must be understood in the light which Christ is. The essence of that light is that He is an Anointed who had to be humble, had to suffer, had to die, and to rise from the dead. He had to do all this because only a reparation of infinite value could undo the infinite offense which man's sins pose to an infinitely Holy God. For all its attention to God's holiness the Old Testament failed to perceive this decisive point of theology.

The point is the difference between a ram, a mere brute, and a Lamb, who was more than mere man. The ram reappeared each year when the high priest laid upon it the sins of the people and chased it into the wilderness where it certainly did not wish to go. The Lamb was the One who appeared only once and a Lamb He was. During His public ministry, He was first pointed out with the words: "Look! There is the Lamb of God who takes away the sin of the world" (John 1:29). Especially revealing of that power of His had to appear His willingness to be led like a lamb to slaughter and make no objection (Is 53:7). It should seem of great moment that in the entire New Testament the strongest emphasis on that difference is found in the Letter to the Hebrews, or more exactly to Jews who became Christians and faced great trials. The heavy use of the psalms by the author of that Letter should seem to be very telling indeed.

While the Letter's author insisted on the Church's essential connection with the Synagogue, it did so by underlining the manner in which the Church is a new essence whereby the old promise is fulfilled. But because fulfillment is not an abrupt new beginning, the Church seized on the psalms as so many prophecies also in that broader sense in which any prayer is a pointer to the future. This is why the Church's sacred writings do not contain a set of prayers paralleling the psalms, although here and there in Paul's letters there are traces of new hymns, usually the restatements of the great acts of Jesus. The Christian praying of the psalms is a refocusing of all the spiritual imperfections in the psalms into the perfection which is Christ's suffering as a step to the fulfillment called resurrection, or the Easter mystery.

Though a mystery, Easter is also a fact, the fact of Christ's bodily resurrection. Nothing is so dear to the secularist press than to propagate in cover stories at almost every Easter the notion that Christ's resurrection is the creation of the faith of the community of believers. The aim of this distillation of the latest "theological" research to the vast lowlands of journalese is to discredit belief in the reality of the supernatural order of redemption. That reality is the risen Christ's existential answer to questions that baffled the psalmists—David and Jeremiah, to mention only the greatest among them—even when it vaguely came within their ken. They could not imagine that the Messiah of the psalms had to undergo, and voluntarily, the unspeakable torments of the crucifixion and thus provide the long awaited clue to all pains, frustrations, setbacks, and devastations. The clue is the new life in Christ, a life springing to eternal life in the believer while still on earth. Without severing the Kingdom of God from the earth, Christ anchored it in the heaven. He came in order to prepare dwelling places for us in heavenly mansions. "The Kingdom of God is among you" (Lk 17:21) He said, though only within a perspective and on a condition best put by Paul who warned Christians that their "conversation" should be about heaven (Phil 3:20).

The unshakable conviction of Christian faith about Christ's resurrection remains alive even in lukewarm Christians. Answers to questions that come naturally to Christians, who are not nominally such, utterly mystify pious Jews. They recoil from considering even for a moment the light which Christians find in the fact that a Jew like Christ, whose Jewishness they are eager to emphasize, had to die in the hands of the impious, who included the leaders of His own people. Jews still want to find answers in *this* life for the great problems of life. And since all too often this life on earth does not provide the answer, they, crestfallen as they are, begin to speak as if they were pagans.

Yet Christians, too, are apt to speak as if they were Jews for whom everything is practically over with death. Having had to go, out of courtesy, to a Conservative Jewish burial service, I cringed on hearing the officiating Rabbi voice his perplexity as to whether there is survival after death and offered this perplexity of his as the hallmark of his tradition. Time and again I found in Catholic wake services something practically equivalent to that perplexity. After the Scripture readings and the recitation of the Rosary, where each of the fifty Hail Marys come to a close with the request that She should pray for us now and at the hour of our death, people linger around the still open casket so that everybody may take a last look at the departed. But as the conversation develops, one hardly hears anything except that the departed loved to live and that he would be missed greatly.

Surely this contrasts sharply with that burial service, where the officiating priest took his place in front of the coffin that contained the body of a Catholic woman who lived almost to a hundred, and began his sermon by exclaiming: "Dear Auntie, tell us, please, what does Heaven look like!" For a virtuous Christian, death, being an entry into Heaven, is the answer to all the excruciating paradoxes of this life, including death itself.

The change of the black vestments to white robes, and from Requiem Masses to Masses of the Resurrection, may not be a pure progress. Surely, the white robes are effective reminders of the Resurrection of Christ, but do they also remind us of the judgment that occurs already at the moment of death? Can a vague fear of God, who is no longer thought of as a Judge, still function as the beginning of wisdom?

This question leads us back to the psalms as Christian prayers or rather the prayers of Christians. Many a Christian will find it difficult to identify with prayers composed thousands of years ago and in conditions very different from those in the affluent parts of the world with its mirage of lasting comfort and security. None of us has ever feasted on "honey from the rock," to mention only one detail from the psalms. Even in this age of Judeo-Christian perspectives, it takes an effort for a Christian to pray the psalms as so many proofs of the fact that the Church is inconceivable without the Synagogue, that Christ makes no sense unless He is a descendant of David.

An even greater effort is to be made to counter the presumption dear to the progressive Western world that its new-fangled categories alone can make the Church relevant. Those categories are not germane to the notion that salvation history is a chain of concrete historic events that had a beginning and move towards an end. Within those categories the reality of salvation is an endless concatenation of ideas about religion that do not even hang together. There everything has to be reinvented or rather refashioned according to momentary preferences. No wonder that John Paul II felt it important to note during a pastoral visit of his to one of the most "progressive" Western nations that "the Church did not invent itself."

The Church is the ongoing salvation history that began with facts whereby God presented man with a chain of *faits accomplis*, as if to suggest that man has not been given the liberty to argue with a show of "healthy skepticism," this hallmark of modern "maturity." The Psalms make it all too clear that it was not given to man to argue with God, who had spoken, although man can and will start an argument at the drop of a hat. Man is free and therefore can proceed headlong into what is nothing short of a free fall in the moral sense. Not being fully aware of this, the Christian's praying of the psalms may become what it all too often had to be to the Jews: a series of misplaced demands, futile hopes, false expectations—that peter out in perplexities.

In other words, unless the Christian knows that the psalms are time and again imperfect prayers, the Christian's recitation of the psalms can become very imperfect indeed. The method of seeing the psalms in their "sensus plenior," in their mystical and allegorical application, may not be as good a remedy as it appears. The mind is heavily dependent on words. Now and then the mind can be alert enough to think of something which the words do not state but merely suggest. That "mere men ate the bread of angels" (Psalm 78:25) should readily recall to the Christian the Eucharist, is a case in point. For even when it does, the same psalm almost immediately makes one utter words that are hard to connect with Holy Communion. The same problem arises if, say, some words in Psalm 23 are to be taken in succession for the seven sacraments. Many other examples can be quoted and in reference to the fact that Christ is the full meaning of words such as anointed, king, son, and servant. In these cases, too, the very words of the psalms all too quickly carry the mind to details whose "full" meaning becomes clear only to minds riveted on allegorization.

It may therefore be better for the Christian to take the psalms as they are in their literal immediacy, provided he knows full well what Christian faith is. Many verses in the psalms—all the words of praise, all the cries for mercy, all the admissions of sin, all the attestations of trust—can be used by the Christian to the greatest spiritual profit. Yet even then the monumental simplicity of the finest lines in the psalms must not distract the Christian from the fact that the New Dispensation added crucially new nuances to that simplicity. Further, even the finest lines are often interrupted by verses that call for caution. Before faith becomes an experience, a psychological state, it has to be a riveting of the mind on the objective facts of salvation history and on the concise propositions of the Creed. In reciting with such a mind the psalms, the Christian will not find in them assurances about earthly things that, after all, cannot be given unconditionally to a follower of Christ.

Above all, the Christian should be keenly aware of the fact that many a precious truth the psalms may proclaim, they are for the most part no doctrinal texts. They were not composed with the aim to tell what one should systematically believe or what one should exactly do in given circumstances. Whatever exultation and inspiration one can derive from the psalms, their use can be such as to leave the Christian very perplexed indeed.

Anyone who browses through shelves full of books on the psalms is in for more than one surprise. The most painful of these is perhaps the manner in which this or that verse of the psalms was seized upon by groups of zealous Christians who denied the benefit of doubt to other groups claiming the same verses as justification of their very different stances and courses of action. Even to provide an example or two of this would unnecessarily open up wounds that in this age of ecumenism may appear to have been healed, in part at least. Still the question of why such phrases were pulled mostly from the psalms must be touched upon because it bears on the manner in which the psalms are to be prayers. The answer lies in the fact that whereas prayers of various lengths occur throughout the Bible, only one Book, the Book of Psalms, is a series of prayers.

A prayer should begin as the raising of the mind to God, but it has to turn into the kind of direct communication with God which is between two persons. Prayer is thought turned into a cry. Not all psalms are such cries to God. Some are plain soliloquia in which the soul addresses and instructs itself. Instances of this are Psalms 62 and 146. Some other psalms are plainly didactic (exhortative), such as Psalms 36 and 105. When the psalms are prayers properly so called, or a direct communication with God, they have especially strong emotive components. But even the former two kinds of psalms are often distinctly emotive which is the mark of a genuine instruction or exhortation. In other words, the psalms illuminate the mind for the purpose of enkindling the soul, indeed to put it on fire.

It may indeed be said that the purpose of the psalms is to turn the soul into a sort of burning bush, into a vague replica of the one which God used to make His presence felt to Moses. For if God found nothing better for that purpose than a burning bush, the soul itself ought to catch fire in order to communicate with God. Perfect as the philosophical definition of God as an "actus purus" may be, it can help the mind only up to a point in its quest of understanding God. Thinking of God as "an act" in whom all possibilities are activated all the time, will reveal its power only if that act is taken for a fire which is burning without consuming itself because it needs no external fuel to keep its flame alive. Therefore God, the "consuming fire" (Dt 4:24 and Heb 12:29) will leave intact all those who unite with Him.

All properly spiritual instructions, however detached, should issue in a light that provides warmth as well. Our Lord Himself explained that it was fire that He came to bring upon the earth and that nothing was dearer to Him than to have that fire enkindle any and all (Lk 12:49). Already John the Baptist distinguished his baptism in water from one in Spirit and fire, or the kind of immersion into water which Christ was to institute (Lk 3:16). On hearing Jesus explain to them the Scriptures, the two disciples of Emmaus felt nothing less than that their heart was burning within them.

But what the Lord could safely do, namely, to enlighten and warm, we poor disciples of His cannot do in a fail-safe manner. Thus it happened time and again that the use of this or that verse from this or that psalm proved to be an incendiary act, precisely because taken not only out of the context of a given psalm but out of the context of all psalms, indeed of the entire Bible. Not the least aim of these commentaries is to draw attention to the whole of each psalm, and beyond that to the wholeness of God's revealed word as concisely rendered in the Creed. In the process the danger that this or that verse of the psalms might be turned into some inflammatory material, may be diminished.

The praying of the psalms should promote the kind of fire in the soul that even in its greatest intensity is controlled by moderation. Whenever one finds the psalmist exploding, one should be keenly conscious of Paul's instruction that the man of God should never lose patience (2 Tim 4:2) even when he has to reprove, and regardless of how much he has to endure in the process. That he has to endure, among other things, the perspective of very harsh contrasts inseparable from salvation history is the very point of Psalm 1, which itself is a summary of all the other psalms and therefore an appropriate starting point for taking the psalms one by one.

Psalms One by One

Book I, Psalms 1-41

Psalm 1

How this psalm came to stand at the head of 150 psalms we may never know, just as it remains a mystery why exactly so many religious songs, no more and no less, were collected, and by whom, into a single unit from previous partial collections. But together those 150 psalms stand and Psalm 1 stands in front of all of them as if it were their summary. Already in the middle of the third century Origen looked at this psalm as the summary of the message of all psalms. Since then almost all major commentators on the Psalms have spoken of this psalm in the same way, often as if they said thereby something original.

Being one of the shortest psalms, Psalm 1 can be taken in almost at a glance. Modern eyes may, of course, readily be drawn to this psalm's middle section which conjures up the image of the just man as if he were a tree standing by flowing waters, shooting ever new leaves, always rich in fresh fruit.

This image should greatly appeal to modern man, proud of having discovered the beauty of stately trees and of a great many other beauties of open nature. Modern man did this all too often in order to draw attention away from the emphasis which the author of Psalm 1 put not so much on that stately tree as on the morally just man it symbolized. To downplay the supernatural by extolling the natural has become the strange privilege of modern man. Even when modern man does not want to slight the supernatural, he may hardly rise above the natural. The dictum that only trees are more noble than cathedrals betrays this type of dubious leveling.

Modern man has also discovered that trees may be the first towering signs of life on earth. Trees were already standing tall before dinosaurs began rearing their fearsome bodies. Modern man knows much more than did men of biblical times about the fact that trees are crucial for life's continuance. Trees replenish the vital stuff called oxygen. Trees are more responsible than was thought until recently for rain, this other main blessing of biblical man, living mostly on arid stretches of land. We now know that there are rain forests and for good reason we worry about their rapid depletion without really doing much about it.

Modern interest in trees is all too often more aesthetic than vital. Modern times, the early part of this century, saw universal applause greet the poem that began with a sentiment taken for truth, "I think that I shall never see a poem lovely as a tree. . ." Were a poll to be taken, Van Gogh's painting of a cherry tree in the rosy splendor of its full blossom, may receive more votes than Mona Lisa's cryptic smile, let alone Michelangelo's "Last Judgment."

Many of us might indeed be prompted by the middle part of this psalm to dream of a tree as its foliage gently swings in the afternoon breeze while the setting sun makes the lawn glow in emerald hue. The experience may carry with it a kind of inspiration, bordering on ecstasy, something equivalent to the lines, "The year's at the spring . . . ; The lark is on the wing; The snail is on the thorn," and draw the grand conclusion: "God's in his heaven—All's right with the world!" Then the even more theological sounding line would be added: "God must be glad one loves His world so much!" This in turn might give one the impression that one has thereby risen to the pinnacle of contemplation, worthy of the greatest mystics, minus their unsparing self-mortification.

In order to avoid this pitfall one would already go a long way by recalling that those lines were on the lips of Pippa, a poor girl working twelve hours a day in a silk factory, with only one holiday, New Year's day, to comfort her. But even if one did not take the trouble of looking up the context of Pippa's song in Browning's drama, *Pippa Passes*, the next section of this psalm may bring some sobering thoughts.

For Psalm 1 would not be a psalm, that is, a divinely inspired poem, if it failed to draw one's attention right away to genuine spiritual reality, which, like all bits and parts of reality, has two sides to it. The arboreal image of the vigor of the just man has for its backdrop the picture, which is no less a part of nature, the picture of chaff blown away with the wind. "Gone with the wind" are the wicked symbolized by that chaff, a far cry from a tree solidly rooted on the riverbank.

Whether we like it or not, our real world—natural as well as supernatural—has all too often the shadow of decay, of wickedness cast over it. The very first psalm offers a contrast in harsh perspectives which many other psalms loudly echo. Life is a painful mixture of the pleasant and of the painful. Individuals evoke not only the image of robust trees but also the image of splintered straw, ready to fragment into dust.

This is why we have prayers called psalms which are much more than religious poems. The psalms bear a signature that bespeaks of more than mere human genius. The fact that the just man, symbolized by a thriving tree, is contrasted by Jeremiah with the wicked man who resembles "a barren bush" that "stands in a lava waste" (Jer 17:5-8), suggests that he, easily the most spiritual prophet, was the author of this psalm. A genius Jeremiah certainly was but much more than that. His signature of a prophet, who proclaims God's views, will be noticed on other psalms as well.

More than any other prophet Jeremiah stood for an interiorized religiosity, for the justness of one's heart. More keenly than any other prophet he knew that only a religion of the spirit can cope with the true predicament of man. He knew, from an often riveting personal experience, that man, even the just man, the man of God, is steeped in a reality where darkness and light, suffering and happiness, trials and peace are forever interwoven.

The psalms faithfully mirror the predicament of the man who seeks happiness, though not in a dreamland but in the midst of continually recurring hard challenge. According to Psalm 1 he must not seek comfort in facile reasoning, in fashionable phrases, churned out relentlessly in the "councils of the wicked." He must not try to talk away absolutely binding obligations so that he may conveniently "linger in the way of sinners." He must not tarry with those who make a sport of scorning whatever is well proven as if there were no truth, but only opinions, be they called societal consensus.

Presenting as it does a perennial philosophy by means of a harsh contrast that accurately sets forth the human condition as long as there is time, this psalm deserves to be prayed in season and out of season.

The man who wants to be just will keep focusing his attention on eternal verities, undiluted by captious reinterpretations. This focusing is the matrix of any true prayer. Not so much an intellectual exercise as a prayerful reflection is on hand whenever the just man ponders "the Lord's law day and night." Such a man, only such, will bring his fruit "in due season," that is, in a season known only to God, and in the measure which He alone knows in its justness.

These last restrictions evoke the perspective of the New Covenant as the very novel fulfillment of the Old, and rightly so because, being genuine prayers, the psalms always look forward. Some of the psalms do this so emphatically as to exude a messianic sense. The very next psalm is a case in point.

Psalm 2

To understand a psalm, it is natural to ask first about the original setting which inspired its composition. Psalm 2 gives no information on that score. It is, however, all too clear that the psalm celebrates the status which God's unfailing Covenant with His people assured to the people's king. He is in a special sense related to God. He is God's begotten, his special son. This special relation is marked by his having received his office through anointment. The kings, in this case possibly David, were always known as "anointed" ("mashiah") and especially was this true of the King to come, who was to usher in final victory. Precisely because the psalm conjures up that future, it has been a messianic psalm for the Jews.

Indeed, this was the very first psalm prominently invoked by those who held that in Jesus the true Messiah had come. The Apostles themselves seized upon this psalm in their first major confrontation with the leaders of their own nation. The circumstances allow a fair reconstruction of the original setting of that psalm's first official invocation by the Church. The place must have been the house of Mark's mother where the Last Supper was held and to which Peter returned after an angel led him out of Herod's jail. It was in that house that the first community anxiously waited the outcome of the first formal confrontation between the Apostles and the leaders of the people. In chapter 4 of the Acts the event is described in dramatic details together with the response which the community gave after the Apostles had reported to them. Something akin to what happened at the first Pentecost was noticed again: the room shook to signal the descent of the Holy Spirit.

It must have been an overcrowded scene, but hardly unusual in a Jerusalem of congested houses and narrow streets. In a large room filled to capacity the exclamations coming from so many mouths could produce a sort of cacophony. It would be foolish to imagine that all spoke in unison. It may be more realistic to think that what happened was more like a revival meeting where the word "Amen" is shouted from the pews after almost every sentence uttered by the preacher.

But here the preachers were Apostles. In view of Peter's prominent role in the first part of the Acts, where he is the invariable spokesman, it is most natural to see him as the one who uttered what is described in that chapter as the prayer of all present. In that prayer the center part is a quotation from our psalm: "Why did the Gentiles rage, the people conspire in folly? The kings of the earth were aligned, the princes gathered together against the Lord and his anointed."

A stunning interpretation to be sure, but there can be no doubt about its emphatically inspired character. All of a sudden a most startling and most authentic twist was given to a psalm, which Peter, like his fellow apostles and all who listened to him, must have known by heart. Now for the first time he and the others saw this psalm in a totally new light. The novelty was not that there would be a ferocious opposition to the Messiah. The Jews knew all too well that whatever the Gentiles' disunity, they were united in their opposition to a faith embodied in a nation that stubbornly refused to worship the Gentiles' gods. By then for almost two centuries, to say nothing of the more distant past, the kings of the Gentiles had done their best to eradicate Yahwism among the Jews, by trying to replace it with a secular culture, steeped in a cult of idols, the cult of the Greco-Roman pantheon.

But now the leaders of the chosen people were also cast in the role of the kings of the earth. Peter himself could not surmise the extremes to which some Jewish leaders would go in stating their antagonism to Christ. In our times the Chief Rabbi of Israel stated on the occasion of Cardinal Lustiger's visit in Jerusalem that it was worse for a Jew to become a Christian than to perish in the gas chamber. The Chief Rabbi of France had much more in mind than the Holocaust and other persecutions of the Jews when he rebuffed the same Cardinal's reference to a common Judeo-Christian heritage. Deep-seated antagonism to Christ transpires from those recent efforts of Jews engaged in interfaith dialogues with the Vatican, who, so Rome concluded, wanted a change in basic Christian beliefs. These beliefs are rooted in belief in Christ, the Messiah, already the basic bone of contention between the Sanhedrin and the Apostles.

Peter, and especially James, the leader of the Jewish Christian community centered in Jerusalem, hoped that the observance of the Mosaic Law could form a unity with faith in Christ. But the first Christians soon perceived the awesome measure of the truth of Jesus' words: The vineyard, the sacred heritage, would be taken away from the original beneficiaries and be given to others, who could only be "the nations," so often the scorn of Jews. Instead of the rituals and practices prescribed in the Law, belief in Christ would be the center of true worship.

According to Psalm 2 the Messiah is also the one to whom God "bequeathed the nations," a decree which the nations would resist, and at times violently. Diocletian minted coins with the inscription: "The name of Christians is being extinguished." He merely provided an opportunity for God, who, in this psalm's almost shocking anthropomorphism, "laughs from heaven" at such presumptions. Robespierre, Hitler, and Stalin also proved to be good occasions for a divine chuckle.

Resistance to the Messiah took its most telling turns in the policy of some Christian princes who had their own ideas about who is really the master in matters not only temporal but also spiritual. Beneath the political character of caesaropapism, there lies resistance to orthodox christology, the touchstone of all Christian theology. Therein lies the reason why of all great historical Sees only one, Rome, was able to resist the efforts of political powers to turn the Church into a servant of the State. Political accounts of that reason should seem futile to anyone who is mindful of Napoleon's contemptuous remark that the pope (he had in mind his prisoner, Pius VII), had no power to wrench the muskets from his soldiers' hands. What the pope could not even dream of, the Russian winter did and God seemed to laugh in heaven once more. Stalin's mocking question, reported by Churchill, about the number of the pope's divisions, ought not to be forgotten. Leaders of The People's Republic of China that try to herd Chinese Catholics into a Patriotic Church are still to learn a thing or two about the history of the papacy.

The strength of Rome derives from the solidity of that Rock on which Christ built His Church, against which the Gates of Hell shall not prevail. Its solidity is a divine reply to Peter's confession: "Thou are Christ, the Son of the living God." Such is the broadest and timeless setting of this psalm. It can be prayed only in a state of mind in which the certainty of faith in the invincibility of the Church is coupled with a humble resolve to meet head-on and always with one's head on, the adversaries of God's Anointed. The year 2000 brings to the mind of thousands of millions all over the globe, that time begins with Christ, the Anointed, born "before all ages," on whom that flow of time, which is history, will forever be centered.

Psalm 3

According to its inscription this psalm was composed by David as he ran for dear life to escape Absalom, his favorite son and heir apparent, who revolted against him. Judging by Absalom's character, full of fault-lines, he would not have spared David's life had he captured him. The chances for this were rather good, because much of the army sided with Absalom. Had Absalom not chosen to delay his pursuit of his father, victory would have been his.

David's question, "How many are my foes, O Lord?" repeated three times, conveys the seriousness of his situation. It seems that as he composed this psalm he was not yet harmed by his pursuers. Perhaps this is the reason why, unlike the authors of other psalms, David does not ascribe his predicament to a divine retribution for his sins.

David is fully confident about being a just man, and therefore protected by God. As he lies down to sleep he expects to rise in the morning hale and hearty, in spite of being threatened from right and left. Our just man seems to have been a bit overconfident. Even Paul of Tarsus needed a special word from above to gain assurance that he would safely weather terrible waves rising around him and his shipmates.

The psalm may not seem to be a timely prayer in times that appear to be peaceful. Yet a little realism would reveal the fallacy of thinking that such times last long and extend over wide areas. The fallacy may be compounded by something even more deceptive than the security consequent on one's being far removed from areas where wars and hostilites rage, where Aquinas' line, "bella premunt hostilia . . .," is literally true. It would be the height of folly to overlook that one was bound to be surrounded by adversaries as long as one was truly Christ's disciple. May not the apparent peacefulness of one's life be a sign that one was not truly the kind of disciple about whom the Lord stated that no disciple is greater than his Master? Do not the lives of saints show that they faced countless opponents not only from without but also from within the Church? And if the disciple does not find himself surrounded by adversaries, should not this give him cause for anxiety about the depth of his discipleship?

Such an anxiety should be more gruesome than the fate which the psalmist implores to be meted out to his enemies. Surely, the mere thought of having one's teeth crushed by heavy blows, to recall a phrase from this psalm, may send chill down one's spine. But one should shudder even more at the thought of being the kind of lukewarm disciple who has no adversaries, who is never hemmed in from every side, but whom, in the end, the Lord would spit from His mouth. Let this psalm be recited for the grace of feeling that shudder.

Psalm 4

In view of David's bitter lamentations over Absalom's execution by Joab, this psalm, which its title ascribes to David, must belong to another, and rather peaceful phase of his life, when he could readily anticipate a good night's rest. The author of this psalm is a just man whose state of mind is free of pressing anxieties. He is obviously not one who has to resort to sleeping pills and esoteric yogi exercises in order to fall asleep. There is not even an indirect sight here of a psychiatrist's couch. Jung, who concluded that all psychiatric troubles stem for an inner conflict within one's religious, moral conscience, could have found in this psalm an illustration of what happens when no such conflict is on hand. And he would have looked in vain in this psalm for even the slightest trace of that panpsychism which he concocted as a religious cure for all psychic troubles.

The psalmist is innocently inconsistent as he states that "sleep comes to him at once." Actually he cannot help pondering, however briefly, the predicament of those caught up in the futility of worldly pursuits and in their inability to find lasting happiness. They cannot refrain from asking themselves the question, "What can bring us happiness?"

The surfeit of material goods, symbolized by feasting on choice bread and new wine, can bring only happiness which is paltry compared with that of good conscience. Not, of course, the kind of conscience held "good" by the world, a conscience which Newman pilloried in no uncertain terms as being but the individual's whim and fancy, a mere travesty of conscience. The conscience, as the psalm states, is a conscience which no sin would accuse. But the psalm also advises caution because sin is always a possibility. One should lie still, ponder eternal verities, and "do not sin."

Whatever the merit of taking Psalm 3 for a morning prayer instead of an evening prayer, Psalm 4 has always been a prayer for the hour when the onset of darkness brings the day to its close. In the old Roman Breviary this psalm was part of each Sunday Completorium. In monasteries that follow the Rule of Saint Benedict this psalm was sung every evening as the monks gathered for that canonical Hour.

Since this psalm was such an integral factor in setting the peacefully mystical atmosphere of that Hour, one may recall the hymn attached to it in the Roman Breviary, because that hymn, "*Te lucis ante terminum . . .*" was equally effective in evoking the same atmosphere. The latter struck the visitor in Christian villages whenever the plain "people of God" gathered for evening prayer in the church. One such village, Undervelier in the northeast corner of Switzerland, was immortalized in Hilaire Belloc's *Path to Rome*. Standing by the village church he saw, as the evening bell rang, all the people come to pray. He followed them into the church: "All the village sang knowing the psalms very well and I noticed that their Latin was nearer German than French; but what was most pleasing of all was to hear from all the men and women together that very noble good-night and salutation to God which begins: *Te lucis ante terminum . . .*"

Belloc continues: "My whole mind was taken up and transfigured by this collective act, and I saw for a moment the Catholic Church quite plain and I remembered Europe and the centuries. Then there left me altogether that attitude of difficulty and combat, which, for us others, is always associated with the Faith. The cities dwindled in my imagination, and I took less heed of the modern noise. I went out with them into the clear evening and the cool. I found my cigar and lit it again, and musing much more deeply than before and, not without tears, I considered the nature of Belief."

But back to the psalm, or rather to its advice: "Lie still and sin not." Surely there is more to this than the folly of going to bed with a cigarette, let alone with a cigar, in one's mouth. The warning is best understood in terms of that hymn's second strophe: "Procul recedant somnia/ and noctium phantasmata,/ hostemque nostrum comprime,/ ne polluantur corpora." With these lines those villagers begged God to keep away from them turgid dreams which the Devil uses to pollute mind and body. Generations of the faithful, who lived before Freud tried to cure libido by counseling surrender to it, found nothing wrong with that supplication. They had more mental health than we progressives can ever dream of, we who have been delivered, with the assistance of some of our theologians and even of some pastoral letters, to our murky subconscious, without being told that only the Truth, writ plain, can liberate and land us in the realm of Joy. But joy remained foreign to the thinking of Freud, who never used the word "Freude" (joy) in all his writings. He was one of those who keep repeating, with ever new twists, the question, "What can bring us happiness?" and fail to find it either for themselves or for others.

Let the praying of this psalm keep us at safe remove from this futility, the cultural curse of us moderns.

Psalm 5

The animated tone of this psalm may fit the context of David's conflict with Absalom. Hemmed in from every side, it was natural for David to burst out with a cry, indeed with repeated cries. With him let us not be afraid, if circumstances allow, to beg aloud our God, our King and Lord, to pay heed to our groaning, to the clamor of our cries. Let then the decibels of prayer blare forth as the wings of dawn begin to flutter, provided one does not break some house rules or some city regulations.

To cry out loud rather than to blink in the face of obvious threats would perhaps be not brave, but certainly very human. Did not Kierkegaard strike a most human chord in remarking that cry is the first sound uttered by man? Young parents may indeed turn into a prayer their infant's crying whenever they endure it with patience, a commodity that may be in short supply in a morning that was preceded by a repeatedly interrupted sleep, perhaps by a night-long vigil over a child's fighting for life or just struggling with a nasty fit of hiccups.

Morning hours, especially the early ones, are certainly conducive to the watching and waiting which, according to the psalmist, is another form of his prayer. Undoubtedly, it cannot be practiced while crying and groaning as well.

But what to do with one's sworn enemies? One can certainly derive comfort from the fact that "the Lord loves no evil, that no sinner is his guest." Evil men will not have a chance to plead their case before God against the just, so our psalmist states. Therefore the just man has an unquestionable advantage if he has access to the Lord's House and bows before his holy Temple.

Muslim worshipers come to mind, who keep an old Semitic custom as they bow their heads to the ground. One may fancy the Apostles in that posture as one follows them up to the Temple for prayer at the crack of dawn.

They or anyone else in good faith and clear conscience could safely pray for the favor that the Lord may keep their way clear from those who lie in wait for them. There will be plenty of traps laid by business associates, by lobbyists, and—may God keep them at more than at arm's distance—reporters, these foremost professional trappers of modern times, in slavish service of editors with no or little conscience. Pulitzer, their patron saint in America, made it a religion to play unconscionable games with truth, games sumptuously rewarded by a huge Prize. That it turned into a "coveted" Prize should tell much to those who are still aware of that word's prominent presence in the last of the Ten Commandments.

Seen from the perspective of the New Testament the psalmist obviously goes beyond the limits of requests which one can prayerfully make as far as bloodthirsty men are concerned. To request as the psalmist does that God exterminate at least one's own bloodthirsty adversaries, to say nothing of all such adversaries of all good people, is not theologically unobjectionable. The Christian's spiritual shopping list is strictly limited even when he or she is surrounded by bloodthirsty enemies. There is, of course, nothing wrong with one's longing for justice, provided it is subject to God's own good time, which all too often is very long in the coming. Long-suffering on our part has to match the tempo of His justice.

One should indeed use a sordino (an artistic forerunner of a muffler, an item better known in this automotive age) as one replays the enthusiasm of the psalm's concluding exclamations: They state that all whom God protects will be glad because God's favor will surround them as a shield.

It is wise to recall that not only shields are made of metal but also nails, lances, and swords. Have not these gruesome tools proved to be, let us just think of Jesus and Mary, the instruments of God's supreme favor and the best shields against the Evil One, this most bloodthirsty among all of man's enemies?

Psalm 6

Since the account in 2 Samuel (13:1 - 19:40) of David's conflict with Absalom does not indicate at all that David was stricken with sickness, it is not advisable to follow the title given in the Hebrew text to this psalm and take it for one of the various reactions of David at that time. Neither this nor other such titles bear on the inerrancy of the Scriptures.

This psalm is the first of seven penitential psalms and the most surprising of them all. Penance and penitence are terms inseparable from the idea and reality of sin, but of sin there is no trace whatsoever in this psalm. It is, however, full of references to sickness that racks one's body with pain and leaves one with no strength at all. The pain is so great as to make the psalmist think that he is on the edge of the grave. He certainly feels exhausted as he keeps groaning on his bed while his tears soak his pillow. On the top of all this, he is also weighed down with that most weighty of all burdens: old age. Worse, he grew old "surrounded by his foes."

A grim picture to be sure, but it contains no reference to sin. The picture is an Old Testament classic of the failure to realize that sickness is not necessarily a punishment for one's sins. The prayer of Hezekiah, as recounted in Isaiah (38:10-20), is an illustration of this failure. Were personal sins the cause of sickness, the entire world might not contain the necessary number of hospital beds.

It is, of course, right to pray for health, it is right to burst out in thanksgiving as done by the psalmist, who seems to feel the first intimations of being cured and of the retreat of his enemies. Did not our Lord say that by asking favors through Him we shall glorify His Father? Did not John Paul II use the occasion of his first visit to Lourdes to urge us to pray more intently for more miraculous cures? Of course, the Pope did not urge us to evaluate statistically the curative power of prayer.

Most of those who pray for such favors will not obtain them, though they may obtain the even greater favor of bearing with patience the cross of their bodily infirmities. Of these few are so trying as the debilities of old age, so many notifications of the approach of the Angel of death.

Psalm 7

As suggested by its title, this psalm could very well have
originated during the confrontation of David and Absalom. Their
confrontation extended over the wild areas stretching from the
northeast of Jerusalem to well beyond the Jordan where in
David's time lions still roamed and roared. Hence David's prayer
that God may rescue him from his pursuer, who, as if he were a
lion, is ready to tear him to pieces and drag him away with no
one to rescue him.

By the time Jerome arrived in Palestine, lions there were few
and far between. Today even hares are scarce there, although
lapdogs and laptops proliferate in witness of affluence. In this
age of safety and comfort it should be useful to remind ourselves
that not too long ago nature was still full of wild life that today
certainly appears harmless from safari buses equipped with
machine guns. While man made wildlife look safe by putting it
on the edge of extinction with his boasted technology, life
became a jungle in big cities that resound with gunfire. Meta-
phorically speaking, animals more fierce like lions are roaming
in ever greater numbers. There should be no difficulty in taking
this psalm for a very timely composition.

Like the preceding psalm, this psalm resounds with the
incomprehension of innocent suffering. The psalmist is ready to
concede that he would have no right to complain had he done
any injustice to his fellow men. Let them in that case drag him
down into dust. But he declares himself to be a just man, and of
innocent heart.

Let us be grateful that many of us can indeed have no reason
to charge ourselves with great crimes. But think of the one who
said that it was easy to go to confession: "I simply say to the
priest: 'I did not kill anyone, nor stole anything, but I declare
myself guilty on all other counts'." Poor confessors who are also
tried by those "saintly" souls who in the confessional assure the
priest that they cannot think of having committed any sin.

The psalmist implores God to sit in judgment. It would be
wrong to think that he has in mind a Last Judgment, although he
begs God to summon all the nations before His tribunal. The
psalmist speaks of a judgment which indeed goes on continually.

One need not comb the newspapers to find almost daily instances of the connection between crime and punishment, the latter often being taken in one's hands.

Anthropomorphic presentations of God, such as the one in this psalm that God is shooting barbed arrows at the wicked, are not so much naive as they may be very misleading. But there can be no doubt about the truth of the fact that the wicked all too often fall into the trap which they are busy digging for others.

Not only about long-term history is it true that history is philosophy teaching by examples. As one hears of unconscionable manipulators of the stock market, of forgers of checks, of falsifiers of lab records, and of phony advertisers being caught in their scheming, to say nothing of politicians who love to lie so much as to become able to love only those who lie to them, one can note short term proofs of that philosophy. One can hardly find a more inspired and encouraging reflection on all this than the concluding lines of this psalm. There those who are busy digging pits for others fall into them in the first place. Let us thank with this psalm "the Lord for his justice," by putting the emphasis on *his* justice which is all too often not *ours*.

Psalm 8

There was a time until not too long ago, when this psalm could be prayed with no nagging concern, indeed with a confidence that had a cosmic breadth, whatever the narrowness of one's idea of the cosmos. Not any more. In this age when Christians are blamed for any real and perceived crime committed against mankind, it has become chic to charge Christians also with crimes committed against the ecosystem. A prominent case of this was the late December 1967 meeting of the American Association for the Advancement of Science. There the distinguished historian of medieval technology, Lynn White Jr., minced no words in voicing that charge. Only he failed to prove it, or even to give the semblance that he had the intention of proving it in a manner befitting a thesis, allegedly corresponding to a fact of history. One wonders whether he and similar accusers would prefer to bog down in marshes which monks would not have drained if animated with a worshipful respect for a pristine nature replete with swarming mosquitos.

Fortunately for some self-righteous modern academics, pampered in their ivory towers, all at a safe remove from smelly marshes, those monks had common sense. This they derived in no small measure from reciting within the span of every week all the hundred fifty psalms. In their daily confrontation with wild nature that challenged them to a life-to-death struggle, Psalm 8 must have been for them a source of great confidence. In carrying on with battles, ideological motivation plays an all-important role.

Now that Darwin has disclosed Nature as a cruel battlefield among species, nothing could give better assurance for man caught in a nature "red in claw and tooth" than an idea pivotal to this psalm. In the words of the psalm man has been made "just little less than a god, with all things put under his feet, not only the birds of the air, but also the savage beasts." The idea is a beautiful elaboration on the injunction given in Genesis 1 to the first couple: "Increase, multiply, and subdue the earth." Neither this injunction nor the foregoing words of this psalm were a command to man to run roughshod over nature. When this began to be done, the chief culprits were the captains of industry of a rising industrialism, who had no qualms about commandeering mere boys and girls to form appalling divisions of child labor. Those captains did not do these things to have the lips of those babes, emaciated by often 14 hours of daily labor, resound with the praises of the Lord of heaven and earth.

To call those captains Christians, just because they were living in still nominally Christian times, would be as much a miscarriage of justice as to take Hitler and his Nazi high command for Christians just because they were baptized as newborn babes. For all his benefactions to Baptist causes, Rockefeller's invocation of Darwin's principle of a ruthless competition was a pagan's act. It was a far cry from the truly Christian spirit of the great social encyclical of Leo XIII, which Rockefeller and his ilk most likely did not deign to take note of. Not recognizing the pagan spirit of a ruthless capitalism, Rockefeller was even less clear-sighted than the Nazi leader, Alfred Rosenberg, who paid his due to consistency as he declared: "When one puts on the brown shirt, one ceases to be a Christian."

So much about some shaky foundations of the charge that Christians are to be blamed for the threat which technology poses to nature and that they in turn have to blame for this their having parroted this psalm for over so many centuries.

Would that each Christian remain steadfast in thinking, in terms of this psalm, of himself as God's viceroy in the universe and as the subject of God's loving care. Champions of an "ecologically sensitive" theology can but resent this psalm. Their resentment is, however, a piece with their rapidly decreasing sense of the supernatural. In the process they invariably fall back on process theology. They can do this in appaling ways one of which bears recalling because of its timing and place.

In May 1990, when the Pontifical Academy of Science held a meeting jointly with the Royal Swedish Academy of Sciences on the preservation of rain forests and related ecological issues, the delegates from Sweden brought along a Lutheran theologian. He claimed nothing less than that the central aim of the Christian message is to save our ecological system, and that man is redeemed, or rather redeeming himself in the measure in which he contributes to that aim. Not only did he not speak of redemption through the blood of Christ, but he also carefully avoided speaking of our psalm. His performance could be justly characterized as one worthy of Judas.

The centrality of man in the universe was, of course, easier to hold when the universe was believed to be centered on the earth. Five hundred years after Copernicus replaced the earth with the sun as the center of the universe, four hundred years after Galileo's telescope began to show the sun to be just one of an immense number of stars, a hundred years after our sun turned out to be a peripheral point in our galaxy, science, about half a century ago, served notice that the universe is centered on man after all. Science did this in a sense that has nothing to do with the triviality of spatial centeredness.

The universe seems to have been designed from the start as if given the task to produce carbon, this basic stuff of living matter. Furthermore, the design had to be finely tuned to an astonishing degree or else the whole process would have never led to stars, known as supernovae, within which carbon atoms and all the heavier atoms are produced. Taking things in a reverse order, it should indeed seem astonishing that man, standing on a platform which is but a speck of dust by cosmic standards, can explore a universe measured in billions of light years. If not anthropomorphic, the universe is anthropocentric, regardless of the resolve of some to hide this fact by some freshly coined words as such as "anthropic." They are no more convincing than those who by inventing the word "teleonomy" hoped to exorcise the word "teleology."

This is not the place to discuss the various meanings attached to the so-called anthropic principle of modern scientific cosmology. But regardless of how one twists words to cover up the theological pointer lurking beneath that principle, there is little scientific reason today for repeating Bertrand Russell's century-old-dictum that man is a sheer accident in this universe. In recent decades scientists stumbled on a number of details that throw indirect support to Aquinas' assertion that God created the universe for the sake of man. There should indeed be plenty of justification for testing new drugs for man in laboratory animals, a new way for man to feed on animal flesh.

Tellingly, in making his assertion, Aquinas mined Christian theology, not Aristotelian science. He never derived philosophical or theological arguments from purely scientific premises. He knew the order of things. He firmly stood behind the idea of a hierarchically ordered universe. And being fully aware of the "sacred" which is part and parcel of the word "hierarchical" (the rule of the sacred), he found in his consideration of God, as he knew Him through Revelation, the basis for man's unique standing.

This order is fully honored in our psalm which begins and ends with the assertion that the entire earth resounds with God's praises, including the ones uttered by mere babes. Such praises, the entire Church history is a witness, have been far more effective in confounding "the foe and the rebel" than mere argumentation. The ideologically hostile and rebellious attitude of some "humanists" obtained a new variant in the comportment of some latter-day "Greens."

This psalm, judged by its almost bucolic style, may be one of the most ancient among the psalms. Yet it exudes a freshness that does not fade as time goes on. It also has a dynamical energy that can be drawn upon by reciting it with unabashed enthusiasm. Psalms are a recasting of eternal truths in a form that should be savored. This psalm should help one to retain the sanity of the view that use is not necessarily an abuse. Man abuses nature most rudely when he fails to find in it a pedestal to praise God and be grateful to Him. After having lived much of her life in voluntary and utter poverty, Saint Claire echoed the gist of this psalm as she whispered just before she died: "I thank you God for having created me."

Only in the measure in which man recognizes his created-ness does it make sense to quote this psalm at moments of great technological achievements, such as man's landing on the moon. Otherwise the act will sound hollow. There was indeed a hollow ring to the applause that greeted the words of two American astronauts who, as they flew around the moon on May 22, 1969, broadcast this psalm toward the earth. Yet even those who would not admit man's created character are apt to wonder, now and then, about puny man's ability to penetrate with his mind cosmic reaches immensely vaster than the distance to the moon. It should remain a mystery for them why that mind, if indeed produced by mere chance, can think of chance at all. Thought is rooted in that rationality which compels us to recognize that "chance" is a mere word for ignorance.

Psalm 9

Those who, for not having their canonical hours, love to recite the psalms in a numerical order, certainly find easy the transition from Psalm 8 to Psalm 9. The former ends, the latter begins with registering one's joy over Nature's witness to God's goodness. But here, as all too often in the psalms, the attention quickly turns from the macrocosmos to the microcosmos, to man and mankind. We now know that in the macrocosmos "violent" forces dominate. As to the microcosmos, we have not discovered anything to refute the old observation that conflict dominates there, the conflict of two men within one breast, as memorably noted by Saint Paul. As to society, it is an ongoing conflict between the just and the wicked who, to make matters really contentious, are never in neatly separate compartments. Crusaders of all sorts would be wise to take note.

Undoubtedly the Bible pays much less attention to nature than to man and society. Yet the fact that the psalms always take nature first and man only afterwards when they speak of both should give pause to those who brandish the Bible against natural theology. Considerations of the external world are basic, though not the main fuel of religious dynamism. A motor's cylinder and piston merely serve the purpose that the fuel may be properly confined so that its explosion may be constructive. Just as without confining tools the fuel would never burn in a helpful way, natural theology, too, remains a solid framework for a theology concerned with a reasoned use of the supernatural as channeled through the great events of salvation history.

As to the conflict between the just and the wicked, this psalm presents it not on the individual level, as in Psalm 3, but on a social, international plane. Part of the moral drawn by the psalmist is similar to the one in the preceding psalm: just as the wicked "are snared in the work of their own hands," so are the nations. This is, however, not to be taken for a call for triumphalism of any sort and not even for a facile invocation of the "moral imperative."

The psalm seems to evoke as its background a major defeat of the nations, or rather, of a major nation and its minor allies that posed a direct threat to Israel. It is not possible to identify that defeat. The author of the psalm seems to telescope several such past defeats into one, looking at them from a standpoint which seems to be post-exilic. Its alphabetical structure may be a proof of this. The same structure is in part responsible for the lack of a clear train of thought in the psalm. It is rather a rhapsodic juxtaposition of ideas relating to the final victory of God over the nations and on behalf of His own poor, orphaned people. The psalm ends with a deeply theological wish that has not ceased to burst forth from the breast of the believer: "Let the nations learn that they are but men."

Profoundly theological as that wish may be, it can also be very human and shortsighted indeed. Few things can be so tempting as to oversimplify matters which in matters historical are always extremely complicated. Good guys and bad guys are almost invariably on both sides, though not always in the same ratio. It was in good part the fault of the Jews themselves that David's kingdom as inherited by Solomon broke up within a few decades after the latter's death. Babylon's capture of Jerusalem in 586 B. C., might have been averted had Jeremiah's counsels of moderation and compromise not been rejected by a goodly part of his compatriots, who madly shouted: Why not victory? Clearly, God was not necessarily on their side. Those who studied *The Jewish War* by Josephus know all too well the enormous role which Jews themselves played in bringing on the destruction of Jerusalem in A. D. 70.

The combination of threats posed by the nations and by the Nation itself to its very survival can also be seen in the history of the new Israel, the Church. External threats were a staple feature in Church history. The Muslim nationhood was hardly more than half a century old when it led a naval assault on Constantinople, in the belief that its capture would mean the end of Christianity. But far more treacherous were the threats which internal dissents posed to the Church. Saint Paul's assertion that heresies need arise so that the faith of the faithful may come to light, is a painfully persisting truth indeed.

Again, whatever the "incomparable good" which, so Newman emphasized, the Church has performed culturally, only a blind triumphalist would now take at face value the dictum, *gesta Dei per Francos,* let alone by Franco, providential as his role may appear in some respects. It is not safe, history has amply shown this, to take the judgment of the nations out of the hands of God, who alone knows the true source of the wealth of the nations and the true measure of their wealth which neither moth consumes nor rust devours. It is not to be expected that, highly desirable as this may be, the nations would ever learn that "they are but men," and especially so when they clamor for the rights

of man at a systematic disregard of God or when they take Him
for nothing more than a "distant hypothesis."

Psalm 10

The estimate of God as a "distant hypothesis" is the characterization by Card. Ratzinger of present-day thinking in most parts
of Germany. The same could be said of wide areas of the affluent
Western world, where wickedness runs rampant to the accompaniment of condescending references to God. There are still some
voluble atheists around, but as a rule God is dismissed with quiet
ease, while a broad spectrum of wicked actions are spoken of
with indifference. Moral relativism rules with an intolerant
absolutism. The decibels of moral indignation are reserved for
genocides, usually called "ethnic cleansing," but not consistently.
Some people are more expendable than other people. And "the
murder of the innocent," an expression of this psalm, is not a
label to be used in "nice" circles in reference to partial birth
abortion.

Psalm 10 would not, of course, be genuine if it contained
anticipations of the modern disease of utter skepticism. Whoever
was the author of this psalm, he would not consider even for a
moment that the wicked might be in good faith. As portrayed in
this psalm the wicked deny God, though they are not really
secure. Although they say that "God does not exist," they are
more intent on assuring themselves that "God forgets," that "He
does not see," that "He will not punish."

The wicked's hollow boasting, "Never shall I falter, misfortune shall never be my lot," might have been exposed by the
psalmist for what it was worth, had he not been overwhelmed by
the wicked's readiness to pounce from his hiding place on any
and all: The poor, the common folk, the ordinary toiler—all seem
to be "devoured by the pride of the wicked."

All this misery reflects an internal affair of the people,
unlike the scene presented in the previous psalm in which the
misdeeds of the nations are the cause of agonizing complaints
addressed to God. But the resolution of the problem points in
this psalm, too, in much the same direction. Here, too, the

psalmist begs God to finish off all the wicked, to save all the innocent, and on a very short run at that. To be sure, even in the New Testament we have to pray that God's kingdom may come and that we may be delivered from the Evil One. But we are not instructed to beg God that He should do wholesale justice right now or even within the foreseeable future.

We are always tempted to pray for precisely that. May the recitation of this psalm, which pleads in an almost naive way for the rapid elimination of all wickedness that rends society apart, be a much needed reminder of the need for a patient endurance of the wicked. This endurance we must turn into a virtue, and all the more so as Jesus himself warned: "In patient endurance shall you possess your soul" (Lk 21:19).

Psalm 11

Since there is no quick fix for societal wickedness, one may be tempted to take a seemingly easy way out, which is to remove oneself from society. Possibly it was David himself who was given this counsel by some who saw that a conspiracy was being hatched against him in Saul's entourage. Would it not be wise for him to flee into the desert as a threatened bird flies to its mountain? This has indeed become a pattern, say in the time of the Maccabees, and one can hardly blame them. They saw the Hellenization of their land shake its divine pillars to their very foundations. When the first wave of Decius' persecution came and all the foundations of a growing Christian world appeared to collapse, Cyprian, bishop of Carthage, went into hiding at the urging of his own flock, only to remain in his post when the second wave came.

He now truly took his refuge in the Lord alone. This in spite of the fact that he could not guess how close at hand was the demise of Decius himself, who, next to Diocletian, was the most cruel persecutor of Christians during pagan Imperial times. Cyprian could not guess the kind of "barbed arrow," a sudden early death on the battlefield, which God was preparing for the one, who—Cyprian was to record this—had a sharp perception of the strength of Christians. Were he not holding the power of an Emperor, Decius was heard to remark, he would aim at becoming the bishop of Rome.

In comparatively much milder persecutions, such as exist today in the world of democracies, where Christians (and especially the Catholic Church) are the only ones who can be mocked with impunity, there is much less ground to take the easy way out. Let this psalm be a call for engagement in the great cultural battle, at least to the extent of showing up unfailingly at the voting booths. If not only fifty percent of Christians voted but, say seventy percent of them, we might have in considerable number political leaders who at least would not try to obliterate the theoretical difference between good and evil. This would greatly protect the very foundations of modern society from collapsing into mere behaviorism.

Psalm 12

The beginning and the end of this psalm may seem contradictory. If indeed all good men have vanished, there remains no ground for begging God that he may "save us from this present generation." It is important to keep one's eyes open to spot the good everywhere, even in this "present generation," which some "good men" flatly denounce as if there remained no saving grace there whatsoever. Good people, who make sweeping denunciation of the evil of the present day, should not be listened to without great reservation.

Apart from this the psalm contains an earful that is applicable to our own "present generation," but especially to its media. If indeed there is a charge that can be laid at the door of the media, it is the very first complaint voiced in this psalm: "truth has gone from the sons of men." To many a media mogul and anchorman the only truth is that there is no truth, only opinions which are sedulously tabulated almost every day in this age of instant poll taking. That sanguine ideologue of the nascent French Revolution who declared that "people are infallible" would now say that infallibility belongs to the media. Editors and newsmen decide what questions to ask from the people and what questions ought not to surface. One finds again and again that lawyers are interested not so much in serving the truth as in saving the hides of plain liars and perjurers. "Lying lips" abound and "false hearts" beat inside more and more men (and women) as they champion the cause of openness.

The world is indeed full of "tongues speaking high sounding words," full of those who mockingly ask: "Our tongue is our strength, who is our master?" Most TV programs are so many proofs of the psalmist's astute observation: "The worthless are prized highly by the sons of men."

But not everything is lost. There remains the Lord to whom one can confidently turn for the favor that humanly speaking appears almost impossible: "Save us from this present generation." But here, too, as with other favors implored from God, one has to do one's own share. It consists in the task of finding all good men and women still left in this generation. The task is not difficult as there remain many such men and women. And this was true of the day when the psalmist wrote, indeed of any day in the history of God's chosen people as well as in the history of the Church. Realism, so often a catchword for pessimism, should be keen in spotting the good, or else there remains no logical room for expecting that God would surely rise. He will, of course, do this in his own good time. No man can act as God's appointment secretary. But we must do our appointed duty.

Psalm 13

In writing this psalm the psalmist thought of only one kind of enemy, the enemy from without. Such opponents have not always been around in many areas even during this century that has witnessed more hostilities than many other centuries taken together. But the enemy from within is always on the prowl. He is within us because our undisciplined urges give him endless opportunities to take a partial and even, which God forbid, an almost total hold on us. Viewed in the light that spiritual death is far worse than its bodily kind, a line of this psalm which forms its very gist, takes on a fearful significance: "Give light to my eyes lest I fall asleep in death, lest my enemy say: 'I have overcome him'." The enemy from within produces most effectively, through the relentless remorse of one's conscience, a grief in one's soul, a "sorrow in one's heart day and night."

The psalm's words about "falling asleep in death" were quoted in Fr. Martindale's insightful book *The Meaning of Fatima*. Surely, they are very germane to the request which Our Lady made that the rosary be recited with a remembrance of the souls who at the hour of death especially stand in need God's mercy. Nothing can save one more effectively from the fire of Hell than the grace of being protected from sudden death. It is also the grace that will enable us to sing, throughout all eternity, psalms to the Most High.

Psalm 14

The most remembered phrase in this psalm is undoubtedly its first line about the fool who "said in his heart there is no God above". Originally, the psalm may have been a taunt of the Pharaoh who kept the Hebrews slaving, while turning a blind eye on the signs performed by Moses and Aaron. The scattering of "the bones of the wicked" could be a reference to the destruction of the Pharaoh's soldiers whose bodies were found on the seashore or, if the psalm was later re-edited, to the sudden demise of Sennacherib's army in 721 B. C., of which more in connection with Psalm 46.

The psalm has, of course, a perennial timeliness. That atheism would hit its propagandists as a boomerang was perceived by Voltaire when he warned his atheist friends to play their tune softly, lest ordinary people would take a liking to it. Then they would soon draw the consequences, rise in revolt, and break the instruments of the atheists on their very heads. Faith in God has long been recognized as a safeguard of social order. Very resentful of this were those who spoke of religion as the opiate of the people. Yet wherever Communism was introduced, lawbreakers quickly grew so numerous that only the heavy use of police could save prisons from bursting at the seams. In a free society, where everyone is free to formulate one's own set of principles, the need for ever more prisons is one of the chief legislative headaches.

One can certainly muse on the fact that Nietzsche's declaration of the death of God went hand in hand with his celebration not of man but of Superman, which then was quickly seized upon by the Supermonsters of the "Herrenvolk." They have been just as short-lived, relatively speaking, as those who turned, among other things, a splendid church into a "Museum of Atheism" in a city that for three generations was forced to carry the name of Lenin. The name of the city not only reverted to Petersburg, but to Saint Petersburg.

Only some specialists of late-nineteenth-century English literature know now more from Swinburne's "Hymn of Man" than its closing line: "Glory to Man in the highest! for Man is Master of things." Yet in the hundred fifty or so lines of that "Hymn" there are some more worth remembering. One is Swinburne's announcement of the imminent death of God, or rather of belief in Him: "Thou art smitten, thou God; thy death is upon thee, O Lord." A strange notice, to be sure, since Swinburne had already declared: "But God, if a God there be, is the substance of men which is man." But if God is dead, also man is to be considered dead, at least according to Swinburne's logic.

Atheism is never logical. Its champions prove themselves fools by settling in that materialist paradise where self-contradictions abound. There they blissfully overlook the fact that they take advantage of their freedom to act whenever they endorse total determinism, without which materialism makes no sense.

Once in that paradise they may also contract some fearful symptoms, such as the one that, according to this psalm, plagues those who "tremble with fear without cause for fear." Today the commodity known as "freedom from fear," seems to be more elusive than it was half a century ago, when the great promise of "four freedoms" was dangled before a mankind in the grip of global fear. Anxiety, which is a form of deep-seated fear, is endemic in modern society full of "village atheists," including their kind who thrive in the village known as academe. Psychiatrists make money hand over fist by trying to cure that Angst by fueling the deception that freedom of religion should mean freedom from religion.

Just as in medicine, where inoculation is often the means to activate the body's resources, one may need to be injected with fear in order to battle the fear of fear itself. That healing fear is the fear of the Lord which is the beginning of wisdom.

With this in mind one can easily cope with some sweeping generalizations in this psalm that remind one of Psalm 12 where one reads about the apparent disappearance of all good men. God needs only a few good men who are ready to heed His call, a point so reminiscent of the recruiting call of the Marine Corps. May we be among the very first to enlist and let the half-hearted moan the absence of all good men, themselves included.

Psalm 15

The reference to God's tent at the outset of this psalm may indicate that it was written before the construction of the Temple by Solomon. Indeed the atmosphere of the psalm, where plain commandments dominate plain reflections, also suggest that it is one of the earliest psalms. Its composition may have been occasioned by the carrying of the Ark of the Covenant to the former stronghold of the Jebusites, which, after having been conquered by David, became David's city and the place of God's Tent. The psalm lists the moral qualities needed by those who wish to live in that Tent's proximity.

In praying this psalm one may profitably think of many upright men and women, indeed saintly ones, who not only kept all the commandments but went far beyond the line of duty. They certainly showed that God's commands are not impossible to obey and that it is even possible to embrace the narrow path of Christ's counsels.

Among the commandments listed in this psalm there are several that do not appear grave but are indeed difficult to live up to. Slurs that soil our neighbors' reputation are sins committed about the second of the two great Commandments. We should not forget that Christ branded a "crime" to call others "fools." There is indeed plenty to look for within one's own bailiwick before one points an accusing finger at those who in public life have made it a virtue to "take a bribe against the innocent." Let us also think of those who think highly of themselves just because they have not transgressed any major commandment.

Psalm 16

This psalm begins and ends on a note that makes one feel in the presence of a true mystic. Only saints can say to God, "My happiness lies in you alone," and they alone had a foretaste of "the fullness of joy" which one has "in God's presence," a remark at the end of this psalm. In between, one finds something even more spiritually elevated, if this were still possible: The psalmist describes God as his "only prize" and his "sole heritage." No wonder that the psalmist keeps thinking of God "who even at night directs his heart and gives him counsel."

All this can be understood even by the faithful who never had any mystical experience. But it takes true mystics to know that one might die of joy as one experiences God. Some of the mystics experienced that joy so intensely as to think that they could not endure it any more.

But what to make then of the lines in which the psalmist, a great mystic to be sure, speaks of his hope, indeed assurance that God will not leave his soul (a part of his flesh and blood reality) among the dead? We know what to think of these lines ever since Saint Peter revealed their meaning under the guidance of the Holy Spirit. He put those lines in the mouth of Christ who knew that God "would not let his beloved know decay." All the mystics—so many beloved of God—died in the full knowledge that their bodies must decay before they are resurrected. Only the one, upon whom God's voice resounded, "This is my beloved in whom my favor rests," died without his body being subject to decay. This is why Christ's mother, that "most favored daughter," was saved from the decay of her mortal body. Her death has indeed been aptly referred to as a "dormitio."

May this psalm strengthen our faith in Christ and increase the favor we are to receive in Him, through Him, and by Him as we see Him raised over the altar at the conclusion of the Canon. His risen body, given to us in communion, is the pledge of our eventual resurrection.

Psalm 17

This is another of those psalms, a dozen or so at least, that one would in vain try to see in its original setting unless one had studied the life of Jeremiah. On more than one occasion he was hemmed in by his enemies, the false prophets. Then as now there were just too many who felt themselves to be the mouthpieces of God. In these days when so many assume the stance of prophets, although they are woefully ignorant of the catechism, this psalm should seem very timely indeed. True prophets and teachers of Truth (especially the one who sits in the chair of Peter), can say that "my foes encircle with deadly intent." So was Jeremiah encircled on more than one occasion. If one wants to know something of a true prophet's state of mind under such circumstances, let him recite this psalm, but first its verses 9-12 that grippingly describe Jeremiah's dire predicament. And if one wants to know also something of a true prophet's peace of mind, let him reflect on the concluding verse. True prophets are not bothered by the thought that, unlike their opponents, they would not "abound in offspring" and would not "leave their wealth to their children." Children and carefully drafted wills give but faint consolation at the moment of one's departure from life. But the true prophet, in his justice, feels sure that when he awakes, he will see "God's face and rejoice in the sight of his glory." This is one of those cryptic phrases in the Old Testament that indicate a faintly visible belief in a life after death which is immensely superior to a shadowy existence in Sheol.

Psalm 18

The dramatic use of the image of a violent storm may in part refer to a real event in David's stormy and victorious career. Undoubtedly the poet king of Israel had a considerable role in creating this psalm, which, however, carries in it touches subsequent to his reign. David certainly could not hear the Lord respond to his cry from the Temple which it fell to his son Solomon to build. Again, the concluding lines that refer to his sons, may seem to refer to a chain of his descendants on the throne, which he had set up.

Insofar as David authored this psalm he may have also taken a cue from a tradition that must have contained more about the storm that helped Joshua's victory over the Amorites than the few lines in the Book of Joshua. Then as later, sudden storms could play havoc with one or the other of the opposing armies, or with both of them. The Jews themselves may seem to have been the target of God's punishment through such havoc on at least one momentous occasion. Such was at least Josephus' view about the storm that raged over Jerusalem during a night, just before Titus and his legions laid siege to it. The storm disarmed the soldiers of the Peace Party who guarded the southern Gate. As a result several thousand Madian ruffians entered the City and turned it into a place of internecine warfare that more than anything else led to the destruction of Jerusalem.

But back to David who might also have thought of the storm that accompanied the passage of the people through the Sea of Reeds. While the particular storm David had in mind could have been accompanied by an earthquake (the Jordan valley rests on a major fault line), it was a poetic exaggeration on his part to refer to the ocean whose bed, indeed the very foundations of the earth, was laid bare.

Poetic minds reciting this psalm may delight in David's use of the billowing head of the storm as an image of God's angry and vindictive face. One can perhaps tolerate the anthropomorphism of God's flying on the wings of black clouds, but one is tempted to pass over quickly the details about God's nostrils from which fearful flashes burst forth.

Two thousand years after the onset of the New Testament there is a distinct urge to think of God as infinitely merciful even of his enemies. This is not to endorse the resurgence, in our times, of Origen as an inspiring theologian who thought up a mechanism whereby even Hell becomes ultimately empty. The Hell as emptied by some modern theologians should seem more frightening than the thick rows of snowflakes which in a vision of Saint Teresa of Avila showed the number of souls heading into eternal punishment. The plain realism of the catechism should generate more confidence than the Hegelian fancy of some theologians bent on rehabilitating Origen.

From the New Testament's perspective a touch of hollow boasting may seem attached to David's explanation of God's sweeping intervention on his behalf. A noble soul in many ways, he was no true saint. The Church would never consider for sainthood one in whose writings the Devil's advocate would find lines such as in this psalm where David claims, with no reservations whatsoever, that he was just, that his hands were clean, that he kept the ways of the Lord, that he had not fallen away from Him, and so forth. Real saints have all too often been overburdened by the thought of their small failures.

No less a far cry from New Testament perspectives is the almost commercial balance which David draws up between his own righteousness and the just reward God meted out to him. One is indeed tempted to pray this psalm by saying its verses 22-26 with a negative: Although I was not just, although I did not keep my hands clean (and there are so many ways of misusing one's hands and soil thereby one's soul), and so forth, yet God showed His great mercy to me, miserable sinner.

There is no problem, of course, in reciting those verses in which David recounts God's manifold benefactions to him in making him grow into a great king of Israel. Anyone can think of events in one's life to which fully apply the lines in which David recounts that God made safe the path before him, that God trained him with care, that God truly girded him for the battle, that God truly helped him pulverize his enemies.

We can think of only one enemy, the Enemy writ large, whom we are supposed to crush to dust. Our success has been partial, and at times very partial indeed. In repeating with David the concluding verses of this psalm, we should thank God for whatever success we have had, but we must not dream that all our enemies (that is all our weaknesses) have been subdued and for good. The Enemy is always around the corner, ever ready to present us with ever new traps. Our final victory over him can only come with a holy death.

Meanwhile let us emulate David in stirring up our love of God. True religion alone can inspire one to exclaim with David: "I love you, Lord, my strength, my rock, my fortress, my savior." He meant love and not merely an appreciation, however profound.

Psalm 19

In his *Reflections on the Psalms* C. S. Lewis declared this psalm to be the most beautiful of all psalms. Surely, there is a lasting grandeur to this psalm's opening verse: "The heavens declare the glory of God and the firmament shows forth his handiwork." Let us not, however, forget that aesthetics cannot forever distract from problems it cannot cope with.

For one, the message of the heavens turned out to be wrapped not in a majestic silence but in violent roars bursting through the entire cosmos and through its entire history. The stellar heavens proved to be a very violent universe. The explosions of its supernovae and the collisions of its galaxies appear harmless only in color photography, even though all that violence still testifies to sparkingly beautiful scientific laws. Looked at in this way, the heavens, the universe, is still a powerful pointer to its Maker. The heavens still declare in a very real sense the glory of God.

But the firmament celebrated in this psalm turned out to be a mere illusion. The firmament does not exist at all. Whatever is nonexistent cannot be the work of anyone, let alone God's handiwork. Gone are forever the days when one could contemplate the starry skies with eyes wide open but with one's mind shut out from the act.

This is not to suggest that poetry has no place in thinking rightly about God. As long as one takes poetry for poetry and not for science, one can still dream about the sun as rising each morning as a bridegroom who exits triumphantly from his tent at dawn, sets out on his day's work, carries out his task in admirable silence, although nothing can escape his influence, symbolized by the sun' burning heat. This is not the silence of infinite spaces that eventually was to frighten the libertine mentioned in Pascal's *Pensées*. The silence of that beauty converts with the true, with the good, and with being itself.

Insofar as the true and the beautiful are inseparable, the first part of this psalm keeps raising nagging questions, which it takes more than literary criticism to answer. And when we come to the convertibility of the good with the true, the second part of this psalm will appear equally problematic. There one is confronted with a problem, which, as will be seen in connection with Psalm 119, triggered in C. S. Lewis the greatest misgiving he had in reading the psalms.

To see that problem in proper perspective, the problem of an inordinate love of the Law that issues in pharisaism, one should recall that Revelation is given to concrete human beings and not to specious abstractions. Even in the Church concrete individuals speak with authority, and grace is channelled through concrete sacramental signs. The Law with all its particulars was a "paidagogos" to the Word become flesh. Just as error has a power of swaying because it appears in concrete paraphernalia, the Word of Truth became incarnate in order to sway men from error which is a lure only when concrete.

One can, of course, pity those whom *The New York Times* contemptuously calls "Ultraorthodox Jews," and especially the young ones among them, who play "ritually clean" rock music. But one must not forget that the depth of the commitment of the Ultraorthodox to the concrete Law is a manifestation of their commitment to the historic, concrete reality of the event called the Covenant. Out of that depth wells up the endurance of Judaism and not from the tracking of the DNA of one's mother and grandmother, a procedure that smacks of outright racism. Hitler might have nodded on reading that paper's joyous headline that one of the grandparents of General Clark, the NATO commander in Kosovo, was Jewish.

Similar observations may be in order about Catholics, who often are lost in all sorts of devotional trivia, who long for the days when one had to fast since midnight before communion, for the time when Friday abstinence was equated with Catholicism, for the time when only boys could serve at the altar. But beneath this apparent legalism there often lies a depth of commitment to Jesus and the Church which some enlightened Catholics, trapped in their progressive shallows, shall never fathom.

Once one ignores Augustine's commitment to a concrete Church that stubbornly keeps legislating in Jesus' name, his dictum, "ama et fac quod vis," may easily become a guidepost to such shallows. Once there, one shall denounce the legalism of the Church in order to cover up one's shame or at least one's confusion. Plenty of the latter was in evidence in the decision of some students at Georgetown University who thought, with the approval of the University's President, that they could learn something about sex by inviting Larry Flint, the country's most notorious pornographer, to speak to them. Imagine Saint Paul dialoguing with the homosexuals of his day (who paraded at that time as the paragons of normal male behavior) so that he might write with greater competence the first chapter of his Letter to the Romans! The approval in question may mean that the certainty of faith's assent, of which Newman spoke so emphatically in his *Grammar*, is no longer an "in thing" at a university that prides itself as being "Catholic," while it replaces that label with "Jesuit," a procedure also in vogue in other institutions of higher learning run by the Society of Jesus in America.

What such "dialogues" cannot achieve, the keeping of the infallibly declared laws of the Church on the use of sex will do: Observance of those laws will give light to eyes confused by lurid billboards and TV screens, will refresh souls dumbed by soulless sex, will prove more valuable than anything that gold can buy, will taste far sweeter than honey, including sweethearts called "honey," who are readily discarded whenever a more delicious flavor comes along. These positive effects of the observance of those laws will be obtained because they protect the soul, when the sudden onrush of temptation leaves no room for the mind to make lengthy reflections on the long-term benefits of doing the right thing.

In the midst of a lawless society, including some ecclesial gatherings where the laws of God and the Church are taken lightly, no prayer can be more timely than the concluding verse of this psalm: "May the spoken words of my mouth, the thoughts of my heart, win favor in your sight, O Lord, my rescuer, my rock!"

Psalm 20

One can safely ascribe this psalm to David or to an inspired scribe in his entourage. All faithful Israelites knew that they needed God's help, and that this was true especially of the king ready to lead the nation into battle. One wonders whether this

psalm was recited as King Josiah was pushed into the fateful
battle at Megiddo, of which one has an epic account in *Hearken
to the Word*, Werfel's biography of Jeremiah. The Book of Kings,
but especially the writings of Jeremiah, are a proof that the chief
instigators of an armed resistance against Pharaoh Necho had put
their chief trust in chariots and horses.

The Papal States and their battalions are now a thing of a
distant past. Yet long before their demise it was clear that the
pope's spiritual power (think of Pius VII) had a strength of its
own which armies (think of Napoleon) could not match. Weapons of spiritual kind must always be on hand because all
confrontations have spiritual dimensions to them. The dictum,
diplomacy is the continuation of war by other means, has
revealed an unexpected twist indicative of this. Diplomats of
democracy are all too often willing agents of a culture war
waged against Christian morals and they do this in the name of
human rights. To cope with such dimensions one needs the kind
of spiritual weapon known as prayer. The latter makes sense
only if one trusts in God much more than in any other means at
one's disposal. Let the recitation of this psalm be a prayer that
the Pope and his closest advisors never trust more in diplomacy
than in God's assistance. And in praying for the Pope, may we
never forget our own need of this psalm's warning as we face our
own battles of much smaller proportions.

Psalm 21

This is another psalm that one may safely ascribe to David who
in the preceding psalm prayed for God's help before battle and
here gives thanks for the help received. The imagery and the
context perfectly reflect Israel's most successful warrior king.
David may have been mistaken in seeing his great conquests as
an immediate pledge of a kingdom to be established forever. One
wonders what was in his mind as he spoke of his remaining in
God's presence forever. From the perspective of the New
Testament, which emphatically proclaims the onset of eternal life
after bodily death, assertions such as the one in this psalm, of an
unlimited future to be spent in the presence of God are covert

expressions of belief in the soul's immortality. This is our chief way of sharing in the eternal Kingdom of God.

It is therefore more than justified to see in this psalm a messianic psalm, a celebration of Christ the King, who declared himself to be a King and who was thus celebrated by Saint Paul (1 Tim 6:15) and even more emphatically in the Book of Revelation. It was no accident that devotion to Christ the King came into sharp focus in this apocalyptic century of ours. The Feast of Christ the King did not become one of the feasts demoted by the New Liturgy, which, on the contrary, turned that Feast into the crowning event of the Liturgical Year. The celestial liturgy, which has its beginning down here, has Christ the King in its eternal focus.

Psalm 22

Behind the lines of this psalm one should see Jeremiah's handwriting and between the lines his much tried heart beating. Of all the prophets none is so much a forerunner of the One to come as Jeremiah, the son of the priest Hilkiah, from Anatoth, a village of an hour's walk to the northeast of Jerusalem. As a child he could not foresee the dramatic and humanly tragic role assigned to him. Later it dawned on him that he was chosen for that role while he was still "in the womb." This expression, so unmistakably the signature of Jeremiah, marks in the variant "from the womb" also Psalm 70, another and equally messianic psalm.

Jeremiah suffered a great deal, but none of his trials (registered in his own writings, in the Book of Kings, and in the Rabbinical tradition) suggests that he was ever literally laid in the dust of death, that his bones stuck out so much from his emaciated body as to be easily counted, and that he was given vinegar to drink. In this psalm painful reminiscences and prophetic foresight mix with free abandon. It took a medical analysis of the physiology of crucifixion to see the full meaning of the phrase about one's heart becoming like wax, about one's throat becoming parched like "burnt clay." The prophet must have seen with his mind's eyes someone being laid in the dust and his robe being disposed of by lot. Other innocent victims could be seen as surrounded by scoffers, but all these details could hardly be seen together before they merged into one single reality on Good Friday. Even on strictly literary grounds quite right should seem the decision of the fifth Ecumenical Council in 553 where Theodore of Mopsuestia was condemned for his claim that Christ cannot be included in the literal sense of this psalm.

Prophetic, that is, humanly unforeseeable (and certainly not within purely Jewish perspectives) was also the prospect that after all this the victim would sit down at a banquet table with his children in a joyful celebration. That in spite of everything the last word will be joy is, of course, incomprehensible in a culture which confuses joy with a smile enhanced by gleaming rows of teeth. A stark contrast with that joy that filled Peter and the rest for having been found worthy of being flogged at the order of the Sanhedrin. Paul, who could list a long array of occasions when he was tormented for Christ's sake, wanted to boast in no one except in Jesus the crucified and considered everything mere dross in comparison with the joy he had in Him.

Jeremiah, who at divine command chose to remain single, could not foresee himself at the head of an ordinary family banquet. But the One whom Jeremiah prophesied about and who had children only in a purely spiritual sense (Heb 2:14-17) repeatedly described the life to come as a banquet, which is hinted at in the verse about "the poor who shall eat and have their fill." When in performing the Last Supper, Christ anticipated sacramentally the total giving of His body, He promised those around the table that when the next time He would eat and drink with them, it would be in the Kingdom of God. That it was a spiritual kingdom was amply signified by the mysterious qualities of His risen body, so tangibly real and so elusively intangible at the same time. That Kingdom is a Kingdom of unalloyed joy, a pure bliss, of which two disciples had a foretaste at Emmaus as He broke bread with them.

Only the prospect of that bliss could satisfy the good thief, the fortunate recipient of the supreme promise: "Today [yes in this very day of this horrid agony] you will be with me in Paradise." The latter is no longer a luxurious garden where plants sprout and wither, but a state of eternal Life and Joy.

Psalm 23

The verse, "Should I walk in the valley of darkness, I will not fear because even there you are with me with your rod and staff," were perhaps most genuinely used when the Poverello chanted them as he crossed, in the summer of 1219, from the crusaders' camp into the camp of Sultan Malek el-Khamil. Sincerity rings through Bergson's statement that from his reading of hundreds of books he had not derived so much light and comfort as he did from that same verse.

Great reservations are called for when one thinks of Kant who spoke of that verse as the most comforting passage in the Bible. Anyone familiar with the gist of Kant's straitjacketing "religion within the limits of reason" would be wary to read real religion into his words. Religion is a re-tying (re-ligare) of man with God but not with that God whom Kant tried to bring in through the dubious backdoor of his *Critique of Practical Reason*. Kant's last great manuscript contained repeatedly the phrase "Ich bin Gott" ("I am God") which has a very modern ring for those who create God to their own image. They make themselves God in the process and want to shepherd everyone else through valleys of intellectual darkness of their making, which they call "enlightenment."

We should not be overawed by the remark that this psalm is so popular in Scotland as to qualify as its "national anthem." But one can recall only with awe the story which I heard with my own ears on a windy mid-morning at a main thoroughfare in Saint Andrews, Scotland. I stopped on seeing a handful of people standing around a revival preacher. What he just said on the top of his voice, I still hear in my ears: "A little Scottish lad was found, frozen to death, under the snow. Some frozen lambs lay around him. They all were caught in a snowstorm. For a while nobody could figure out why the lad's right hand was holding fast to the little finger on his left hand. Then somebody heard his own little boy recite this psalm. As he went from word to word in reciting the line, 'The Lord is my shepherd,' a total of five words, with his right hand he grasped first his left thumb than the left index finger and so on until he reached his little finger. Then he started all over again, as he came to the next line:

'There's nothing I shall want.' Then all became clear," the preacher added. "As the little lad began to freeze, he remembered the words 'The Lord is my shepherd'. Jesus, the great shepherd of souls, then carried the little shepherd to pastures that shall forever remain green and warm under the light of the Eternal Sun." Standing on that street corner and buffeted by the wind blowing from the North Sea, one could not help feel some inner warmth run through one's chilled body.

Compare with this the blasphemous defiance of that drug addict who wrote: "The heroine is my shepherd, there is nothing I shall want. He lays me to rest by the brooks, he leads to sweet insanity, and destroys my soul. He leads me along the road to hell for the love of its name. Even if I walked in the valley of the shadow of death, I would fear no evil, because the drug is with me. My syringe and my needle bring me comfort." But perhaps even more important to note is the innocent looking antecedent of this disaster: "The Lord is my external-integral integrative mechanism. I shall not be deprived of gratifications for my viscerogenic hunger or my need dispositions. He motivates to orient myself toward a non-social object with effective significance. He positions me in a non-decisional situation. He maximizes my adjustment." The passage is an antecedent because some time before drug addicts roamed around, the academe celebrated hollow sophistications and misplaced categories as signs of superior insights. Once more it became true that those who rejected God's word would be deprived even of the sane use of purely human words. Truly there is need for a Good Shepherd who is ready to go into the wilderness after the lost sheep, including their professorial kind. Let the praying of this psalm turn us into His unstinting teaching assistants.

Psalm 24

This is one of the few psalms that may have been generated by some Temple function. The psalm could have been an exhortation by the priests to those ready to enter the Temple precincts to pray to the One who is above all the Lord of all. The priests reminded the would-be worshipers of some moral conditions needed by those who want their prayers to be heard.

It is not so easy to imagine the liturgical circumstances of the second part of the psalm as it does not refer to the entry of worshipers but to the Lord's passing through the Temple's gates. Possibly the psalm is a combination of two different songs, originally independent of one another.

As the psalm now stands in a total separation from Temple functions, nothing can distract from the nature of its second verse, which speaks of the earth as being firmly set on the sea. The statement is a piece of the Hebrew world picture: a cosmic tent erected on a flat earth which, though it floats on the seas, does not wobble. Beneath such a primitive view there lies, however, a profound perception independent of the details of any world picture, however scientific. The classic setting forth of that perception in the Bible is Genesis 1. Its author listed the main parts of that cosmic tent to convey that God, whom he set up as the model of observing the sabbath rest, took His rest only after the making of *all*, the greatest conceivable work.

Such is, of course, a spiritual approach to the Maker of the Universe, an approach embodied in this psalm, whose author goes from the universe to the Lord's Holy place, though with a warning about the moral prerequisites for doing so. In these times when the stock market feeds on man's desires of "worthless things" and prompts man to soil his hands with unethical deals, this psalm should seem to be more timely than ever.

On the onset of the year 2000, when all Catholic churches and institutions display the banner, "Open your life to Christ," nothing would be a better response than to say "yes" again and again as one recites the second half of this psalm: "O gates lift high your heads; grow higher ancient doors. Let him enter, the King of glory." Compared with this opening up in full the recesses of our mind and heart to Christ, it is utterly irrelevant to speculate, as many commentators do, whether this psalm is really a trace of an annual feast called the feast of Yahweh's enthronement of which the Bible knows nothing and the Rabbinical tradition is entirely silent. On seeing that some scholars still write books and learned articles on that "feast" one can merely sigh, "Some feast, some scholarship."

Psalm 25

Being an alphabetical psalm, it is a fragrant bouquet that does not call for a systematic approach to it. One should enjoy each verse of it in the manner of bees tasting one flower after another. But no one who grew up with the words and melodies of the Tridentine Liturgy, can fail to think of Advent as one begins to recite this psalm. Its first verse, beginning in the Vulgate's rendering as "Ad te levavi animam meam . . ." served as the Introit of the Mass for the First Sunday in Advent. Few things make one more nostalgic than memories of long-gone Christmas Days toward which the misty days of Advent move, at times very slowly indeed.

Nostalgia then brings back one's past in more than one way. Various phases of the path of one's past begin to drift into the focus of memory. Some of those phases will stand out with a sharpness that cut deep into one's heart. Still the word, "path," four times repeated in this psalm, deserves special attention. It should remind one of one's course of life and of the many smaller and longer paths in it: some going forward, some sideways, some in circles, and some backward, perhaps at times precipitously in reverse. And if some of the picture is very dark, there is all the more reason to say in the words of the old Introit, which comes to a close with the words "non erubescam." They mean more than just not being disappointed. They mean trust even if one's face is covered with the blush of shame.

Psalm 26

The old saying, *quotidiana vilescunt*, may come to mind to any priest, now fifty or older, if he muses about his having started saying Mass in Latin. This psalm, because the priest recited it while he washed his hands after the Offertory, became therefore known as the *Lavabo*. And since often repeated prayers are bound to be recited at an ever speedier rate, lay people can also muse about their vain effort to keep pace with the priest.

About the purity of soul proclaimed (and demanded) by the recitation of the *Lavabo*, Thomas Aquinas elaborated on a remark of Dionysius: The priest needs to wet only his fingertips because he should begin the celebration of the Mass with nothing more than mere peccadillos on his conscience.

May no priest ever have to accuse himself of anything more as he acts more really than in any other of his functions in the person of Christ, that is, when he makes Christ's supreme sacrifice once more present on the altar. But we know only too well the extent to which we would like to exclaim with Peter: "Depart from me Lord, because I am a sinful man!" Or we may further insist with the impetuous Peter: "Lord, wash not only my feet but also my hands and my head!"

One has to have the sensitivity of a true saint to be taken aback by the self-confidence of the psalmist. Of course, since he, an inspired author, could not lie, he must have been a saint. But even if we cannot live up to the psalmist's firm confidence that the Lord may indeed "test his heart and mind," we should at least be able to say that we were not in cahoots with liars and hypocrites; that we did not seek the evil-doers' company; that we did not align ourselves with bloodthirsty men going around with profuse references to the innocence of nature; that we did not sit down with those whose right hands are filled with gold. Such handouts, let it be noted, are to be repaid at compound interest.

Far more difficult it is to implement with the psalmist the resolve that one should avoid the company of liars and hypocrites. Are we not all one of them, even if not systematically and professionally so? And what about the pharisees? Some verses of this psalm, such as "I have not wavered," could easily flatter them, but some other verses, such as "I trust in the Lord," could hardly comfort their brazen self-confidence.

This is a psalm that sorely tests one's mind and heart, and especially of those who love churches and chapels where the Lord's glory dwells bodily. Since we must be resolved to "walk the path of perfection," let us, after each verse, cry out, "Redeem me and show me your mercy!", as if this were the psalm's anti-

phon. Then with trembling and fear we may continue: "My foot
stands on level ground, I bless the Lord in the assembly."

Psalm 27

Not so much a commentary is needed for a real grasp and
appreciation of this psalm as the experience of having gone
through situations to which brief references are made in it. For
anyone who lived his life in safety and comfort this psalm largely
remains a closed book. This is also true of those whose mind is
locked in thinking about comfort and ever novel amenities.

Even if one has not had the experience of being approached
by someone ready to devour one's flesh, even if one did not find
himself threatened by a hostile army camped all around, even if
one has not found himself on the brink of being ambushed, even
if one has not lived through the outbreak of a war—one may try
to picture oneself in at least one such dire situation. It may to be
too much to ask that one should try to relive all four of them,
briefly referred to in this psalm.

To suggest that one should see movies like "Titanic" and
"Jurassic Park" may be counterproductive. A very few people
cannot endure such movies without being utterly drained as they
are unable to forget that what they see is no deeper in reality
than the screen itself. Most moviegoers have grown so blasé
about hair curling situations that they need not care about
grasping this psalm. It is neither for the faint-hearted nor for the
hopelessly insensitive.

But much benefit can still be derived from praying this
psalm (not merely reciting it) if one is ready to savor some lines
of it. All psalms contain one or several lines that can be savored at
length. One such line in this psalm explains why the psalmist,
most likely David himself, would like to live in the house of the
Lord all the day of his life. The reason: to savor the sweetness of
the Lord.

The place where the House, or rather the Tent of the Lord
stood, was a notable stronghold. David could not forget that it
took special effort on his part to conquer it. But in addition to its
strategic position, that spot stood for a far superior strength,

which derived from the special presence of the Lord, the Lord of hosts. It is well to recall from Josephus' *Jewish Wars* that even when Titus' soldiers were literally at arm's length from the Holy of Holies and resistance to the Romans appeared utterly senseless, there were still some Jews who held that the Temple was unconquerable precisely because of that presence.

David longed to be near the Lord's Tent, because he wanted to "see the face of the Lord." For someone, like David, or other Jews, for whom it was a supreme blasphemy to draw or sculpt the face of the Lord, such a longing for the divine face could only be a spiritual act. The words, "God is spirit and those who want to worship Him must do so in spirit and truth," come to mind.

For David the seeing the face of the Lord was an assurance of being protected by Him. Dangers could mean that the Lord turned His face away, the worst thing David could think of. We may not do any better than nurture this thought as we *pray* this psalm and do so facing the Lord's tent called "tabernacle" and savor the Lord's real presence and find protection in Him.

Psalm 28

This psalm also has David's signature on it, though not so much of David the mystic as David the warrior who faces dire threats. No king of Israel was so much a warrior as David was, and no other king of Israel came from the lowly rank of shepherds, who even much later were the epitome of backwardness in Jewish eyes. The psalm's concluding prayer, "be their shepherd and carry them forever," could naturally be born on the lips of one who himself must have carried more than one lamb on his shoulders or in his arms. David also emerges as the psalmist asks God's blessing on "his anointed." Anyone who, like this psalmist, is ready to give thanks to the Lord and have his heart rejoice in Him, can safely ask for further blessing from the Good Shepherd, who went after the lost sheep and carried it in His arms.

The reference to those who "plan evil in their heart but speak peace to their neighbor" has received in our times just too many illustrations to need elaboration. They also bring out the truth of the verse: "They ignore the deeds of the Lord and the work of his hands." More than a generation has now gone by since Pope John XXIII surprised the world, frozen with fear into the coldest of all cold wars, by issuing his encyclical *Pacem in terris*. Since then the world has seen more wars than for centuries before. The most outstanding deeds of the Lord, of His salvation history, are systematically discounted by the learned of the world. As to the works of His hands, man and the universe, they are spoken of as random events.

The old truths stated in this psalm, which belongs undoubtedly among the oldest psalms, should seem worth pondering in their undying timeliness.

Psalm 29

In reflecting on this psalm the old saying comes to mind: those who want to learn to pray should embark on a stormy sea. The psalm gives us the prayer which was inspired by the passing of a heavy storm over Jerusalem. One need not picture the people thoroughly drenched, although some may have relished such a rare event in the middle of the hot season. But it was no fun to see lightning strike and hear thunderbolts shake the air. At times fatalities must have occurred as no one knew that lightning was attracted by tall objects, such as the Temple's cornices and the towers of its walls. Even Benjamin Franklin was surprised that the kite which he let fly into a thunderclap, almost proved to be his undoing.

Now that we know why lightning hits tall objects pointing sharply upward, why mountains tremble, why volcanos erupt, we no longer need to turn our thoughts to God out of ignorance. Still whatever our modern defenses against the forces of nature, these (suffice it to think of tornados and earthquakes) should be especially useful to remind us of life's fragility on this earth. Life is no less fragile today than in the times of the psalmist whose vistas were limited by the cedars of Lebanon and the wilderness of Kadesh, the point from which Moses sent scouts to the Promised Land to gather information about it. Danger or not, there remain plenty of lasting pointers in this world to prompt us to say on the top of our voice: "Glory, glory—to God in the highest." Then men of good will may even have Peace, which they seek by belligerent means and mostly in vain.

As to those who take their lukewarmness in matters religious for enlightened moderation, they should recall that the first of the two great Commandments is to love God with all our heart, with all our strength. They should take care not to fall behind those who keep shouting from the depths of their heart: Glory!

Psalm 30

This psalm is obviously a thanksgiving for recovery from grave sickness. Otherwise, its author would not voice his gratitude that God "raised his soul from the dead" and restored him to life by separating him, for the time being, "from those who sink into the grave." The soul, of course, means here not so much a strictly immortal entity as the totality of life in man. Similarly total is the psalmist's reaction to his transition from sickness to health. In sickness he is caught in utter despondency, symbolized by wearing sackcloth, typical of mourners. As he regains his health, he sings and dances with free abandon.

The reference to dancing strongly suggests David, who danced with no restraint as the Ark of the Covenant was carried to his city. The Davidic authorship is further indicated by the psalm's exuberant tone.

The psalmist's cure is experienced with the coming of the dawn, which is often the case with recovery. Fever usually rises as evening comes and a good night's sleep often brings a drop in one's temperature. Keeping this in mind is part of natural wisdom which should be resorted to all the more so as God usually works through natural means.

It is imperfectly supernatural to take sickness for a sign of God's anger, instead of taking it also for a token of God's favor as a means whereby one gains a closer union with God. This reflects a New Testament mentality, of which there is little anticipation in this psalm.

People of both Dispensations are, of course, subject to the illusion of overconfidence which health (and prosperity) often generate. When everything goes smoothly, one is apt to think, as the psalmist does, that "nothing would ever disturb" one's tranquillity. Expectations of this type can prove illusory at a moment's notice.

Even if one acknowledges that health and prosperity are God's favor as if He had placed us on a "mountain fastness" impregnable to adversity, we are not allowed to assume that such a state will last forever and possibly not even for too long. Also, while one can safely hold that God rejoices in one's health, a point aptly made by the psalmist, one has to go well beyond the perspectives of this psalm to see that sickness and death faced with full trust in God bring Him as much glory and at times much more.

Psalm 31

This psalm derives its fame from a line in it which Jesus himself uttered on the cross: "Into your hands I commend my spirit." But the author of this psalm, most likely Jeremiah, did not exactly mean the same. Jesus knew He would die, whereas the psalmist commends himself to God so that he would be rescued quickly from a precarious situation.

The situation of the psalmist does not closely resemble that of Jesus on the cross. Unlike Jesus, who was literally surrounded by a jeering crowd, the psalmist merely states that he heard of a hostile crowd's slander. It is not so much the enemy itself that engulfs him as his fear of the enemy.

In fact the psalmist states that God has already removed him at a safe distance from his enemies by "setting his feet at large", though he is still the target of their hostility. Jeremiah certainly could present his life as a "life spent in sorrow and sighs," and speak of his bones as "wasting away." The old Jeremiah could rightly say that he was largely abandoned, that he was avoided, that he was treated as "being dead, forgotten in men's hearts, like a thing thrown away."

In a manner strongly evoking Jeremiah the psalmist speaks of his enemies as the wicked to be put to shame by God. His characterization of the wicked "who speak haughtily against the just with pride and contempt" has a very modern ring to it.

Trust in God may provide one with the feeling that one is in the shelter of God's presence, where one is protected from plotting tongues. Yet this trust cannot necessarily issue in a deliverance from one's enemies. Contrary to the psalmist's tacit expectation, the just may never see that his enemies, "who act with pride," are indeed repaid by God "to the full." But regardless of the outcome in this life, one can take for a safe guideline the closing verse of the psalm: "Be strong, let your heart take courage, all who hope in the Lord." Only this kind of hope deserves to be spoken of as the hope that "springs eternal" and therefore is a truly Christian hope.

Psalm 32

Long before the cultivation of psychology began to turn into a cult of it, insights into the deepest recesses of the soul had been clearly glimpsed. Psychology, distrustful of religion, had then to discover anew those insights and fumble with them.

Repression of one's sense of guilt is a case in point. Its psychological effects are described in uncanny accuracy in this psalm: "I kept it secret and my frame was wasted." One, of course, has to live in a hot and arid climate to appreciate the telling force of the observation that almost immediately follows: "Indeed, my strength was dried up as by the summer's heat."

Relief from all this came with the admission that one was indeed guilty. After holding out for long in his presumed innocence, the psalmist came to realize that there would not be a way out of the anxiety that consumed him, unless he confessed his offence to the Lord.

By admitting his sin and confessing it the psalmist found deliverance. He suddenly felt as if deadly floods had receded from him. He found a new hiding place, God himself.

For it was God himself to whom he confessed. He certainly did not hold God to be a product of his own mental powers and suppressed desires. Modern man, who turned his back to the idea that he was shaped by God in His very image, has no choice but to think that God is the product of man's own imagination. Hence the confessional has been replaced by the couch.

About the latter as a piece of furniture, one can certainly say that it is far more expensive than a kneeler in the confessional. Whereas the use of the couch costs the earth, the confessional is available for the mere asking. In this latter remark there is, of course, an irony which is not at all unintended. In some progressive parishes, confessions are available only by appointment. Their progressivism fails to include the old truth, prominently rediscovered by R. Coles, the Harvard psychologist, whose course "Guilt 101" proved to be a runaway success among the Crimson. One may presume that in flocking to that course a few of the "ten thousand men of Harvard" blush now and then.

But even in parishes where regular hours are still set aside, though hardly generously and conveniently, for confessions, the number of those who take advantage of them has fallen sharply during the last decades. It is not an exaggeration to say that belief in the sacrament of confession is being abandoned (a form of denial) by the practice of not using it.

This is to be kept in mind if one is to see the awesome timeliness of the concluding instructions of this psalm. The psalmist could very well think of his own former reluctance to confess as he urges others: "Be not like horse and mule, unintelligent, needing bridle and bit, else they will not approach you." For as long as they do so, they will be like the wicked who indeed "has many sorrows." In times that are caught in mad and vain pursuit of joy, the best thing is, like in many other contexts, to see clearly the first step to be taken before one engages in the pursuit of whatever. With respect to joy, sadness is the first thing to face up to.

But the sadness ought to be seen for what it truly is. Man is sad not because he lacks this or that, but because he lacks that ultimate good and goal which is best called God. Only when man sees this will he go to the bottom of his problems where he finds God as the ultimate. Then, and only then, he can say goodby to sadness. If the once famous book *Bonjour tristesse* by Françoise Sagan fell into oblivion, it was precisely because she, as so many others, tried to cope with sadness by eliminating God from the equation. They merely found that "many sorrows has the wicked" and failed to experience that "he who trusts in the

Lord, loving mercy surrounds him." Last but not least, only such a soul will keep exclaiming, with no false pretense of having found joy: "Rejoice, rejoice in the Lord." Preliminary to this is that one confesses and receives absolution. One thereby acquires the state of grace, which alone justifies that one should call on any and all: "O come, ring out your joy, all you upright of heart."

Psalm 33

This hymn of thanksgiving has a structure, or a train of thought, which should be worth noting. The thought or the principal theme is, of course, the trustworthiness of God's work, the chief reason for which man should be thankful to Him. Of the two main classes of God's work the one which is considered first is his work of creation. More than any other psalm that has the created world for its theme, or at least a part of it, this psalm praises the trustworthiness of that creation not so much from the viewpoint of its benefits for man, but from the perspective of the superior ease with which God produces things, indeed all things.

That ease comes very close to the idea of creation out of nothing in the verse: "He spoke and it came to be. He commanded and it came into being." Unlike in Genesis 1 where God begins with a *tohu v bohu*, there is not the slightest hint here that God merely shaped a nondescript material already on hand. Nor is there any hint of any science whatsoever. The psalm does not refer to some physical factor, such as a spherical bowl, that would keep the waters of the ocean together. God himself stores up, He himself "collects the waves of the ocean." But, again, there is no hint either of a special act on God's part as different from his primordial act of creation. Creation and conservation form a unit, though not a confused one.

The chief concern of the psalm is, of course, to stir up thankfulness for God's actions among men. Those actions have a specific design, a purpose that stands forever: "The plans of his heart endure from age to age." Within the Hebrew perception the heart not only performed emotive actions, as it does in modern perception, but also the action which we moderns ascribe to the brain.

Further, God is always present. He closely watches all human actions. In a charmingly anthropomorphic way God is described as one who "gazes on all the dwellers of the earth." This statement about God knowing all is not surprising, nor the fact that He considers the deeds of all. But immediately preceding this is the phrase about God as one "who shapes the heart of them all." The phrase is a generalized form of the specific declaration in Exodus that God hardened the heart of the Pharaoh into obduracy against the evidence.

Both the specific and generic statements reflected sound theological logic. Insofar as a human action is a reality, it can exist only as something which God himself caused "to come to be." No determinism is suggested thereby. Theology as a good science is both inductive and deductive. Here, too, the starting points are plain data, the immediate, obvious evidence about man's ability to act freely. One cannot even try to deny meaningfully this ability, unless one does it freely. It is equally obvious, though in a deductive way, that no reality, be it a free human act, can exist unless God, the supreme reality, gave it existence. One is faced here not with a contradiction, but with the mutual irreducibility of two equally sane lines of reasoning. Chafe as we may, we cannot get away from this irreducibility. We, of course, can unnecessarily mystify it by calling it "mystery."

It is not in reference to this irreducibility that the Bible, the New Testament in particular, speaks of "mystery." The Bible endorses both the freedom of human actions and the total sovereignty of God over all existents, of which free human acts form a most noble class. The latter received a pregnant expression through Saint Augustine, the Doctor of grace, who said that "we are nothing without our freedom."

Nothing would therefore be less biblical than to feel anxiety over the fact that God indeed "shapes the hearts of them all," including those who sing the psalms. We should sing them freely and with full trust. We should sing them all the time with a freshly renewed resolve that should make for a "new song." We should play them loudly with all our skill. Anxiety should arise in our soul only if we trust our own power, "our horses and chariots," rather than the Lord's Holy Name.

Psalm 34

In this age which resounds with the noise and publicity of all sorts of rescue operations, this psalm may appear very timely. It may indeed be taken for "a call to God the rescuer." The "poor man" of this psalm may be anyone of us. And anyone can walk with a radiant face on considering the many ways God has rescued one "from all his distress," an expression which may stand for one major distress. At any rate, neither this psalm nor any other psalm is a divine pledge of a Utopia on earth even if it reads as such on a superficial look.

This is the point to keep in mind as we ponder the promise of the psalm that "those who revere God will lack no blessing." They can count on plenty of blessings, among them, persecutions and adversities. Insofar as it related to a spiritual enlightenment, the verse, "Look towards Him and be radiant; let your faces not be abashed," received a special touch in the Vulgate's Latin, "Accedite ad eum et illuminamini, et facies vestrae non confundantur," through the presence of the word *illuminatio*.

It was not the spurious light of private inspiration, let alone an advance mirage of the Enlightenment that prompted John Fisher to utter that verse when, as he mounted the scaffold, the sun blinded him briefly. It was rather his attachment to Christ, the Eternal Light who illumines the world through His Church, that prompted the martyr bishop of Rochester to act as a martyr, that is, a witness to Light. With that verse on his lips he climbed the remaining steps to the spot where his witness would kindle a light that would shine in the darkness of an England that for centuries tried to snuff it out but in vain.

This superior perspective should be kept in mind, lest this or that phrase in this psalm might give illusory hopes. Prosperity and length of days, or ripe old age, must not be construed as something that necessarily devolves on anyone who "keeps his tongue from evil, speaks no deceit, and strives after peace." Saint Benedict, who quoted with much emphasis these verses in his Rule, and right in its Prologue, knew that monasteries do not necessarily become oases of peace. He wrote a Rule for monasteries, because there, too, unruliness can raise its ugly head at a moment's notice, and therefore constraints are in order.

None of us shall necessarily live to the moment when the Lord "destroys all the remembrance of the wicked." That moment will come only with the cessation of all moments, with the end of that mysterious thing called time.

But we can trust that the Lord will find comfort (of His choice) for any of us whenever we find our spirit crushed. Meanwhile we shall see plenty of evidence of the claim of this psalm that those "who hate the good are doomed," and that "the Lord ransoms his servant." But this happens in His way and not in our ways. This is why the last line of this psalm, "those who hide in Him shall not be condemned," is applicable to the reception of the Eucharist, this most unique way of hiding which only God could think up. The phrase, "In thy wounds I fain would hide," in "Anima Christi," a prayer composed by Saint Ignatius and recited after communion, may very well have been suggested to him by his praying this psalm at least once a week. To communion he went daily for years before he was ordained a priest. Long before there were Jansenists frowning on daily communion, the sons of Loyola urged that holy practice.

According to that gem of patristic literature, the *Catechetical Instructions* of Saint Cyril of Jerusalem, this psalm was sung as the Body and Blood of Christ was distributed during the Eucharistic celebration. Saint Jerome referred to that last line as he encouraged Lucinius, a wealthy Christian from the Iberian peninsula, to go with confidence to the Lord's table every day as was the custom in Rome.

Psalm 35

As one reads this psalm one can hear once more Jeremiah's voice. Indeed, one would do best to shout each line of this psalm in order to have one's soul reverberate with all the vigor of what may best be called Jeremiah's spirituality. In facing his elemental longing for justice, we should not, of course, follow him in his request that the wicked be "like chaff before the wind," that they be "scattered by the Lord's angel," that "their path become slippery and dark," that "ruin may fall upon them," that "they should fall into the pit they had hidden."

Again, we must not be carried away by the psalmist's wish that God may put on his armor, "his buckler and shield," and grab his "javelin and spear." In imagining such postures on God's part the psalmist was as imperfect as we would be by thinking of Him as busy launching cruise missiles, or piloting stealth bombers, or dropping graphite bombs.

But whenever we are betrayed, when "lying witnesses arise against us," when we are "accused unjustly," we may certainly voice our confidence in God with Jeremiah's vehemence: "Lord who is like you who rescue the weak from the strong and the poor from the oppressor?" This happened all too often in history. Yet, God does not necessarily listen to those who clamor: "Why not victory?" However, He will not let the wicked ever achieve universal domination.

Our joy may safely be in the Lord, if we can sincerely say that we kept praying for those who turned against us as if they were our brothers. The psalmist in fact attended them when they were sick and felt so sorry for them as if he were mourning his own mother. Jeremiah seems, however, to be more intent on seeing them punished.

One should, of course, sympathize with Jeremiah. Lying witnesses arose against him, they thought that they had made their charges stick and rejoiced at his misfortune, indeed at the prospect of seeing his very end. Such is hardly a situation easy to bear. Only saints can really cope with it. Their privilege is that peace of which the psalmist says that God himself takes special delight in noticing it.

Psalm 36

This psalm is a gripping study of a stark contrast: the cunning of the wicked and God's protection of the just. What modern historiography has documented in great detail about the thoughts and plans of some notoriously wicked figures, is summed up in the first part of this psalm in a few brief lines that can hardly be improved upon. Being caught in the vicious logic of sin, the wicked lose wisdom to the extent of no longer having a distinct sense of guilt. The state of mind of the wicked becomes *Darkness at Noon*, to recall a now largely forgotten portrayal of some professional plotters of evil who wanted to achieve universal peace by fomenting universal class warfare. Their hopelessly entangled state of mind is unfathomable to those who refuse to see even the most grievous crimes as an offense to God. In vain they probe the abysmal depths of Hitler's thinking in terms of a psychology and sociology that have no room for true equality among men, which is on hand only if all men are created in the image of God. This inability is germane to the perspective of those who take the psalms for their "national" inheritance, though do not want to inherit the faith of the psalms.

This faith reaches almost mystical heights in the second part of this psalm. Many a Christian mystic found a vehicle to the highest levels of union with God in the verse: "They feast on the riches of your house, they drink from the stream of your delight." Some of the most elevated utterances of Saint John the Evangelist seem to be anticipated in the verse: "In you is the source of light, and in your light we see light." Also some texts of Saint John of the Cross should come to mind.

Most of us can admire those spiritual heights only from a great distance. But we all should find expressive the description of God's love and truth as both reaching to the heaven, that is, being beyond measure. In the same mystical perspective God's protective love appears in the metaphorical guise of some mysterious wings hovering over us. Jesus' fondness for this image came through when He spoke of His effort to gather all God's people as the mother hen gathers her brood.

We may pray without any reservation that God may keep loving those who know Him and that we may not be "crushed under the foot of the proud." We may even register the fact that evil doers do indeed fall, but we must not take the line, "flung down they shall never arise," to mean that still another wave of the wicked would never again raise its threatening crest.

Psalm 37

This psalm may be said to describe itself in that line where it speaks of the mouth of the just that "murmurs wisdom." It may not be unjust to picture the wise man who is muttering to himself. Wisdom cannot be shouted at the top of one's voice. In fact, all too often one can preach it only to oneself. It can hardly be taught, and all too often one learns it only at one's own painful expense. The memory of one's resistance to the wisdom of one's parents can cast painfully long shadows over one's life.

Wisdom is, of course, a many-splendored gem. A psalm, even if it is relatively long like this one, would become easily incoherent, if it tried to enumerate all those splendors. Just as it is self-defeating to gather all flowers into one bouquet, equally futile would be to disregard the particular shape of a vase the bouquet calls for. Since flowers are of many kinds, vases, too, have to be of many forms. And so it is with the manifestations of wisdom. No psalm that celebrates wisdom can list all of them.

The wisdom of this psalm is limited to a great insight which itself is very sharply defined. The psalmist tries to deal with the natural impatience felt over the ascendancy of evil people, about which one can justly remark: nothing is new under the sun. Newspapers devoted to reform have a section or two where those are glorified who keep deforming themselves and society, and provoke the kind of discontent which is the rumbling of revolutions in the making. Was the reckless burning of trailers at the conclusion of the latest Woodstock "festival" necessary to air other forms of reckless selfishness at such and similar celebrations of the "soul" of American youth captive to their bodies?

The desire naturally arising in the frustrated soul that people who take rank advantage of society be restrained, must not, however, turn into envy. This point is made by the psalmist right at the outset: "Do not fret because of the wicked, do not envy those who do evil."

Anyone who has not thrown to the wind a fair measure of sanity, can but fret on facing the delay of justice. But what antidote can the just find to their impatience with a state of affairs that ruggedly maintains itself? The psalmist describes that antidote as a patient waiting for the moment when the wicked's fortunes quickly come to an end. They fade quickly like grass, like the green of the fields, like the beauty of the meadows, so evident in Palestine (or even in California) as spring turns into summer. Then he refers to the sudden vanishing of smoke.

This idea of a quick end, by which the psalmist does not mean so much a short-term change as a sudden one, sums up the wisdom offered in this psalm. Indeed recent history provided some monumental examples of the sudden shift of fortunes. In the late 1980s it was still a widely received wisdom to think of the Soviet Union as a superpower to endure well into the 21st century. Gurus of political science, such as Kissinger and others, merchandised this view as the hallmark of sound prognostication. The downfall of the Evil Empire came with suddenness, although the process was hardly a fast one for those who had to live through long and tense months while the outcome was still in the balance.

But the psalmist has in mind no so much nations as individuals. Instances are a dime a dozen not only of the sudden downturn in the fortunes of the wicked but also of cases when the just experience a sudden turn for the better in their conditions. The latter case is compared by the psalmist to the sun's rays breaking through a cloudy sky. One may think of Newman's reaction to the official word from Rome that he would be created a Cardinal. He felt as if clouds of suspicion and distrust suddenly lifted from over him. Yet for months he had to live with a nagging uncertainty for which he could blame himself no less than he could blame Manning, already a Cardinal, who had some excuse in Newman's penchant for double negatives.

Most of the time "sudden" changes come at a snail's pace which may test all our reserves of patience. History, individual, social, and ecclesiastical, shows that the sudden shifts for the better are not universal shifts. Plenty of trouble remains. Old problems do not fail to reappear in new guise.

Some of the psalm's statements are outright exaggerations, but the kind which all of us are apt to make. We all have seen many a just man forsaken, and many children who, though they had upright parents, go "begging for bread." It is also a gross exaggeration to say, as the psalmist does, that the just shall inherit the land as far as the immediate sense of that statement goes. Even if the psalmist is not taken literally in reference to his promise that the just shall live "forever" on the land, we know only too well the shifting earthly fortunes of exemplary families.

Their list begins indeed with families that belonged to the "poor" or the ordinary, pious Israelites.

To sum up, the wisdom offered in this psalm should be greatly complemented by a wisdom which is not the wisdom of this world, but a wisdom which Paul set forth in his Letter to the Ephesians for the benefit of the new Israel. That superior wisdom is not merely a rebuke of the unwisdom of this world but also of the very narrow wisdom of this psalm and of the Old Covenant. Once on the lips of the Church, the melody of psalms have become very much transposed in order to serve spiritual needs that reach far beyond momentary needs even when moments are taken for a few years, or even for a full lifespan.

Psalm 38

As is the case with some other penitential psalms, this one, too, is long on details of physical pain and sickness, the presumed effects of sin, but very short on details of the sin itself. In fact the psalm leaves the nature of sin committed utterly unspecified. One can, of course, state in the psalmist's defense that at that time it was not possible to say that the transgression of a particular commandment could issue in a specific form of corporal aggravation.

It was only in modern times, from the discovery of America on, that one could see a direct connection between illicit sexual union and the contacting of, say, syphilis. There is no hint in the Book of Genesis that most of Lot's neighbors had ruined their bodies by their unnatural lust. The beginning of AIDS in humans may have been triggered by the eating of the flesh of a certain monkey in Africa. The timing of this with the coming into the open of gay people and the sudden spread of that disease among them will be seen as an act of God only by the believer whose sights enclose more than "random occurrences." Yet even the believer should pause, as undoubtedly a great many innocent people have also been victimized.

The symptoms of AIDS victims, who courted disaster and did so at times defiantly, may come to mind as one reads the verse: "All my frame burns with fever; all my body is sick." But one should rather think of the shining example set by the Cardinal Archbishop of New York who joins for half a day every week those who do volunteer work in hospital wings filled with AIDS patients—he carrying their bedpans. He certainly has some first-hand knowledge of how many of those AIDS victims, all of whom "are spent and utterly crushed," would "cry aloud" in the kind of "anguish of heart" that is indicative of true repentance. We know of the bitter anger which some of them felt about the one who, in exchange for their votes, promised crash programs of medical research to find a quick cure to that terrible disease. They obviously looked for that cure so that they might go on "safely" with their "alternate" lifestyle.

AIDS or not, this psalm should be a medicine against taking our sins lightly. Once we feel tortured on account of our sins, as the author of this psalm did, we may safely believe that we are on the road to genuine spiritual recovery.

Psalm 39

The task of commenting on the psalms imposes the duty of finding in them a touch of modernity, and expressing it with an appropriate turn of phrase. This psalm may indeed have been written with a view of those who leave no stone unturned in their resolve "to catch up with the Joneses." Once seen in this light, this psalm will appear timely forever. Only the "Joneses" will have to be identified differently, though always in such a way as to serve as perennial mirrors in which we can see our own hardly flattering moral physiognomy. We must not be so blind as to smooth out with pseudo-spiritual cosmetics the heavy lines drawn by the desire of the eyes and by the pride of life. Though we try not to be of this world, we all are in this world. But the deeper moral of this psalm lies not with greed that seems to tear anyone apart who tries to catch up with the Joneses but with the far from deep solution given by the psalm. The psalmist seems to accuse God for not seeing the obvious: the shortness of human life. He seems to want to remind God that even He can run out of time if He really wants to redress the balance between the haves and the have nots. Worse, the psalmist hardly appears to be one who is one of the have nots. His problem is that he does not have as much as some others, the Joneses, who, to wax modern again, are making a killing on the stock market, this latest version of the temple of Mammon.

The manner in which the psalmist portrays the short span of life, valid for the rich and the not so rich, is a literary gem. Verses 6-7 would have done credit to the greatest poets. Those verses are about the short span of one's life, which is but a passing shadow, the riches hoarded up are a mere breath, and, to make a bitter pill even more so, one cannot know who would ultimately have one's possessions of which nothing can be carried beyond the grave.

In order to resolve the problem on hand one may take the worldly wisdom which is to register with William Blake that we shall "never know what is enough, until we have more than enough." Unfortunately, few in the world would then start implementing the true reform which always begins at home. The world always wants to reform the otherworldly. Meanwhile the world keeps wasting the earth's rapidly dwindling energy resources. To crown the comedy, many of those who try to forestall this, turn for money to those who derive their fat profits from making more and more waste by flooding the market with ever new products many of which we don't really need.

The other and far better way is to let verse 12 remind us of the moth about which Jesus made a pointed remark. In the same breath He also referred to the remorseless corrosion effected by rust. Only if we take this in utter seriousness shall we have a cure against the desperate urge of "catching up with the Joneses" and against other urges that tear us apart. The cure takes more than what is offered by this psalm which does not help us see the incomparable riches waiting for us beyond the grave. Only the view of eternal life, stressed in the Gospels, can resolve the agony that prompted Augustine to conclude: "Restless is our soul until it finds its rest in you, O Lord." He meant, of course, the Lord of the eternal sabbath, who is Life itself, because, as Jesus said, God is not the God of the dead but the God of the living. The riches of that "living" are ours for the asking, which we, however, cannot do with the words of this psalm so restricted to

life on earth, unless we recite its verses as so many stark
contrasts to the Gospel's words of everlasting life.

Psalm 40

One's situation can be so grim as to allow only the thought:
when you are at the bottom, you can only go up. But when the
bottom is the floor of a deadly pit and the floor itself is a shifting
miry clay, such thought cannot give even the semblance of hope.
Although this psalm is in its title ascribed to David, it contains
phrases that are identical with some in Psalm 69 that clearly has
Jeremiah's signature on it.

Details about what happened to Jeremiah will be given in
connection with Psalm 69 which deals more of what he felt while
in that pit. Here in this psalm he mainly offers his profound
thanks to God who rescued him from there. Jeremiah's eventual
rescue is conveyed with his reference to his feet having been set
on a rock. He seems to have implied much more than that his
feet touched at long last a layer of rock beneath masses of miry
clay and sticky mud.

An experience like that of being lowered into a pit so that
one may slowly die there of hunger, never leaves one. But it takes
more than the usual measure of sensitivity to remember one's
gratitude which issued in a new song. Of ten lepers whom Jesus
cured only one returned to Him to give thanks. Jeremiah recalls
only the essentials of that new song, which may be one of the
deeply religious songs that did not become a psalm. He sang of
his joy for not having "gone over to the rebels, who follow false
gods." One need not think of idolatry. It is enough to recall that
the rebels were false prophets who precisely because they
resisted God's true prophet, rebelled against Yahweh Himself.
One can safely surmise that all such prophets eventually slid into
the worship of false gods. Slopes have no half-way houses.

His miraculous escape from the deadly pit appears to
Jeremiah as one of God's various wondrous designs. They appear
to him countless, which is indeed the case as long as one keeps
counting them. The phrase, "count your blessings," should be an
ongoing operation, partly because one can always find ever fresh

instances of them, and partly because one can grow utterly oblivious, and indeed insensible to them.

Gratitude for them constitutes a part of true worship. Another part is the resolve to obey God's will. Such resolve is the true sacrifice demanded by God, a sacrifice that one finds, so Jeremiah argues, set forth clearly in Holy Writ. No wonder that the supreme manifestation of that obedience by Jesus will be commended with a reference to the words in this psalm: "In the scroll it is written that I should do your will" (Hebr 10:5-7)

The scroll to which Jeremiah refers may be either the first Book of Samuel (15:22) or Isaiah (1: 10-20) where obedience to God's will is extolled as better than any other forms of sacrifice. But it is Jeremiah, more than other previous prophets, who insisted on the supreme value of an interiorized service of God. His own calling began with a response to God's voice: "Before I formed you in the womb I knew you" (Jer 1:5). The echo of that voice in his ears helped Jeremiah confront the great assembly, the political and religious leaders, a task hardly comfortable. Humanly speaking it would have been easier for Jeremiah if he had hidden, if he had kept to himself, what God had told him.

Such are the reminiscences of a prophet now grown old, who once more finds himself buffeted right and left. On seeing the great number of his mishaps he thinks that they indicate many sins committed by him. They appear to him as numerous as the hairs on his head. Elevated as Jeremiah's spirituality is, he is unable to see that suffering is not necessarily caused by one's own sins. The notion that one may suffer for others' sins is not within Jeremiah's ken. Herein lies the great imperfection of this psalm, which it shares with much of the Old Testament. The suffering Servant of Yahweh, as described, and rather mysteriously, in Deutero-Isaiah, does not find a further elaboration in Jeremiah. Or rather, he does not anticipate it because that description quite possibly postdated his ministry.

In praying this psalm, let us imitate Jeremiah's undaunted trust that past favors of God should strengthen our hope that He would once more come to our rescue. And as we look forward to that moment of great rejoicing, let us repeat with him, with an eye on our own wretched predicament: "O God, do not delay."

This we should do even when we find God delayed to no end. Whatever dark phases are contained in His plans about us, our motto should remain: "Dum spiro spero."

Psalm 41

Once more Jeremiah speaks. This time we find him a sick man, confined to bed. Once more he attributes his suffering to sins committed by him, which he does not specify, perhaps because they were hardly proportionate to his suffering. The inability of the Old Testament to solve the problem of the suffering of the innocent once more stares us in the face.

Jeremiah's particular complaint is about having been betrayed. The traitor was his best friend, who shared his table with him, who broke bread with him. Jeremiah's hope for a solution is once more a mixture of a vaguely perceived ideal and of a far from ideal expectation that God would punish in full the one who betrayed him. It is difficult to specify what was exactly in Jeremiah's mind as he voiced his hope that God would put him in His presence ever-more. He clearly could not expect to live forever. Was he thinking of life after death?

For us Christians, who look at bodily death as the very beginning of eternal life in God's very presence, a life of beatific vision, the recitation of this psalm should be of great moment. It should stir up our sentiment of gratitude for the enormously great gift which this faith of ours secures for us.

Christians know that this gift comes to them through Jesus' redeeming death and His rising from the dead, events triggered by a betrayal. Christian commentaries on the psalms have not failed to point out that Jeremiah's reference to his own traitor prophetically anticipated what happened at the Last Supper.

For this and other insights given in this psalm, such as the meritoriousness of being good to the poor and the weak, and for all the inspiration coming from this first book of the psalms, let God be praised with the last verse of this psalm which is also the doxology concluding that book:

> Blessed be the Lord, the God of Israel
> from age to age. Amen. Amen.

Book II, Psalms 42-72

Psalm 42

This and the next psalm are variations on one and the same theme or experience—a combination of utter dejectedness, of visceral longing, and of firm hope. This combination is told in Psalm 42 in images some of which reoccur verbatim in Psalm 43. No wonder. Both psalms obviously have the same author who was either David, or possibly a Levite who went with him into hiding in the country of the Jordan's headwaters, just below Mount Hermon. The psalmist specifically names the Hill of Mizar as his hiding place. Then and now the area was famous for its waterfalls, not large to be sure, but still places of oasis in an often barren landscape.

For all the similarities between the two psalms, there are some notable differences. One finds only in Psalm 42 the image of a deer in a restless search for a stream. The Levite uses this image to convey his own intense desire to see the face of God by which he obviously means the facade of the Tent housing the Ark of the Covenant. But the verse in which the psalmist pictures himself as leading once more a deliriously happy crowd to that Tent may fit David better.

Only in this psalm does the psalmist compare his inner torments to the roar of rushing waters, to torrents sweeping through his very being. These torments are so intense as to issue in the question repeated twice: "Why are you cast down my soul, why groan within me?" Such torments are made even more painful as the psalmist (once more David would fit the bill better) seems to hear his enemies ask him, all day long, "Where is your God?" a question that pierces him to the heart.

The psalmist voices full trust in God in spite of the fact that God, his safety, his rock, seems to have abandoned him: "Hope

in God, I will praise Him still." We must echo all this with the
words of the prayer which was not the psalmist's privilege to
learn: "Your will be done on earth, as it is in heaven," the only
place where God will be seen face to face.

Until then let us admire those, the saints, who could
genuinely say that their sole desire was to see the face of God.
Unlike the psalmist, who too closely tied the face of God to the
facade of the Tent, a Saint Teresa of Avila surely spoke in terms of
the highest mystical experience when she wrote in her
Exclamation XV: "O Lord, how long will this exile of mine last.
The thirst to see God fills my heart with bitterness. Life appears
long to anyone who wants to see his God. Why stay in this sad
exile? . . . Hope, hope, therefore, my soul; you do not know the
day and the hour; watch carefully, all will pass rapidly."

For those of us who are too imperfect to have such an
experience, there remains the Face on the Shroud of Turin. It
bothered atheists so much that shouts of joy went up in their
camps when carbon dating assured only about five hundred
years to the Shroud. An atheist scientist in Oxford, involved in
that dating, gladly received a huge reward from an equally
atheistic Foundation for having helped discredit another pious
fable and false relic.

But the Shroud has several facets, which no honest scientist
should try to ignore. The Shroud itself is a negative image,
which, when first photographed in 1897, appeared as a positive
image on a negative plate. Negative images were not appreciated
before the advent of photography around 1830 and certainly not
around 1400 or so. Then there is the perfection of that negative-
positive image, which in addition is the only surviving specimen
of a technique, if indeed such a technique flourished at that time.
Could any technique begin with a perfect product? Would it
make sense to assume that the making of airplanes began with a
Boeing 747 or with a Stealth Bomber? Further, there are some
anatomical details, such as the nail wounds in the wrists and not
in the palms as generally pictured then or before and later.
Finally, there is the incomparably moving Face. Its contemplation
on plain holy cards already gave to millions of simple faithful a
far better grasp of the face of God than our psalmist could

convey. Jesus himself assured us that those who saw Him, saw the Father Himself. The Shroud shows that this holds true even of Jesus' lifeless face as if to bring out the dogmatic truth that Divinity was never separated from Jesus' body.

Psalm 43

In this psalm the psalmist (David or a Levite) seems to focus more on his eventual return to Jerusalem than on his torments while in exile. To be sure, those torments are still acute, otherwise he would not ask twice the question, "Why are you cast down my soul, why groan within me?" the very same questions he also asked twice in the preceding psalm. He still bemoans the connivance of cunning and deceitful men.

Still his sight seems now more firmly set on the day which would find him coming "to the altar of God, the God of my joy." This phrase, "the God of my joy," could be mined to no end. The psalmist, possibly David, does not declare joy to be God. David does not celebrate joy for joy's sake. He is not a prophet of a happiness severed from God. For him God is the source of joy. Had Schiller appreciated this psalm in a way befitting a religious man which he was not, his "Ode to Joy" would have gained in depth and Beethoven himself might have risen to greater heights as he put that Ode to music for the great finale of his Ninth Symphony. The joy exuding from that Ode remains a treat to a relatively few, who listen to it while sitting in plush chairs in concert halls or while running their daily miles with a CD player tied to their waist and microphones fastened to their ears. For the vast majority more true joy is on hand in the Poverello's illustration of it. It is the image of a friar standing drenched at the door of his own convent and receiving rank abuse instead of welcome. This may send a chill down one's spine, but in the end may bring the kind of warmth which is the touchstone of true joy born in faith.

This is not the place to elaborate on joy and mysticism. Still one cannot help noticing a mystic strain in the request that the following verse of this psalm be engraved, and in Latin, on one's tombstone: "Emitte lucem tuam et veritatem tuam, ipsa me deduxerunt et adduxerunt in montem sanctum tuum et in tabernacula tua." Those who read Father La Farge's autobio-graphical *The Manner Is Ordinary* know that I am referring to his mother, who sometime after her son's ordination converted to Catholicism. In that book one finds also delicate hints about the kind of exile she had to suffer through much of the second half of her life. It was a most searing kind of exile for a woman who at the same time remained at home. David presented his own experience in two variations, as if to hint that many other variations as well are indeed possible.

Psalm 44

If there is a theologically instructive psalm, this is it. It is one of the paeans of God's grace, that is, of his goodness which precedes and in fact generates all our good responses to it. The psalmist does not tire of referring to God by using "you" and "yours" as opposed to "we" and "ours" in reviewing the past history of the people. In the first nine verses the psalmist uses "you" and "yours" a dozen times in order to leave no room whatsoever to the notion that either "we" (the psalmist's own generation) or "they" (all his forefathers) should be given any credit for the miraculous transplantation of the Israelites from Egypt to the Promised Land and for their no less unlikely survival there.

Such an unstinting appraisal of God's unmerited goodness reaches impressive theological, indeed mystical heights as the psalmist states: "It was your right hand, your arm and the light of your face: for you loved them." The psalmist shows no inclination to take anything back as he credits God and God alone. Nor would he suggest ever so slightly or indirectly that God loves the Israelites in response to their lovableness. God's grace is sovereign.

But the vision of grace and love becomes suddenly over-shadowed by the specter of a total disgrace: God's people is found at the mercy of their enemies. God himself appears to offer them up for sale and to ask nothing in return. The people are like sheep destined for slaughter or at least scattered among the nations. The people become a byword, a thing of derision. The psalmist finds himself overwhelmed with despair: "All the day long my disgrace is before me."

He sees nothing but disgrace, he finds no explanation. He is convinced that all this could not have come as a punishment from God. After all, they have not forgotten Him, they have not strayed from His path, they have not withdrawn their heart. The psalmist is not inclined to look way back into the past for evidence of infidelity. As to the present he cannot find anything wrong done by the people. He also knows that God would have easily found out even their most secret deeds.

The verse, "it is for you that we face death all the day long," might have contained a remote clue to the problem if it could be taken to mean that it is for God's own unfathomable designs that one has to be in that cruel situation. No, the phrase is rather a reproach to God. The psalmist seems to say: You made us believe in you, and this belief of ours is the cause of all our troubles.

Were this psalm a mere human composition, it might end in a revolt, in an anticipation of Nietzsche's boasting that announced the "Death of God." But even the lowest theological level of the Old Testament is a high ground with respect to mere human wisdom and reasoning. In spite of everything, the psalmist still cries out to God for help as if to testify to some agonizing residue of faith in his heart.

To appreciate this residue of faith, which at least manifests itself in desperate cries to God, one has to recall that the unspeakable miseries of Hitler's concentration camps dissipated in the hearts of many Jews even that residue. The Holocaust turned many Jews into atheists, an outcome all the more paradoxical as Erich Fromm, a notable survivor of the Holocaust, testified to the saving power of faith in those circumstances. It is another matter whether a very generic faith in human goodness would qualify for faith in God. Anna Frank's testimony comes to mind about her rugged belief that there always remains something good in all men. Let us hope, against hope, that this kind of belief in humanity somehow can pass in God's eyes for belief in Him. It was not a faith in humanity that enabled Maximilian Kolbe to offer himself as a replacement for a married compatriot of his slated for the gas chamber.

It often happens that the faith of a Christian diminishes into a desperate outcry to God. Let us cherish that strange flicker of faith. In spite of the exacting demands He posed to us, Our Lord Himself wanted to be remembered as one who does not quench the smoldering wick. And in the midst of all our agonies, let us be grateful for the light He brought us through His own suffering. For man caught sight of the sole explanation of human suffering only when Christ endured the agony of crucifixion so that God's infinite holiness may truly be expiated for our sins.

A generation or so later tens of thousands of Jews were crucified by the Romans outside the walls of Jerusalem after they had tried in vain to escape the hell, so vividly described by Josephus, into which some Jews turned life in the Holy City. From a certain point on the Romans offered no clemency to those who escaped form the City, although many of them would have said what Jacob Eisner did in our times. Only sixteen years old as he watched the Warsaw ghetto go up in flames, Eisner recalled that all the Jews there would have been willing to be slaves, even to become converts, if only they would have been allowed to live.

The agonies of all of those Jews crucified outside Jerusalem only increased the sense of despair and disgrace in the ones inside who nourished the last flicker of hope for a mere survival. One wonders how many of them, or among those who lingered on half-dead in the concentration camps nineteen hundred years later, found solace in the seemingly hopeless cries to God that bring this psalm to a gripping close.

Psalm 45

This psalm is a royal wedding psalm, and to say this is to say something obvious as well as puzzling. Weddings celebrate the tying of a union between two human beings. The etymology of the word "religion" (from the Latin *re-ligare* or re-tying) may give a glimpse of the religious aspect of that union. For men and women seem to be eager to include religion, and therefore God, however vaguely, in their union as they tie it in some ceremonial way even when the ceremony is not distinctly religious.

But if one takes that part of the wedding celebration which usually lasts far longer than the religious rite, one is hard put to think of religion. One hardly ever hears of God as one listens to speeches delivered during the sumptuous wedding banquet, let alone during the dinner which on the eve of the wedding is offered in honor of the bridegroom.

Matters could not be much different in the context that gave rise to the composition of this psalm which reveals nothing about the actual circumstances. One makes a mere guess if one ties this psalm to the wedding of Solomon, a guess which makes the interpretation of this psalm even more problematic in view of the notorious proliferation of women in Solomon's household.

Originally a royal wedding song, full of pomp and circumstance, full of exaggerated praises of the royal bridegroom as an invincible hero, as a paragon of beauty, as a bulwark of justice and truth, the song eventually became a psalm, a song touched with divine inspiration, indeed a messianic psalm. This happened because the bridegroom's beauty, sense of justice, and heroism were portrayed as having a superhuman measure.

In spite of the ribaldry that often goes with weddings, the total and mutual commitment between man and woman remains intrinsically noble. As all good things, that union, too, derives its goodness from God, the source of all good. Therefore, marital union should naturally serve as a pointer to the union that man is destined to have with God. As C. S. Lewis found—read his *A Grief Observed*—this union begins to count much more than any human bond as one's hour of death approaches.

Being a covenant, the marital union is the Bible's favorite simile for describing the covenantal union between Yahweh and His people. This is why the Bible brands the worship of idols as sheer adultery committed against Yahweh. In the New Covenant the relation Yahweh-people reappears in the relation of Christ to His Church as His Bride, a relation even more mystical than the former. Within the Church as Christ's bride a special role is filled by Mary as the bride of the Holy Spirit, "who is queen and mother, and who stands above all the choirs of angels in her golden dress, gilded by the divinity; not that she is God, but because she is the mother of God." So wrote Thomas Aquinas who echoed many and who was followed by many more in extolling the mystical privileges granted to Mary.

This mystical sense will forever have a special appeal to virgins who consecrate themselves entirely to God's service. They have since the earliest times been the finest manifestation of the spiritual power at work in the Church. Evidences of this have not been lacking even in times which historians are apt to dismiss as lacking in spirituality, indeed as wholly overwhelmed by the desires of the eyes and of the flesh.

One such evidence deserves to be recalled partly because it is so cryptic. Few residents of Edinburgh suspect the full story tied to Sciennes Road, just south of the Meadows. They would be surprised if told that the name is a deformation of Siena, the name of the Italian town which owes its fame in no small extent to a famous virgin, Caterina Benincasa, better known as Saint Catherine of Siena.

Her mystical union with God worked historical miracles in a phase of ecclesiastical history usually described as far from spiritual. Not even a stone is left of the convent of the Dominican nuns on that road who had a great repute throughout Scotland for their holiness. On June 29, 1559, "the rascal multitude," so goes a contemporary account, "leaving behind them the smoking ruins of the monasteries of the Black and Grey Friars, rushed out in their thousands along the Cowgate, the Candlemaker Row and the other southern outlets of the city to the Sciennes, where, without opposition of any kind, they completed their vengeful work of destruction." The nuns escaped because people mindful of their virtues warned them in the last minute about the imminent disaster. Those virtuous nuns must have derived much spiritual sustenance from reciting this psalm week after week.

Those lacking in virtue, especially the virtue of purity, should not poke fun at this psalm's nuptial realism. They should, however, take note of instances of strange contrasts that occur again and again in public view. Surely, even for a jaded eye there should appear a clash between the almost naked thighs of a young woman perching on a bus seat and the white robe, whose sole decor is a wide brown scapular, of a woman of the same age standing next to her in the isle. One merely stares ahead, the other is absorbed in a prayer book in her hands. One face is already spent and blasé, the other fresh and sweet like a bloom=ing lily. To my question, "Which order do you belong?" she answered: "The community of the Queen of Peace." It is one of the many new shoots appearing everywhere in the Church in proof of her spiritual power to inspire many to vow themselves to a spiritual wedding, void of clamor but full of the joy of an unalloyed peace.

Psalm 46

A famous psalm, to say the least. In Luther's translation, "Eine feste Burg," it turned into a battle hymn of the movement he triggered and over which in later years he had more than one moment of tormenting second thought. It cannot be gainsaid that Luther's movement further lowered the already low morals of a notoriously immoral epoch. Whatever reasons Luther may have had for ignoring Augustine's dictum, "There can be no just cause for disrupting the unity of the Church" ("Dirimendi unitatem ecclesiae nulla datur justa necessitas"), the immorality of some ecclesiastics in Rome could not be such a reason. There was as much of it in Germany where Luther approved of the bigamy of Philipp of Hesse, a most lecherous prince, but also most support-ive of Luther's movement, which greatly enriched the princes.

The psalm's verse, "God is a stronghold for us," calls for a remark about Calvin who turned Geneva into a fortress of religious repression, employing spies that peeked through the keyholes of private homes. He could, of course, see divine intervention behind the sudden lifting of the siege which a Catholic prince had laid earlier on Geneva. One wonders what Calvin would think today on seeing Geneva under the tyranny of "enlightened" civic comportment taken for religion. I cannot help thinking of the words of a prominent Reformed theologian, who once whispered into my ears: "Protestantism leads straight into naturalism."

It is never safe for an individual to declare a particular historical configuration to be the embodiment of God's turning into a stronghold for us, especially when it amounts to the breaking up of the unity of that sole true stronghold which is the

Catholic Church. There one has at least a clear perspective between vice and virtue, which no theologian can put better than Jackie Gleason, the comedian. To the reporter who asked him why he, twice divorced, remained a Catholic, he said: "While I might not carry out my obligations in any manner to be commended, at least I know where I stand" (*Time*, Dec. 29, 1961). There is more logic to this stance than to Luther's "Here I stand."

But back to the psalm which is about the sudden lifting of a siege against Jerusalem. Being a poem, the psalm's meaning may be distorted if taken for a historical document. It would be unsafe to take the narrative in 2 Chronicles (ch. 32) for a specific event. Historical evidence assures us that in 721 B. C. Sennacherib's army suddenly collapsed near Pelusium, the city of entry to Egypt. The cause of collapse may have been pestilence brought about by the invasion of mice (rats) that also chewed into tatters the leather components of weapons and gear.

While not surrounded directly, Jerusalem, too, must have been under dire threat regardless of the underground water conduit that could greatly help in sustaining a prolonged siege. The sudden relief is celebrated in this psalm with poetical exaggerations. As long as history lasts, there will be no total victory for the just, the kind of triumph conjured up in this psalm, although the wicked often collapse just when they appear to be wholly victorious. God is a stronghold with a groundplan that assures victory only *sub specie aeternitatis*.

Psalm 47

This psalm, a victory psalm, carries no less the mark of exaggerations than the preceding psalm. Even the most victorious moments of Jewish history could not justify the tone of this psalm that shows no trace of realism. Poems are never meant to be mirror images of reality, let alone of a reality which divinely inspired poems try to grasp. This psalm can be justified only as an eschatological declaration. Its triumphalism is not to be attached to anything historical. In moments of triumph one should rather temper one's exultation with Job's remark, "militia est vita hominis super terram" (Jb 7:1, Vulgate) on the drudgery of soldiering. As we labor on behalf of the Kingdom of God, let our spirit be kept vigorous by an unshakable trust in the final outcome that will show that God is truly the king of all the earth, that all princes and rulers will be assembled with God's people.

Psalm 48

This psalm was most likely born from the same experience that gave rise to the composition of Psalm 46. An unbridled optimism exudes from all lines of this psalm, very much riveted in the material strength of the Holy City, Jerusalem. One wonders whether in counting the towers of Sion the psalmist thought of the disaster that befell David after he had ordered all his subjects to be counted (2 Sam 24). The psalm offers no clues as to the particular siege laid against Jerusalem. That only the people of Juda are mentioned to rejoice suggests that the composition of the psalm postdates the annihilation of the Northern tribes. Perhaps once more Sennacherib's sudden defeat is in the back of the psalmist's mind. He certainly uses strong similes to indicate God's power over Sion's enemies. One such simile is about the ships of Tharsis, or large merchantmen that carried goods between Phoenicia and its distant colony, Tharsis, in Spain. Yet even such ships were powerless against the gale winds that blew on occasion from the inland mountains to the east. To keep in check the unbridled sense of power exuding from this psalm it is best to shift to eschatological perspectives, partly because eschatology connotes great trials with great triumphs. Those unwilling to contemplate those trials, would do well to ponder the very next psalm.

Psalm 49

It would be rather naive to think that this psalm simply recommends some music as a cure for one's perplexities as the psalmist states: "With the harp I solve my problems." Saul, who sought relief for his worries by ordering David to play the harp for him, was not saved by melodies, however comforting. The melodies that carried the words of psalms in Old Testament times were not substitutes for long and hard thinking, nor are their modern musical settings. The psalms keep conveying harsh truths that may sound very dispiriting, humanly speaking. A case in point is this psalm, almost a poetical echo of the dirge in the Book of Ecclesiastes, where even between the lines one but hears the words: "Vanity of vanities, all is vanity."

For a Christian, whose Creed is riveted on the certainty of eternal life that sets in immediately after death, it is especially painful to be exposed to the absence of any such certainty in this psalm. One can at most find a vague intimation of the soul's immortality in the verse that in death the just become the rulers of the wicked. It is no less dissatisfying to be exposed to the psalmist's perspective that because those whose names resound all over the world do not carry their wealth beyond the grave, one need not feel downcast over one's poverty. Would not this perspective be more fearful to the one who prior to his approaching the grave enjoyed no wealth at all?

This perspective is not really overcome by the verse: "God will ransom me from death and take my soul to himself." Life beyond death, as something more than a shadowy existence, is not asserted clearly in the Old Testament until the Book of Daniel, which this psalm almost certainly antedates. This psalm anticipates no crisp assertion that after death the soul would have more than a shadowy existence in Sheol.

Yet this psalm contains sobering instructions for these times of ours when the acquisition of riches is becoming a science; when man manipulates with inebriating and maddening skill the stock market; when people are eager to be driven free of charge to gambling casinos where they even receive money to start gambling. Our psalm tells us about "the malice of the rich," about their having everyone else "at their beck and call," and, to wax modern, about their ability to buy social respectability if they have a plenty of the almighty dollar. The psalmist tells us that the rich "like sheep are driven to their death," even if he is not really clear about the sense in which "the just will become their rulers." But the just should know much of the plain truth that "in his riches man lacks wisdom." Many are those who bartered the sanity of modest circumstances for the madness which was awaiting them in positions of affluence. Appalling cases of this are reported almost daily in our papers. Surely, it would be wise to ponder Paul's rule of life which is the abundance of mere sufficiency.

Psalm 50

A grandiose scene is offered in this psalm. In that respect, too, only a few other psalms can match it. Psalm 148, which calls on all the major figures in heaven and on earth to join in God's praise, has perhaps a greater sweep, but it does not reverberate with the drama which this psalm unfolds under our eyes. The drama is suited for a stage production. The stage is God's judgment seat as set up in Sion, but His courtroom spans from the rising of the sun to its setting. The universality of this divine court is further stressed by the fact that the entire earth is summoned to witness the judgment. The court is also frighteningly splendid, as befits a truly divine court: It shines with a perfect beauty, and a fiery tempest announces that God takes His seat of judgment.

As measured against the grandeur of this psalm, puny may appear the dimensions which mere aestheticism can provide. For the finely cultured Fénelon, easily the most outstanding bishop of early-eighteenth-century France, this psalm surpassed anything Greek literature offered in the way of sublimity.

This was indeed so, but also for a reason which Fénelon did not notice. While all human drama is a judgment where the accused or the guilty have some say, here the party under judgment has only one right: to listen in silence. For man has to fall silent when God speaks and this is no less true of God's own people when under judgment or of anyone else for that matter. At that judgment no defense attorneys will be present to have the case dismissed on sheer technicalities. There will be no chance to compose hung juries, no editors to sit in judgment apart from the judge, no pollsters to create the perception that there is no crime if the people's majority sees no crime. There will be no appeal to the justice of the three little monkeys, however popular.

At any rate, it would be daringly foolish to speak up when the charge is laid out in an impassioned tone which may appear even more unbearable and unanswerable as the charges are specified one by one. Further, the charges may seem all the more devastating as they declare utterly worthless what the people considered most valuable.

But God keeps stating that none of the bullocks, none of the goats offered to Him in sacrifice are of any value to Him. For one, God makes it absolutely clear, in an almost contemptuous tone, that He needs none of those animals, for He owns thousands of them, indeed all of them, whether they live in the fields, in the forests, or in the air. In a manner evoking a dramatic courtroom proceeding, where the judge seems to rub salt into wounds inflicted by a heavy sentence, the psalmist lays bare the fallacy in the thinking of the accused: They lured themselves into thinking that their sacrifices provided God with something He did not have. But God mockingly asks them whether He is ever hungry for the flesh of animals, or thirsty for their blood.

If God needs anything, if He needs any honor, any recognition, it is the sacrifice of thanksgiving, so the psalmist declares in God's name. It is not the first fruits offered on the Feast of the Tabernacles, the feast of thanksgiving for a bountiful harvest, that God has in mind. It is rather man's mind, provided it is animated with the recognition that all he has he owes it to God. It is in that state of mind that man not only submits totally to God, but also with a totality which grateful love can alone convey.

The value of that sacrifice, as emphasized in this psalm, was a favorite theme with some of the prophets. But one had to wait for the New Testament to see the rarity of truly thankful souls in order to reveal the infinite measure of gratitude which God deserves. That only one out of ten lepers cured by Jesus returned to give thanks to Him, revealed a numerical proportion that should make us shudder. God forbid that it should prove itself a "constant" of an empirical science of spirituality. As to the infinite measure of gratitude, it was displayed in that moment when Jesus gave thanks, broke the bread, and gave His own body and blood to us by offering it to God. Such was His thanksgiving. It instituted that most awesome and unique Christian rite called Eucharist, a powerful echo of the only prayer He is recorded to have uttered during His ministry public. On seeing the good results of the first missionary round made by the Twelve He exclaimed: "Father, Lord of heaven and earth, to you I offer praise; for what you have hidden from the learned and the clever you have revealed to the merest children. Father, it is true. You have graciously willed it so" (Mt 11:25-26). So was a supreme thanksgiving combined with a supreme judgment.

The seriousness of the judgments set forth in this psalm is further driven home as the psalmist makes his grand conclusion. In view of man's proverbial readiness to let painful details fall into oblivion, God lays bare the specifics of the false mentality that lies hidden under a religion reduced to mere externality. Ritual sacrifices were so many cover-ups for inveterate habits of sin: contempt for His law, scoffing at His words, going in cahoots with thieves, associating with adulterers, making a sport of telling lies, of plotting crimes, of slandering others. Is it possible not to think of the flood of deliberately misleading advertisements, of sinful entertainment, of specious expressions aimed at presenting vice as virtue?

God the judge holds back nothing, which should be a fearful reminder in these times when catechetical and theological celebrations of God's love drown out even the few remaining reminders of the fact that God is a Judge after all. Surely, we cannot be grateful enough for parables about the merciful father of a prodigal son, about the good shepherd in search of the lost sheep. God is not the head of a celestial morals squad. But woe to us if we take it for a license to continue in sin. Lest we do so, we should take in all seriousness the verse: "Mark this, you who never think of God, lest I seize you and you cannot escape."

The daily timeliness of this psalm found a telling illustration of a merry gathering where a well-known priest-poet was present. His *bon vivant* comportment made the others think that he would not care much for the difference between right and wrong. For a while he listened silently as one joke followed another, all of them ridiculing virtue. Then suddenly he blurted out: "I kept silent. Did you think that I am one of you?"

Hopefully he did not say this too late. Socially popular priests all too often deprive themselves of the stage where one can effectively recall Paul's exhortation, "Brethren (and sisters) offer your bodies in spiritual sacrifice to God" (Rom 12:1), which no "progress" in theology dare rewrite.

Psalm 51

In praying this psalm one may only hope that one never becomes guilty of David's sin, although his sin—almost every issue of a newspaper is a proof—is not a rarity. Actions triggered by lust almost invariably lead to worse sins. Adultery often leads to obstruction of justice, and even to murder. To give the order that a brave, innocent soldier be put in a spot of deadly danger, and then abandon him to the sword of the enemies, was a despicable act. Had David not been intoxicated by his lust, he would not have given that shameful order. The one who spared Saul, though he could have slayed him in self-defense, now found himself deprived of sane thinking. His sin was iniquity indeed, which defies rational explanation, although leaves intact personal responsibility. "Who understands sin?" asks the Bible itself (Ps 19:13, Vulgate). Apart from gambling and drinking (and the pursuit of glory and power) nothing deprives one so much of the use of one's right mind as the mind's yielding to the lure of lust.

All this squares with the frightful perspective of man's fallen status, so forcefully suggested by David's remark that his mother conceived him in sin. If one wishes to see some of the timeless arguments on behalf of the view that conception, or rather the sexual act as its means is indeed the transmitter of original sin, let him read chs. 16-26 of Book XIV in Augustine's *City of God*. There the saint, formerly a lecher, reflects at length on the inordinateness inherent in that act. One need not waste time on those who dismiss David's remark as a biblical proof of original sin. They had already written off original sin itself.

David's begging God that He may create a pure heart in him should be a prayer not merely on our lips but a prayer welling up from our heart. We should pray for a most elementary yet precious insight, namely, that to cope with lust presupposes a change of the heart in addition to a change of the mind.

Augustine's famed experience comes to mind. After years of struggling, and in vain, with his lustful self, he suddenly found his mind changed as he opened at random a copy of Paul's Letters and read the passage: "Not in rioting and drunkenness, not in chambering and impurities, not in strife and envying: but put you on the Lord Jesus Christ, and make no provision for the flesh in its concupiscences" (Rom 13:13-14). From that moment on the impossible seemed very possible. Surely, God's grace alone could bring about this complete turning around. However, focusing on the role of grace ought not to slight the role of man's mind. The unfolding of the drama began with Augustine's hearing the words: "Tolle, lege." Take the book and read it. Of course, the right book is to be taken, an act which may be very difficult to take when an "enlightened" spirituality disdains of *The Imitation of Christ* and spiritual classics of the same kind.

The request for a rebuilding of the shattered walls of Jerusalem is an obviously post-exilic addition to what David himself had composed half a millennium earlier. It should be enough to think of the shattering impact of the sins of impurity over all society, if one is to see the enduring constructiveness of that request. If growth in spiritual life is not to turn into a dream, it ought to be a construction that cannot start with specious debates about interior decoration of the tenth-floor apartments at a facile disregard of the state of the very foundations. Sex is a most basic but also a very touchy foundation of human life, biological as well as spiritual, that needs close supervision.

Psalm 52

This psalm can hardly be taken for a generic proposition about masters of deceit. Still the particular individual, who is under consideration in this psalm but whose identity remains a mystery, represents a type as well.

It is all the more difficult to keep one's eyes focused on that type as it has become a cultural trend to distract from seeing the plain evidence. It is now bad manners, indeed inexcusable in trendsetting circles to refer to the once widely read book, whose title, *Masters of Deceit*, was obviously taken from this psalm.

The organization, "Accuracy in Media," fights an uphill battle. While wide publicity is given to news releases by the "Anti-defamation League," those issued by the Catholic Defense League go largely unnoticed. The protests of the American Family Association are heeded by manufacturers, publishers, and moviemakers only when they are hit on the pocketbook. Those who take pride in the motto, "All the news that's fit to print," are masters of studied selectivity. They succeeded in creating the impression that Mao and Castro were agricultural reformers. Such is their way of calling a spade a spade. But they show their worst when they try to present *1984* as a parody of capitalism and they do so by drawing heavily on their capitalist investments and using to the hilt the freedom of the press.

On the comforting side of the ledger one can find time and again that some notables, safely ensconced in their ill-gained prosperity, are "suddenly uprooted from their tents." Still, if the just want to become "a growing olive tree in the house of God," they must not allow its being besmirched by willful newsmaking. Pleased as they may be with moments that allow them to "praise God for evermore," they should not for a moment forget that there will never be a shortage of intellectuals, who live on deceiving themselves so that they may continue deceiving others. The Father of Lies knows how to recruit ever fresh battalions so that lies may flourish as never before.

Psalm 53

Any commentator on the psalms, especially if he lived beyond the seventy years which Psalm 90 allots to a man who is not particularly strong, comes to the task with a heavy baggage. The latter may contain a few valuables and a few curiosa. Among these in my baggage is a reference to the first verse of this psalm to illustrate the incorrect use of the Bible. To make matters even more hilarious, if not tragicomical, I found the reference in a thick book on homiletics, or the art of preaching. According to the author it would be wrong to prove the claim that God does not exist on the ground that the Bible says so. But in the Bible, in the first line of this psalm (which echoes Psalm 14), it is the fool who says in his heart, there is no God. It would have been more appropriate to say that even the Devil can quote the Bible.

Those, too, would misuse this psalm who would take literally its statement that "all have left the right path; [all are] depraved, every one [of them} . There is not a good man left, no, not even one." Sweeping denunciations border on the hollowness of universally negative statements, such as "all men are liars," except, of course, the one who offered this statement as a truth. Bitter conservatives (and their Catholic camp followers), who cry over having lost the culture war (which they waged with Bible in hand), may take note.

The author of this psalm ought not to be taken for a facile mind. He, of course, delighted in emphases, which do no harm provided one knows them for what they are. Emphases differ from exaggerations, let alone from sweeping generalizations. It is just not true, even psychologically, that all atheists, all hardened sinners are "trembling with fear and without cause for fear." Often they do, but not always. Otto Stern, the psychiatrist who converted to Catholicism, emphatically noted in his *Pillar of Fire* that he had known more than one atheist who had a remarkable balance of soul. It is not always evident that "the bones of the wicked are scattered." The remains of many saints were scattered by the wicked, whereas Lenin's mummy still lies undisturbed and so do the bones of Voltaire and his ilk. God's mills grind indeed slowly and finely, which is not merely a word of wisdom, but also a biblical truth. This is to be kept in mind as we sigh: "Oh that salvation might come from Sion!" It is not for us to know the moment when "God delivers Sion from bondage" so that "Jacob may be glad and Israel rejoice." Partial deliveries should not give us bold expectations.

Psalm 54

This brief psalm is all too clear to call for anything but some brief remarks. It should be obvious what to think of the psalmist's wish that the "ruthless men" who ganged up on him may receive their just desserts. The faithful, that is, consistent God has His own way of letting evil run its own logic and recoil on those who cultivate evil at a rank disregard of God's law.

One would be tempted to ascribe this psalm to Jeremiah were it not for the psalmist's readiness to "sacrifice with a willing heart." Although from a priestly family, Jeremiah was a prophet and as such did not do what was the privilege of priests and of kings. Does this mean that David composed this psalm? Let us not probe at length into the sole obscurity in this brief psalm. We can do something infinitely better by implementing the psalmist's words, "I will sacrifice to you with a willing heart," whatever the nature of the sacrifice, which God demands from us.

Psalm 55

The psalm contains a phrase, "fear and trembling fall upon me," which Kierkegaard made famous for those who had already let Paul's injunction, "work on your salvation with fear and trembling," drift out of their spiritual focus. The psalm is so full of vivid references to an ominous situation as to allow questions about its Sitz im Leben. Was the psalm composed in the context of Absalom's rebellion? Or, in view of the psalm's style, should we rather think that it shows Jeremiah sitting in a dark corner and expecting his enemies to cart him away? He hears the shouting, the cries of the wicked, as they prepare what they hope to be a final assault on him. Jeremiah is seized with nothing less than "death's terror," he is overwhelmed with horror.

Only in thought can he think of escaping. It is as impossible for him as to turn into a dove and fly into the desert, and find a shelter from the destructive storm of plotting tongues. But he finds himself locked in a violent city, whose walls are patrolled day and night by the guardsmen of iniquity. The streets of the city are ruled by tyranny and deceit.

All this is terrible enough, but what really devastates Jeremiah is that it is not his enemies who are responsible for his torments. There is no sorrow more excruciating than the one inflicted by one's best friend—in this case by one with whom one once walked in harmony in the House of God. Now the friend appears in his true color as one whose "speech is softer than butter but war reigns in his heart." The traitor friend and his confederates even boast that "they have no fear of God."

One can certainly admire Jeremiah who despite all this turns to God as the One who "would never allow the just man to stumble." Jeremiah obviously has more in mind than protection against making an infelicitous tactical move. He hopes that God will not allow him to come to grief. Once more Jeremiah's trustful recourse to God is coupled with an elemental request that God should finish off his enemies, to shove them "into the pit of death."

It is that request that cannot be voiced by anyone who, in reading this psalm's reference to a traitor who turned against his friend, cannot help thinking of what happened in the Garden of Gethsemane. There a kiss from a friend was the means of betraying One who just a few hours beforehand had told the Twelve that henceforth He would consider them as His friends.

There is no commentator of this psalm who would not have seen in this psalm a prophetic prevision of Judas's act. Of course, Jesus was willing to forgive Judas. Those who still do not wish to think of Jesus, while they stand at the foot of the Wailing Wall, can hardly chase from their thoughts some terrifying pages left by Josephus. In fact Josephus was possibly a traitor. Those pages relate to the very last months of Titus' siege of the City when some still tried to walk in harmony in the Temple, although it was in the grip of some worse than traitors. They were the henchmen of their own. By patrolling day and night the city wall, they made it impossible to almost all to escape into the desert, to find, if not peace, at least some wretched roots to still their excruciating hunger.

As for us, we can do no better than repeat the words which Jeremiah muttered to himself: "Entrust your care to the Lord" and add, even though He may not seem to care at all: "Lord I trust in you."

Psalm 56

Possibly David, on the run to evade his enemies, wrote this psalm. Thoughts similar to the line, "You have kept an account of my wandering, you have kept a record of my tears," must have arisen in many who had to taste the uncertainty and bitterness of living in some sort of exile. Their number has reached new heights in this age noted for its progress and notorious for its vast refugee camps. Tellingly, refugees who drag themselves along the road are never said to be progressing. The century of space exploration and instant communication has become a monumental pilgrim's regress. True pilgrims shall march on and so does God's entire pilgrim people. They do so in the firm belief that progress is inherent only in salvation history.

Meanwhile as one much publicized death march recedes from memory, another emerges in all vividness owing to new ways of reporting. From the comfort of their couches millions watch emaciated victims of ethnic cleansing as they head into the uncertainty of a homeless future. One wonders how many are strengthened by thoughts similar to the one which David voiced: "In God I trust, I shall not fear, what can mortal man to do me?"

Even a momentary reflection is enough to realize the vast amount of harm that mortal man can inflict. Words are forever distorted, one (or one's company or business) is ambushed at every turn in a style of life in which blessings are taken to be proportional to success in a cutthroat competition.

Faith as strong as David's is no longer newsworthy, although it comes to the surface more often than a secularized society dares presume. Vows are still being made, in signal witness to the faith from which they spring. There are startling stories of escapes from death's grasp which human wisdom ascribes to luck, lest one should face up to the presence of God. Yet as the closing line of this psalm states, those who "walk in the light of the living," do so because of God's presence everywhere. All remains fully utilizable in this psalm except the unrestrained request that one's enemies be given exemplary punishment: The lines, "repay them, God, for their crimes; in your anger cast down the peoples," are to be repeated with a twist in their meaning: all evildoers will be repaid in a measure which is set not by man's anger, not even by God's anger, which is often but the projection of our anger into God, but by God's justice which, fortunately for all the "good" people, is always tempered by his mercy and forgiveness.

Psalm 57

A few months before his arrest by Stalin's henchmen, Cardinal Mindszenty quoted this psalm in a public speech to give his assessment of the state of affairs: "In the shadow of your wings I take refuge, till the storms of destruction pass by." He stood in the eye of a storm that was making increasingly clear that while the war was won, peace was lost. So he became one of the most famous prisoners of the Cold War. Those who thought of Stalin as an "Uncle Joe" would never take kindly to the Cardinal, whom they labeled, following his death, as a chief among the Cold War warriors.

Fully applicable to him were the lines of this psalm: "My soul (that is, my entire flesh-and-blood reality) lies prostrate among lions, who would devour the sons of men." He was the relentless target of "tongues that were so many sharpened swords." Four full decades had to pass, and well over a decade following the Cardinal's death, before one could see the psalm's words fulfilled: "They laid a snare for my steps, my soul was bowed down. They dug a pit in my path but fell in it themselves."

Many other heroes could be quoted from the history of the Church. They saw only with the eyes of their faith the day of their vindication. Think of Saint John Fisher, or of the Carmelite nuns of Compiègne, or of priests who died in Hitler's gas chambers.

It may be that our psalmist was, humanly speaking, more fortunate. The concluding verses may suggest that he was given to see the dawn of better days. Evidence on hand about a turn for the better seems to be behind his eagerness to have his lyre and harp ready for the first rays of the rising sun. Indeed he wants "to awaken the dawn itself."

Such are the thoughts of one who already sees the first signs of the outpouring of God's love that "reaches to the heavens" and of God's truth that reaches "to the skies." He eagerly asks for the full daylight of the coming of God's glory. But this will come only when the heavens themselves pass away.

Psalm 58

Corrupt courts of justice are the target of this psalm whose "violent" style makes shudder anyone who is not a saint, or who has not been the victim of such courts. Saints, of course, are such who have mastered their indignation, although some of them, a Saint Jerome, for instance, or a Saint Peter Damian, had ever fresh supplies of holy ire. As to those, who saw only others victimized by brazenly unjust legal systems, they should not have too easily counseled a "moderate" reaction. In doing so they all too often hide their infuriating selfishness.

Fury may be the only reaction to those who keep uttering the venom of lies and brazenly ignore evidence to the contrary. Snake charmers baffled by the viper that pretends deafness as an excuse for not heeding commands can be seen nowadays only in some parts of Asia. Politicians and publicists who pretend not to be aware of this or that are more numerous than ever in our civilized world. Our frustration with them can indeed reach the level of fury. Furious indeed is the tone of imprecations and of curses that make this psalm almost unique among the psalms.

The curses are voiced in graphic similes that assure a literary quality to this psalm, though disqualify it as a prayer that can be recited by a Christian, unless he transposed in thought the imperative tense into the indicative. Indeed it happens that the ultimate fate of unconscionable judges will be that of water that runs away, of grass that is trodden underfoot, of a snail that dissolves into slime. Pro-lifers will find rather disturbing the next simile, the dissolution of a woman's miscarriage. Unfortunately, this happens all too often for no fault of anyone and may be a consequence of man's (and woman's) erstwhile fall. Still it is a tragedy. This the psalmist seems to have sensed and he did so not only in respect to the pregnant mother, but also to the being she carried in her womb.

This psalm was composed long before the onset of times that began with the utterance: "Let it be to me according to thy words," which made any violently induced miscarriage an affront to the mystery of the Word become flesh. His prayer on the cross for those who crucified him, "Father forgive them for they do not know what they are doing," is the farthest conceivable cry from the violent curse and almost insane exultation that brings this psalm to a close: Let those unjust judges be swept away before they produce their thorns as if they were so many brambles, and let the just bathe their feet in the blood of the wicked. May we never entertain such wishes about the fulfillment of God's justice on earth.

Psalm 59

In reading this psalm one cannot help thinking of Psalm 55 where the psalmist, most likely Jeremiah, bemoaned the patrolling of city walls by guardsmen serving the interest of the wicked. This time those guardsmen also search the houses for food and do so as if they were stray dogs that roam around howling: "They prowl in search for food, they snarl till have their fill." They also rub salt into wounds: They laugh on a scornful tone, their words full of insults, they gabble full-mouthed: "For who, they say, can hear us?" Not for them the perception of the author of Psalm 139 who knew that even the darkest night is full daylight for the Lord.

Many years later Josephus was to describe scenes eerily reminiscent of this verse. His was, of course, too shallow a piety to quote this verse. As one who subordinated all other considerations to the pursuit of his own advancement in the world, whether it was the Jewish world or the world of the pagans, his mind was hardly tuned to the psalms, although he must have known many by heart. And so are many today who denounce evil, though at a systematic disregard of the good against which alone does the evil truly appear for what it is.

Some devout readers of this psalm may be as alone as the author of this psalm, who looks for rescue, but can only turn to God. He apparently finds himself totally isolated. God alone is his sole stronghold. But his chief concern is not so much his own fate, as the fate of his people, the people of God.

And so should it be our concern on seeing that our own people, members of Christ's body, are seduced, and in much the same way as the manner deplored in this psalm, by a flood of lies generated by the proud. While we cannot follow the psalmist who wants God to show no mercy to evil traitors, we may readily imitate him as he acclaims each morning God's love, which is certainly not a matter of sentimentalism. Let us have God as our real stronghold, the God who shows us His love. Its strength best reveals itself in its greatness which far surpasses the range of our own heart, so intent on easy triumphs, and—God forbid—on quick revenge. It is best to strengthen one's heart with God's grace (Heb 13:9).

Psalm 60

Israel's defeat must have been stunning. All seems to have been shattered as if an earthquake had hit the land. To the psalmist who knows that nothing happens unless God wills it, the debacle appears as if God had made Israel drink a cup of toxic wine. God himself seems to have given a signal to his own to flee the enemy's archers. The nation feels bewildered as if rejected by God. The same idea seems to have crossed the psalmist's mind that occurred to Philip V on being told of the defeat of the "invincible" Armada: "One cannot fight against God."

While nothing specific can be learned from the psalm about the time of that rout, its place may have been in the general area of Shechem and of Succoth, a town not far to the east. Shechem guarded a strategic pass on the road from Jerusalem to the north. A rout in that general area could evoke in the mind of the psalmist some past military glories as tokens of a recovery from a major defeat. Both Shechem and Succoth were connected with military victories under the leadership of Gideon. Shechem was also the place where Joshua made the people reaffirm their covenant with Yahweh at the end of a victorious conquest of much of the Promised Land.

With all this in mind one may try to reconstruct the psalmist's line of reasoning. Precisely because everything is willed by God who certainly willed something most important about Israel, hope for a better future should remain unshaken. And since the future is the child of the past, promises which God had already carried out in the past are recalled to stir up trust in the future. The tribes of Gilead, Ephraim, and Manasseh, who settled in that general area, must have served well under Gideon. Therefore they could be expected to rally again to God's cause. Still, God's promise that Moab and Edom would be humiliated by being used as God's washbowl and footstool seems but partially fulfilled. The psalmist's question—"Who will lead me to conquer the fortress? Who will lead me face to face with Edom?—" may have been a reference to the difficulty of confronting Edom, and its citadel, Petra, ensconced within precipitous cliffs.

The final requests made to God in this psalm rise to a high spiritual level as they state that unless God helps, "the help of man is vain." Only with God's help "can man do bravely and trample down his foes." This is especially to be kept in mind in view of ongoing warfare about man's very mind. There should be much food for thought in that Darwin viewed the mind as the very citadel which his theory of the mechanism of evolution ought to conquer. That theory, in itself sheer science, had Darwin's virulent materialism for a broader matrix.

But the mind is a citadel of spiritualism in a sense that goes beyond philosophy and metaphysics. The mind is an eminently spiritual, that is, morally oriented entity. The mind is meaningless without free will. Even our most abstract thought processes contain a factor called intentionality. Intentions in turn have a target, a goal, a purpose, which can be legitimate or not. In other words the citadel is a moral citadel as well.

That citadel is threatened as much from within as from without. The enemy within is our chief weakness that we must forever try to keep under control. Nothing would be more self-defeating than to let our guard down even for a moment. But with trust in God we can always ask on a tone of hope: "Who will lead me to conquer the fortress?" and add with Newman: "Lead kindly light amidst the encircling doom."

Psalm 61

This psalm, so simple, yet so full of longing, fits the atmosphere we meet in psalms that without any doubt can be assigned to David. A telling, though hardly foolproof, indication of this is the reference to the Lord's Tent in which the psalmist wants to dwell and be protected as if he were under God's very wings. The massive and splendid Temple of Solomon is still to be built.

David the warrior is also hinted at by the reference to the rock, the sharply rising precipice, which is the traditional stronghold of guerilla fighters in the Promised Land. Massadah was the largest and most memorable of such rocks that were turned into fortresses. They could be conquered only if their defenders were deprived of food and water. Titus' legions literally had to seal off Massadah by building a wall around it.

David now wants God to lift him to a high rock, too high for him to reach on his own strength. He seems to be in dire

need, his heart is faint, a natural state for one on the run. He tries
to derive comfort from thinking about God's faithfulness and a
long future which it alone can assure: "May the king's life be
lengthened over many generations, may he sit enthroned before
God." To his credit, David keeps in mind his duty as a ruler: He
should "rule in love and truthfulness be his protection." He also
recognizes his obligation to praise God's name day after day and
fulfill his vows as well. Such is also the standard obligation of
anyone with baptismal vows united to Christ.

Psalm 62

This psalm is not so much a prayer addressed to God as an
admonition addressed to oneself. Meditation is often a sermon
where the same person is the preacher as well as the audience.
When we use the words of a psalm like this to meditate, we can
be assured that we stay on the path of orthodoxy, hardly an easy
matter nowadays, when Zen rules as the model of meditation.

Nothing can indeed be more sound theologically than to say
to oneself with the psalmist: "In God alone is my soul at rest; my
help comes from him. He alone is my rock, my stronghold, my
fortress, I stand firm." That this is indeed a self-exhortation is
very clear from the variant of these two verses when repeated as
verses 6-7: "In God alone be at rest my soul . . ." Such is hardly a
popular point of view at a time when man's self-confidence,
sheer will power, and sundry techniques for standing up under
stress are acclaimed as if to distract from the strength which only
belief in God can convey to man.

Verse 4 poses an intriguing problem: Who is that lone man
who is attacked by all so that they may bring him down, "as
though he were a tottering wall, or a tumbling fence?" Possibly,
he was Jeremiah, whose calling included, among other things, to
function "as a pillar of iron, a wall of brass against the whole
land" (Jer 1:18). In that role Jeremiah had to practice day in and
day out what he now counseled to others: "Take refuge in God
all you people. Trust him at all times. Pour out your hearts
before him for God is our refuge."

This is a marvelous way of touching the very heart of
religion. Surely God is our safety, but only if we let our heart

become God's sole possession. This happens when one's heart is truly poured out before God. In that act all is made bare, nothing is kept back.

The psalmist gives some valuable reasons why such a surrender to God commends itself. For who are the others to whom man may entrust his fate and fortunes? The people, the common folk? They are only a breath, says the psalmist in a devastating indictment of some future democratic illusions. Such an illusion would have been the reference of the Declaration of Independence to the equality of all people, had it not started with the declaration as a self-evident truth "that all men are created equal, that they are endowed by their Creator with certain inalienable rights." Compared with the provenance of this equality of theirs, all their differences are ephemeral. Among such differences is the one between great and unimportant people. In the words of the psalmist great men "are merely an illusion: placed in the scales, they rise, they weigh less than a breath."

Editions of the Psalms often carry on their cover the image of a harp. Well enough. Psalms are words composed for melodies, instead of being compositions without words, a sort of religious matching part of the compositions known as "Lieder ohne Worte." And if one wants to convey in one image the conceptual message enclosed in the psalms, one wonders whether the tilted balance conjured up in this psalm would not be a perfect choice. After all, each psalm stands, in one way or another, for the perception that man is an utter lightweight without God.

But if even great men are illusions, one should be wary of trusting oppression whether implemented by military machines or by political parties or by that cultural juggernaut which the secular academe has grown into. They all are bent on plundering in the name of equal rights, of equal remunerations, and of equal talents and abilities.

God should seem a far better choice. After all to Him belongs all power, and love as well, a point that must sound inconceivable in a world where love runs amok as it turns into brazen self-seeking.

Psalm 63

The order of the psalms takes at times a sharp turn in tone and message, but on occasion one may feel that a psalm calls for precisely the kind of psalm that immediately follows. Pondering the great conclusion of the preceding psalm and sensing its profound truth, nothing can be more natural than to exclaim with the opening verse of this psalm: "O God, you are my God, for you I long, for you my soul is thirsting." The psalmist claims nothing less than that his very body pines for God as a dry, weary land waits for water.

Only mystics can understand this. They alone can say to God with no exaggeration that His love is better than life itself, that thinking of God fills their soul as if treated to a sumptuous banquet, and that their very lips reverberate with joy as they praise God.

Mystics often spend their nights in musing about God. They feel as if overshadowed by God's protective wings. No mystic could really put much better and more concisely the sense of total union with God than the psalmist who addressed God with the words that may sound hollow except on the lips of true mystics: "My soul clings to you, your right hand holds me fast."

From this high point, the psalmist suddenly returns to the earth. As he does so he reveals his own identity: King David. Knowing his often checkered life, his failings, his earthiness, one may be tempted to take his foregoing utterances for rhetorical hyperbole. But the saints of Israel should not be judged by later standards. Though the father of all believers, Abraham remained the astute chief of a small desert tribe. He was no mystic, though once he was in a trance when he saw a smoking brazier and a flaming torch pass by him as darkness fell and a terrifying darkness enveloped him (Gen 15). Only when he showed readiness to sacrifice Isaac, did Abraham rise to the heroic summit of a total trust in God. So let us not be surprised that King David, the mystic, was far more often absorbed in daily clashes than rapt in union with God. Were we to deny him occasional mystical experiences, the closing words of the psalm, "for the mouth of liars will be silenced," words often applied to the guards of Christ's tomb, would apply also to us.

Psalm 64

This psalm, too, is a sort of soliloquy of the soul, rather than a prayer uttered to God himself. Jeremiah may have composed it in any of the many instances when he found himself threatened by "false" prophets and officials who thrived on false promises and perspectives. They rely on twisting words, on schemes whereby they want to trap their opponent in an unguarded phrase. Such are the "secret snares" they keep laying. To Jeremiah all this evokes the soldiery of his day, whose chief weapon is the bow and arrow whenever they do not want to engage in a hand to hand combat. Today he would speak of muffled handguns, of illegal wiretaps, of crisp banknotes with no fingerprints on them. In one respect the script remains unchanged: Perpetrators of such secretive tactics are apt to think that nothing will come to light as they ask themselves: "Who will see us? Who can search out our crimes?" After all, is not the practice of law being turned into an art of throwing endless roadblocks along the road to truth?

Today, when psychoanalysts and cognitive psychologists are alone expected to search in the deepest recesses of the human soul, the psalmist's reaction may appear outright anachronistic. The search, he states, will be done by that very God, who keeps searching the mind and who alone knows the depths of the heart. God is now set up as the archer who keeps shooting his arrows and inflicts deep wounds. God does so in a subtle way. God lets man's own tongue destroy him. A very biblical view indeed. A notable occurrence of it is in Psalm 36. Another is in James' Letter where almost the entire ch. 3 is about the wounds which the tongue inflicts on its user as well. Ominous should seem the remark there that while animals can be tamed, "the tongue no man can tame."

The concluding verse of the psalm celebrates the relief of the just, of the innocent. Let their chief joy consist in catching sight of the subtle ways in which God achieves His victory. And let this insight be coupled with the somber realization that the conflict will be renewed as long as there are men. For the psalm also states: "Then all men will fear," as "they tell what God has done." When man sees that God is manifestly at work, even the happy outcome should fill one with the kind of fear called awe.

Psalm 65

One has to ignore deliberately a great deal in this psalm in order to present it as a clarion call from above to commune with nature in an ecstatic mood. The hills, so this psalm states, are "girded with joy," indeed "they shout for joy." Nothing would then be more tempting than to read some superior aesthetics into the vision of this psalm about meadows covered with flocks and valleys decked with wheat. Hillsides against which the slowly moving fluffy furs of lambs look like little patches of clouds (if not cotton candies) are undoubtedly most pleasant to watch, though only from a distance. The thoughts of the shepherd who had already been beaten down from early morning by the blazing sun may be different. The ploughman, too, may rather think of his aching back as he makes ready to apply his scythe to the rolling waves of wheat covering the valleys. Gentlemen farmers are never without those whose skill is hard labor.

This is not to suggest that either the ploughman or the shepherd would not be happy. But their happiness is full of sobering realism. It is not they who write poems about the joy of husbandry and agriculture.

For this reason alone one should be careful not to read the spirit of New Age into this psalm, a spirit which is so readily triggered in those who make contact with nature from well appointed tourist buses and all-comfort caravans, have a sumptuous breakfast under their belt, and have at arm's length a portable frigidaire.

A far more important reason for caution is that the psalm sees God's intimate involvement in the joyful workings of nature. And when the watering of the earth is said to be the direct work of God who Himself fills the land of sunrise and sunset with joy, who Himself and not merely the atmospheric forces release a much needed precipitation, one should rather feel as Moses did when he saw the burning bush or when Peter saw the nets breaking for the magnitude of the catch. Moses prostrated himself in worship, whereas Peter, also in a posture of worship, begged: "Depart from me Lord, for I am a sinful man."

For the God, who according to this psalm, works so intimately in Nature, is a personal God, indeed the most Holy

God. And the psalmist makes no mistake about it. Such a God first of all deserves our praises and gratitude. The vows which we believers pay to God are a principal form of acknowledgment of our sense of indebtedness to Him for everything. In addition, the very thought of the presence of God, especially as present in the Temple, should fill man with the sense of his utter sinfulness. All flesh, that is, each and everyone, comes to Him with his or her burden of sin.

The biblical use of "flesh" for man (or woman) is indeed most penetrating. Our flesh has not ceased to pull us down toward nature, and our sins of flesh have always been a main motivation to call our sins virtues and then celebrate them as if they were means of worshiping God. Prostitution as temple service was a notable form of warped thinking. Today the old Pan with his leery smile is having a major comeback, and with frightening consequences. The mood of our times is not receptive to the information that the cult of Pan gave rise to the word "panic." Orgies performed in his sanctuaries, usually located in some very scenic spots, resounded with the shrieks of women who are always the first and chief victims of the illusion of taking nature for God.

Let the tone and thrust of this psalm be in the back of our minds as we see nature displayed in splendid photos in the pages of our magazines. Those photos talk to us of the wonders of nature, though never of their evanescent character. They are never made to refer to God who produces His wonders so that we may see Him as the One who keeps His pledge, that is, His Covenant with man. One of the ways He does this is to provide countless instances of a nature full of wonders. It would be wrong to see in them miracles, or special interventions of God in nature. But they are still genuine reasons for wonderment, which is the beginning of philosophy, indeed of metaphysics, or the art of seeing far beyond to what physics or any form of natural science can show us. Yet, as the very next psalm shows, wonderment, in the best sense, is far more effectively promoted by events that are not so much those of nature as of human nature that more than anything else has time, called history, for its lifeline and lifeblood.

Psalm 66

Just as the wonders of nature, the wonders of history, of which none are so powerful as those of salvation history, should make one break out in shouts of joy. But here, too, the joy is not merry-making. The deeds of God, over which we are supposed to be filled with joy, are "tremendous deeds." It was not possible for an Israelite, as he walked dry-shod across the Sea of Reeds and the Jordan, not to feel some terror. On seeing walls of water rise and stay must be a source of fright even when one firmly believes that God's hands hold them in place. Did not Peter begin to sink when he looked at the stormy waves around him instead of keeping his eyes fixed on the Lord?

Those wonders were given so that by keeping them in mind one would be able to bear with plain torments. The psalmist first of all considers such torments as were connected with the servitude in Egypt: "You (God) laid a heavy burden on our backs." But the reference to being tried as silver is purified, directs attention to trials that are forever connected with serving God and are the daily fare of any sincere believer.

The psalmist evokes those past experiences that involved the entire people, as a background and solution to a specifically personal trial he had to undergo. To assure God's help for a happy outcome, he made a vow which he brings to the Temple that serves as the focus of salvation history. And we do the same as we light a candle in front of the statue of our favorite saint and deck out grottos with votive offerings, often in small silver replicas of limbs miraculously cured. In doing so we merge our gratitude into the great river of salvation history which now is not limited to a people, but washes over the entire globe in a truly Catholic manner. But whether in the Old or in the New Covenant, the basic condition that should precede our fervent requests for divine favor, is the purity of soul. If God listened, it was mainly with an eye on the sincerity of our resolve not to sin again and avoid the proximate occasions of sin. Otherwise, "God would not have listened." Very biblical indeed is the prayer we use as we confess our sins in the confessional and voice our resolve not to sin again after we laid bare our sins to the priest who has the power to absolve.

Psalm 67

This psalm begins with the prayer which Moses prescribed to Aaron as the blessing to be invoked over the Israelites. And since the blessing is a divine blessing it has to have no limit: even the nations, indeed all the nations, must have a share in it.

This blessing is more needed than ever as all nations of the earth become more and more connected and try to cope with problems, though in a futile way evoking the specter of Sisyphus, who had to start all over again and again. May this blessing give us confidence that the nations will learn more and more that God alone can rule with fairness all the people, and that He alone can give safe guidance to them. Diplomats, who churn out endless phrases while disregarding the role of religion, should be listened to warily.

We shall not live to see the moment "till all the earth will revere Him," but we must take heart in the fact that our missionaries go out farther and farther. Until then let us not get tired of repeating the words of this psalm: "Let all the peoples praise you O God, let all the peoples praise you." Let us also ponder the all-important role of God's praise. Next to Francis Xavier, the contemplative Thérèse Martin is the chief patron saint of the missions. Her lasting renown reveals the utter hollowness of the remark of a once famed leader of the United Auto Workers of America who held that it was no more possible to add by prayer some splendor to God's glory than to enhance by candles the sun's brilliance. The flashes of atomic bombs, brighter than a thousand suns, had to come to awaken a great many to man's need to praise God.

Psalm 68

This is a psalm which, possibly more than any other psalm, landed its commentators in endless perplexities. There will be no time, so it seems, when the summary, which a noted commentator gave a hundred years ago of this psalm's earlier interpretations, would lose its validity: "Every conceivable occasion and date have been suggested for this psalm, from the age of Joshua to that of the Maccabees."

Less perplexing may be the task of suggesting ways of praying this psalm, so many centuries after its original composition and in a perspective very different from the one that determines the torrent of strong images.

The psalm had its origin in the conflation of a bold look into the distant past, of the actually felt joy over a fresh major victory, and of its being taken for a token of a sweepingly victorious future.

A look into the future opens the psalm, and does so with a verse that was used and misused in battles both noble and dubious. Saint Anthony of desert fame was heard to shout that verse, "Let God arise and scatter his enemies," as he felt that hordes of devils tempted him, a scene that titillated the kind of imagination which Hieronymus Busch pampered with his palette and brush. Now that belief in devils is hardly strong, the paintings of Busch are objects of admiration especially for those who try to cover up their nagging suspicion about the Evil One and his cohorts. To assure themselves they are ready to quote instances of the dubious uses of this psalm's first verse. One such case, the crusaders' use of that verse as their marching song, comes all too handy for them. They still have to see the enormous difference between lances and cruise missiles, as they heap scorn on the crusades and write thereby another chapter in Catholic bashing, this great cultural pastime of the age.

The psalmist's look into the past was a piece of the wisdom of hindsight that alone could paint the wandering in the desert as a triumphal advance. As to the victory just achieved by a "numberless army," referred to in verse 12, it cannot be identified even with the boldest imagination. The reference to women who make the most of the spoils of war seems to indicate some prosperous times of the Davidic kingdom. As to Mount Zalmon, it is mentioned in the Bible on only one other occasion. The name comes up in the Book of Judges (9:48) in connection with the campaign of Abimelech, one of the Minor Judges, against Migdal, a town in the Shechem area. Abimelech and his soldiers went there to cut brushwood which they then piled up and lighted at the entrance of a crypt where all the citizens of Migdal hid themselves. This was hardly an operation involving countless soldiers.

But historians of old were wont to inflate numbers. Herodotus and Thucydides come to mind, and Josephus, of course.

If the psalmist had in mind the exploit at Migdal, we have another problem on hand. Was it usual to have snowfall on that nearby but relatively low mountain? The Masoretic text has verse 15 in the following form: "While the Almighty scattereth kings on her [Mount Zalmon], it snoweth on Zalmon." Should this mean that a snowfall helped the Israelites to win? Or does the snow stand for the scattered bones of the defeated kings? Or did the enemies fall like snowflakes?

All these three interpretations, and some others, were proposed by learned exegetes. They should have perhaps considered Newman's rule of thumb about the development of doctrine: "History is not a creed or a catechism; it gives lessons rather than rules . . . Bold outlines and broad masses of colour rise out of the records of the past. They may be dim, they may be incomplete; but they are definite." One may, however, say one thing on behalf of exegetes bent on clearing up everything: Truth comes out much more readily from saying something than from saying nothing at all.

No better rule than the one just quoted from Newman can be given about how to pray the psalms and especially this psalm. Its great contours stand out clearly. It would be perilous to let oneself be lost in small details which no one may ever clear up to general satisfaction.

At any rate, there should be no mistake about the psalmist's violent wish for a crushing victory. No one with plain Christian common sense can read without shudder the following from Luther's commentary on this psalm. Luther's dicta are all the more shocking as, according to him, had "the psalmist chosen plain German," he would have spoken as follows: "O God, punish all those who push and press their way into the office of pope, bishops, cardinals, priests, monks, clerics and do not wait an urgent call to the office. For they assuredly seek only honor and wealth, gluttony, high living, and good days, and become bulls and tyrants of the people. They fabricate human ordinances to suppress Thy Gospel. They are actuated by the prospect of riches in the church donated by kings for the sustenance of the poor. O punish, punish, resist, resist them, dear Lord, lest Christendom perish!"

To speak in this vein was rather incongruous on Luther's part. First, he should not have forgotten his approval of the bigamy of Philip of Hesse. No justification for this could be sought in the need of the Gospel-based Church for being protected from the secular arm of the Holy Roman Empire whose laws ordered decapitation for bigamy and for connivance with it. Luther seemed to prefer not to think of the gravity of calling the evil good, which is the sin against the Holy Spirit. Jesus called it the only unforgivable sin (Mt 12:31). Second, why was it right for Luther to hold high "the urgent call to ecclesiastical offices" which he had already pilloried in his *Babylonian Captivity of the Church*? Finally, and most importantly, he, who staked everything by the Bible, should have recalled the Letter to the Ephesians where Paul sees an anticipation of Jesus' triumphal ascension into heaven in verse 19: "When he ascended on high, he took a host of captives and gave gifts to men" (Eph 4:8). But that triumph was not of this world, but over this world. If it was dangerous for the Church to accept the help of such a semi-convert as Constantine, of such a moral weakling as Charlemagne, and even of such a saintly king as Louis XII of France, it took sheer perversity to see benefits in allying the Gospel with the kind of moral monster Philip of Hesse was.

So much about the danger of entertaining on this earth hopes for the vindication of the right cause and of its full implementation. The final triumphant procession, so vividly described in the concluding part of this psalm, should best be left to the onset of a New Heaven and a New Earth. Meanwhile let us be ready to sweat and toil on behalf of the Kingdom of God, while singing its surpassing beauty.

As we trudge through this psalm, with a shudder felt now and then, we may at least think that even with respect to theological content the psalmists all too often did much better when they did not go to great lengths. Examples of this are numerous among the psalms. Brevity, which is the hallmark of genius, is something worth pondering by the theologian. The parables of Jesus are always to the point because they are brief.

Psalm 69

On hearing Jeremiah's dire prediction that those who refuse to go over to the Chaldeans but stay in the City would die of pestilence, the princes told King Zedekiah that unless Jeremiah was put to death the soldiers defending the city would be demoralized. The king handed Jeremiah over to the princes who then "threw him in the cistern of the Prince Malchiah, which was in the quarters of the guard, letting him down with ropes. There was no water in the cistern, only mud and Jeremiah sank into the mud." So goes the narrative in the Book of Jeremiah (38:6) which is relevant also to Psalm 40.

A dramatic elaboration of that harrowing incident is given in *Hearken to the Word*, a biography of Jeremiah by Franz Werfel, who earned a much greater fame by his *Song of Bernadette*. The latter is, in a sense, a success story which has a far greater appeal than the story of a disaster (Jerusalem's destruction). It does not pay to keep in print a reminder of a disaster that could have been averted. Worse, it foreshadowed an even greater destruction (on the same day of the same month as Josephus tells us) that also might have been avoided.

Psalm 40 resounded with Jeremiah's thanksgiving for his deliverance. Unlike there, where he took his plight for a punishment for his sins which he thought to be more numerous than the hair on his head, here he uses the same figure of speech about the number of his enemies who hate him for no reason.

About this psalm, so clear in its structure and diction, and so explicit about the mud into which the psalmist is sinking, one note at least should seem to be in order. Among his sufferings Jeremiah recounts the fact that he was sentenced to a slow death as he was given some food, though not much better than poison, and some vinegar for drink. Christians saw, of course, from the start, a prophecy fulfilled in what happened to Christ while on the cross. Jesus himself seemed to evoke verses of this psalm when He taunted the pharisees by saying that whether He was drinking or whether He was fasting, whether He was joyful or dressed in sackcloth, they invariably refused to listen to Him. Already in the early third century St. Hyppolitus of Rome, the first antipope and a martyr, interpreted this psalm as being full of pointers to the conflict between Jesus and the Jews and their respective coming out of it.

Without cursing the Jews among his contemporaries who still heavily felt the sweeping restrictions laid on them by Hadrian who built a pagan temple on the spot where the Temple once stood, Hyppolitus saw in their factual fate what was in store for the enemies of Christ whom the prophet represented. He also saw the resurrection of Christ and the triumph of the Church as events that gave full meaning to the concluding part of the psalm where Jeremiah speaks of a bright future for those still in chains. Perhaps the prophet added those verses after all leading classes were put in chains and deported to Babylon.

Once more one may sympathize with Jeremiah's elemental longing for justice, but not to the point of calling down God's punishment on one's enemies. We should keep in mind the harsh reprimand which Christ meted out to James and John as they asked his permission to call down fire on a Samaritan town: "You do not know of what manner of spirit you are" (Lk 9:55). Even if these words were not actually spoken by Our Lord, they well reflect His mind. If Marcion inserted that phrase, it only shows that not everything heretics say is heretical. But Our Lord certainly insisted that we must not judge, lest we be judged, a point which heretics in particular would do well to heed.

And we certainly must not forget the chief lesson given by Christ to us all about the need to suffer, with no consideration of whether the measure of suffering far exceeds the measure of our own personal guilt. Since in Christ absolute sinlessness suffered for the sins of others, sinners justified by Him have the privilege to help expiate by their suffering the sins of others. Paul himself looked at his suffering as bringing to completion what was lacking in Christ's suffering (Col 1:24). This is one of the aspects of the truth of Jesus' words about John the Baptist that the least in the Kingdom of God is greater than very great ones prior to the onset of that Kingdom. Among them were giants such as Jeremiah who reached no greater heights than when he was sinking into the mud and found no foothold there except his unshaken trust in the God of Israel: "In your great love, answer me, O God, in your love that never fails."

Psalm 70

This short psalm is an almost identical replica of verses 14-18 that bring Psalm 40 to a close. Standing by themselves as a psalm, they should bring into sharp focus something that has already been observed repeatedly: Psalms are prayers where perfection all too often goes hand in hand with imperfection. It is not, of course, possible to excise verses 3 and 4 that invoke divine vengeance on those who threaten one's life, although God often disposes of the enemies of His friends and servants in a dramatic way. Further, even those lines of the psalm, where the psalmist begs God for a speedy rescue, should be voiced only with the proviso, "Your will be done on earth as it is in heaven." The One who taught us to pray in such a way set the example with His own prayer as He knew that his enemies were about to arrest and deliver Him to death: "My Father, if this cup cannot pass away unless I drink it, thy will be done" (Mt 26:42). Most importantly, as He hung on the cross He prayed for those who put Him there. He sat thereby a pattern which it fell to Stephen to implement first and fittingly so for a protomartyr.

Psalm 71

Most likely Jeremiah composed this psalm. There can be no doubt that the psalm owed its origin to that experience, old age, which no old man, however much he may wish, can teach to the young. It is also a vain wish that one had the liberty to excise from this psalm verse 13: "Let them be put to shame and destroyed all those who seek my life. Let them be covered with shame and confusion all those who seek to harm me." In that case this psalm would be a perfect prayer for Christians who, like the rest of society, may expect to reach old age in ever larger numbers. As more and more of them become "old and grey headed," they will feel increasingly abandoned whether they are really so or not. The decline of one's physical and mental powers cannot but help create this feeling even if one is not "in the grip of the enemy, of the unjust." Some indeed will see evil spirits everywhere, when they have to contend only with their infirmities.

When "senior citizenship" becomes more and more a pursuit of "relaxation" in which one becomes exhausted as one cannot think up ever new forms of card parties, the praying of this psalm should spark the desire to be useful for the Kingdom of God even in one's declining years. Few are, of course, given the grace and the cross which is to be a "driven" man which Jeremiah certainly was. As befits a true prophet, his overriding desire was to prophesy, that is, to proclaim God's immeasurable greatness: "Let me tell of your power to all ages, praise your strength and justice to the skies."

Jeremiah did not suddenly try to be a prophet, unlike many today who, seized by some popular trend or some new fad, take their "prophetic" insights for a standing or falling matter for the Church. Jeremiah was a prophet, that is, one proclaiming in an emphatic way the praises of God since his youth. He never ceased praising Him: "My lips are filled with your praise, with your glory all day long." It was not a moment's fervor that made him say: "I will always hope and praise you more and more. . . I will declare the Lord's mighty deeds proclaiming your justice, yours alone." He wanted to tell of God: "You who have worked such wonders, who is like you?"

In an age of vain efforts to create a globalized good feeling, it may be difficult to persuade ourselves that there is a unique series of wonders, God's great deeds of salvation history, that stand apart from all other "wonders." To stand resolutely by the unique greatness of those wonders is what makes a true prophet and also makes his life precarious, especially in old age. Jeremiah feels that his stance sets him apart from main-line thinking. And so do many elderly Christians today, who see that line rapidly widening into that broad avenue that leads, in Christ's words, to perdition.

The fact that Jeremiah did not perish "has filled many with awe." Old age makes survival even more precarious. Jeremiah begs God: "Do not reject me now that I am old; when my strength fails do not forsake me." We old (or young) should resonate to Jeremiah's happy anticipation of things turning for the better: "You have burdened me with bitter troubles but you will give me back my life. You will raise me from the depths of the earth; you will exalt me and console me again." Let many more of us be filled with Jeremiah's desire to give thanks to God for His faithful love, to sing to Him "with the harp," to Him "the Holy One of Israel." And let more of us have our very "lips rejoice" as we sing to Him.

But we must go beyond Jeremiah who on seeing his being liberated from the grip of death, also looked forward to seeing all who tried to harm him "put to shame and disgraced." Jeremiah lived long before the onset of the age of grace where one has to consider it a blessing, a privilege, to suffer unjustly for the just cause. In praying this psalm two verses from Peter's First Letter ought to be recalled by Christians, who, of course, should take care lest anyone of them suffer for having destroyed the rights of anyone else: "If anyone suffers for being a Christian, however, he ought not to be ashamed. He should rather glorify God in virtue of that name" (4:16). And if this were not enough to put Christians well beyond Jeremiah's perspective, another injunction of Peter puts them immeasurably beyond it: "Rejoice, instead, in the measure that you share Christ's sufferings" (4:13).

This rejoicing bespeaks of the onset of the truly New Age. Only within that perspective can one see the usefulness of Jeremiah's reference to his having been the object of God's special attention already when he was in his mother's womb. Christians who have relatively lately discovered the usefulness of this for their crusade against abortion, would do well to pause and reflect. Their visceral revulsion to abortion stems from their Christian being, which is inconceivable without the Word having dwelt among us from the very moment when He was conceived, by the Holy Spirit, in the womb of a maiden, who was and remained a Virgin for reasons far transcending mere biological considerations. Once they ponder this, they would not only drop their antagonism to what they call the "mariolatry" of Catholics, but also perceive the deepest reason why Vatican II called abortion an "abominable crime." Catholics, engaged in Pro-Life activities, cannot, of course, reflect long and hard enough on the deepest reason for their opposition to abortion.

That reason, Mary, or rather her reply, "Let it be to me according to thy words," to the angel, is recognized at times in a truly roundabout way. Think of Marina Warner, a convent-educated apostate from the faith, unable to shake off the perception that Mary is indeed *Alone of All Her Sex*, the title of a book of hers. Of course, she does her best to shake off or discolor that perception. In connection with a new book of hers she claimed that her Catholic upbringing impaired her powers of imagination (*Time*, May 24, 1999). In view of the pre-eminent patronage which the Church has always given to artists, she must have given a holiday to her fancy in making that claim of hers. It takes little imagination to see that the proclamation of the full truth about Christ remains strong only as long as one views the maiden from Nazareth as one truly "alone of all her sex" and not merely unique because she cannot be fitted into stale and narrow literary categories. Such is truly a wisdom for one's old age, if one has not nurtured it from one's youth on.

Psalm 72

A beautiful psalm, which, like all beauty, can be a distraction, indeed a trap. The psalm may date back to the days of Solomon, the king legendary for his wisdom in handing down justice. The psalm may have been written in the closing years of David's reign with Solomon looming ever larger as the next king. Reference to the kings of Sheba and Seba, who carry tribute to Jerusalem, evoke Solomon's reign. The same is also indicated by the portrayal of the kingdom as extending from the Great River (Euphrates) to the bounds of the earth, that is, the Mediterranean and by the reference to the kings of Tarshish (possibly Tartessus in Spain) and of the sea coast (Phoenicia) as Solomon's vassals. Such was the extent of Solomon's world, actually a puny stretch on a globe of which no one at that time had any idea. When during the reign of Pharaoh Necho (c. 600 B. C.) some Egyptian sailors sailed around Cape Horn and found the noon sun shining from the "wrong" side, neither they nor anyone else asked any question. By the time Strabo, the first-century geographer, reported that observation indicative of the earth's sphericity, the latter had been established for centuries by the learned among the Greeks. So much for the psalm's wistful evocation of the "whole earth lying prostrate" before the king celebrated in this psalm.

Those concerned with the population bomb may not find to their taste the prospect of a kingdom in which men will flourish in the cities like grass on earth, even if food (corn) is so abundant as to pile up to the top of the hills. There are limits to messianic hopes as long as they remain very earthbound. The kingdom in which all the poor and needy are saved, where all the weak will be the object of kindness and all the lives of all the poor will be saved, is, of course, not of this world. Those who look askance at the fearsome prophecy that the poor will always be with us, may ponder the invariable failure of socialists to equalize everything and of the inability of capitalists to provide equity funds for everybody. Science has been available to both sides, only the funds of good will are stubbornly running short.

Surprising as it may appear, science, or rather its indispensable background, is hiding between some lines of this psalm. The psalm declares that the rule of the king comes about unfailingly. But in order to convey this outcome the psalmist does not refer to Israel's unshakable trust in God's assistance to the people as manifest in His great deeds, the "magnalia Dei." Rather, he refers to the unfailing operation of nature. The kingdom shall endure as unfailingly as the sun and the moon endure. The same idea is conveyed with a reference to the (unfailing) descent of "the rain on the meadows, of raindrops on the earth."

The idea of God's unfailing, providential assistance would not have been conveyed with a reference to the stable working of nature if nature had been looked upon as a sort of capricious deity. Yet only the perspective of a nature stable in its processes could provide the conceptual matrix for the eventual rise of science. There is indeed far more to the fact that when it comes to considering nature, the psalms reflect a perspective very different from that in the canticles of the great and small neighbors of Israel. The reason for this difference is not a national genius, let alone some genetic superiority of the Jews. The reason lies in their being selected to be the carriers of belief in the Maker of Heaven and Earth.

Prime victims of racism, Jewish intellectuals failed to protest when C. P. Snow traced to genetics the unusually large number of Jews among Nobel laureates. Of course, today one need not believe in God (most prominent Jewish scientists do not) to do science well, indeed very well. But belief in God was indispensable for science to be born. This, however, happened at a time when the Old Covenant had been long supplanted by the New in which there was no place for dreams about a Messianic Kingdom. Yet science came in fulfillment to the promise of the Gospel: "Seek ye the kingdom of God and the rest will be given to you." But if science, included in that surplus, is taken for a key to a heaven on earth, the earth itself may turn into a sheer hell for mankind. Such is a sad truth about the power of science to work wonders that dazzle man and dull him into false expectations. About the latter nothing is so expressive as the words of a Nobel laureate physicist: "To assume that science may find a technical solution to all problems is the road to disaster."

Surely, great caution is needed to pray this psalm with true spiritual profit. For it is not earthly glory which is the true meaning of the concluding doxology of this second "book" of psalms:

> Blessed be Lord, the God of Israel,
> who alone works wonders,
> ever blessed his glorious name.
> Let his glory fill the earth. Amen! Amen!

Book III, Psalms 73-89

Psalm 73

"The problem of innocent suffering" is the caption given to this psalm in the Grail translation. A subtly but gravely misleading caption indeed. Of course, within a perspective where justice is expected to be dealt out in this life on earth, the envy which tortures the psalmist may seem justified. After all he considers himself pure of heart, yet he finds himself at the same time strongly disadvantaged in comparison with some who in his eyes are plain wicked people.

On reading the psalmist's description of the wicked, one cannot help thinking of the old saying, nothing is new under the sun. It would indeed be difficult to improve on lines that describe the good fortunes of the wicked as "the lot of those for whom no pain exists." The psalmist seems to have anticipated the smiling faces that fill our billboards with their gigantic display of bodies "sound and sleek." They never seem to experience sorrow, they are "not stricken like others."

But this is just the beginning of modernity in this psalm. The wicked are described as ones "who wear their pride like a necklace," and show no remorse for running roughshod over anyone who stands in their way. Ruthless competition is good for society, they claim, and ignore that society exists only on paper. Individuals alone bear the brunt of the "laissez faire, laissez passer."

The successful wicked "scoff, they speak with malice," they plan their power moves to mow down others in their way. The psalmist proves himself a first-rate social critic as he portrays the wicked's bully pulpit: "They have set their mouths in the heavens, and their tongues dictate to the earth." He has in mind something far worse than the open crudity of dictators. Carefully staged press conferences of any "democratic" leader fit the bill extremely well. To make the picture perfect, the psalmist adds: "So the people turn to follow them and drink in all their words." For all their professed respect for religion, those prosperous wicked seem to say to themselves: "How can God know? Does the Most High take any notice?"

To such incisive vignettes lengthy exposés of corrupt leaders in such classics as Juvenal's *Satires* or Sallustius' *Lives of the Twelve Caesars* cannot hold a candle. Nor can anything expose one's misjudgment of the state of affairs more subtly than the psalmist's own complaint addressed to God: "Look at them, such are the wicked, but untroubled they grow in wealth." Deep in his heart the psalmist knows that his complaint may indeed be very misplaced as he feels that his complaint may make him disloyal to God: "If I should speak like that, I should betray the race of your sons." For if that race had any obligation it was the rule that God's loyalty to that race should never be questioned.

Still the psalmist cannot shake off his perplexity. The solution he finds to it is both ingenious and inadequate. True enough, one finds it again and again that coasting on success may end in a sudden downfall. God seems to have set the prosperous wicked "on a slippery path," they are often found "to slide to destruction." They are often seen to meet their ruin "suddenly." Their success story often ends as abruptly as dreams do. The waking hours are no friend of phantasy mongers.

Such observations are remedy for the psalmist's embittered soul and a cure for his "being cut to the quick." He now suddenly sees that his complaints showed him to be no better than a stupid beast. He now realizes that God never forgot him, that he was always in God's presence, that God has "always held him by hand." There is a mystical touch to this, nowhere to be found in the religious literature of Egyptians, Babylonians, and Canaanites even when their rulers were portrayed alongside with their gods.

The psalmist now seems to rise to mystical heights. He now knows that he has only God in heaven, a symbol of man's highest desires, and that there is no point in having anything on earth except God. His entire being, body and soul, seems to reverberate with the joy of possessing God Himself and "possessing Him forever."

But is truly such the case? Is that "forever" truly a reference to eternity? The last two verses do not seem to confirm this. They show the psalmist descend to distinctly earthly perspectives. He specifies his solution to his erstwhile perplexity in that he would one day stand as a substantial citizen on the market place, that is, at the city gate.

The Old Testament found it indeed very hard to surpass itself and show something convincingly of the perspective of the New. One need not wait as long as the coming of the Poverello. It is enough to re-read Paul's parting words to the community of Ephesus where he labored for three years. He earned his sustenance from hard work without ever setting his "heart on anyone's silver or gold, or envying the way he dressed" (Acts 20:33).

Let the praying of this psalm be a reminder that our Christian prayers can be of very low level even if full of sharp observations and consoling half-solutions. Too many of us will not see the sleek and prosperous wicked slide headlong down the slippery path. To be near God will be our happiness only if it makes no difference to us whether we shall or shall not be recognized as God's friends at the Gates of Sion or at the steps of the City Hall, and face the flattery of reporters who could not care less about God even when they write about religion.

Psalm 74

Only an eyewitness of the destruction of Jerusalem and of the Temple in 586 B. C. could have written this psalm. One would destroy the psalmist's graphic description of what happened by trying to paraphrase it. Great poetry, especially when steeped in concrete reality, should be savored in its own terms.

Something may, however, be added to the psalmist's reference to the fact that not only the Temple but other places of worship have as well been destroyed. In spite of the efforts of prophets and Yahwists of lesser rank, Israel worshiped in a number of high places, including ones dedicated to pagan gods. Here, too, the ideal failed to shape reality in full, or even remotely so.

Just as noteworthy should seem the fact that the psalmist, Jeremiah, takes recourse to the power of God as evidenced in his primordial act of creation. He does this in order to derive hope for a better future, for a future that would show that God's covenant is trustworthy indeed. In order to convey God's over-whelming power, it is described as victorious over the hostile forces of nature. Those who view biblical creation as a cosmic struggle between God and Chaos, a Chaoskampf, found in verses 12-15 their chief support, although for no good reason. The Bible is more than a few of its phrases taken out of context and in rank disregard of many other of its utterances. The absence of any trace of a struggle on God's part as His creative work is de-scribed in Genesis 1 should come to mind.

But even this psalm contains lines that run counter to seeing God the Creator as being embattled by cosmic powers. Suppose the psalmist had taken Leviathan for a real opponent of God, whose head God had to crush in a bloody encounter, reminiscent of Marduch's gory dismemberment of the body of Tiamat, the great Mother. In that case the psalmist would have hardly spoken with utter calm about the sun, a chief deity for pagans and the object of Akhenaton's alleged monotheism. In the psalmist's eyes the sun is wholly subordinate to God: "Yours is the day, yours is the night, it was you who appointed the light and the sun."

Surely, some such considerations should be of great help in times of great distress, indeed of total social upheaval. Add to this the times when chaos is celebrated by those, scientists, who invariably fail to define that term. One can but throw up one's hands in despair when a major political Party can be described, without much exaggeration, as "thriving on chaos" (*The Wall Street Journal*, May 19, 1999).

The result is the spread of violence, prophetically anticipated in the verse where the word "caves" may be replaced by "dens" with screens of TV sets as their sole illumination, with the sets themselves showing murderous acts round the clock. The same sets also abound in programs that thrive on denouncing the hawks while they pretend to promote the cause of doves.

Jeremiah would wonder but he would hardly be surprised. He would certainly cry out and we can but join him in crying out to the Lord: "Remember how the senseless revile you all the day." Only we should refrain from thinking even for a moment that He would ever forget the "clamor and the daily increasing uproar of his foes." Unlike Jeremiah we should know that the clamor would never die out until the end of time, and indeed it may turn into a deafening uproar as time approaches its very end. Still we must look forward with joyful expectation to the Lord's coming.

Let us derive strength from praying this psalm. Our greatest troubles have not been as great as the agonies of those who had to watch axes batter the door of the Temple and foreign emblems set up in it. Even when French troops raised a huge altar to the god of Reason and Liberty in Saint Peter's Square in 1797, they did not touch the Basilica itself. They did not seem to have forgotten completely that the Basilica towered over the tomb of a fisherman who answered to the name Simon until the Lord Himself changed it to Peter or Rock, to serve as the foundation of a Church never to be overcome.

Psalm 75

Were we still in the middle of the Cold War between East and West, it would be tempting to enlarge on this psalm as an implicit warning against lining up God on one or the other side. Moreover, instead of East and West, one could just as well write North and South as Aldous Huxley did in his *Brave New World.* Why the psalmist did not refer also to the south and the north, but only to east and west is somewhat puzzling if one thinks of Egypt and Assyria, two of Israel's chief enemies.

But the psalm raises more important considerations than partly political. There is a never ending applicability to the verses that render God's warning to the wicked: "Do not boast, do not flaunt your strength, . . . do not speak with insolent pride." Pride is difficult to bear, but when pride is insolent even God's patience may seem to wear thin.

It is difficult to fit God into a role in which He seems to hand out a cup "full of wine, foaming and spiced" which "the wicked must drink to the dregs." Such a wine could serve either to deprive the guilty of his senses in order to endure cruel punishment or to convey its full measure.

To be sure, it remains rightful even within the New Covenant to long for a satisfaction of one's sense of justice. We were taught to pray that God's kingdom come and that we may be freed from the grip of the Evil One. We must keep our faith alive in the fact that, all appearances to the contrary, God is the sole guarantee of stability, that His perspectives will remain in place even when "the earth and all who dwell in it may rock."

But we, who also have been taught not to judge, lest we be judged, can repeat only with reservations the psalmist's confident anticipation of a total vindication of the just: "The power of the wicked will be broken and the strength of the just will be exalted." This vindication on earth is only partial and even then its true measure often remains partly hidden. We should keep recalling God's wonderful deeds, without ever trying to nudge Him to come up with the next one, let alone trying to impose on Him our notion of what is wonderful.

Psalm 76

This psalm most likely was composed in circumstances similar to the ones that gave rise to Psalm 46. Here, however, the event, possibly the sudden demise of Sennacherib's army, is brought much closer to Jerusalem than in the other psalm. If a huge horde of mice caused the havoc of the invading army, then one can see the work of millions of mice at play in the verse, "horse and rider lay stunned," as the mice chewed into pieces harness and thong. If they were rats, carriers of bubonic plague, then one can see the reason why "the warriors, despoiled, slept in death," and why "the hands of the soldiers became powerless."

In the light of faith for which nothing happens by "accident" the outcome is readily ascribed to God. Indeed it is better to invoke God, who by definition is the ultimate and all pervading "cause," than to write otherwise interesting books on history under the title *Chance*, or the like. The astronomical improbability of events described in such stories can hardly be evaluated mathematically. Take, for instance, the case of Napoleon's envoy in Madrid, who got into a carriage no sooner had he learned from Paris that he should instruct the French Navy in Cadiz not to leave port. Before long a peg fell out of one the wheels. By the time he arrived in Cadiz the French Navy was out on the high seas to meet its fate in Nelson's hands. Had the French ships stayed in port, they would have been spared the terrible storm that maimed Nelson's fleet the day after the battle of Trafalgar. History would have been very different.

We may, of course, rejoice at some most incredible turns of events. Bishops, who were taken to Nicaea by Imperial post in 325, thought they were dreaming. It also should be a cause for rejoicing that time and again "the kings of the earth" seem to be struck by terror, or at least by that fear of God which is the beginning of wisdom. Time and again it happens that "man's anger" boomerangs on him while at the same time it serves God designs. But instead of trying to write history on behalf of God, we should concentrate on fulfilling our various vows all of which are legitimate only if they try to implement the vows made at our baptism and renewed at each Easter vigil. There we pledge ourselves to resist the continual scheming of the Enemy who never tires of slighting, with the help of leading newspapers, the magnitude of Christ's victory at Easter.

Yet at the dawn of that day a new phase of history dawned on mankind. From that moment on a wholly new dimension was taken on by the first line of this psalm: "God is made known in Judah, in Israel his name is great." A new Israel began to penetrate to the four corners after the risen Lord commanded eleven plain men to preach in His name, beginning from Jerusalem to the ends of the earth. The astonishing results should strongly suggest that He would indeed remain with them until the end of the world.

Psalm 77

Obviously, this psalm was composed at a time of a great national calamity. The psalmist is totally perplexed. He groans at night, he finds no comfort, and desperately tries to get to the very root of his perplexity. He bemoans the calamity mainly because it poses a painful contrast between the past and the present. The contrast suggests nothing less than that God himself has changed. A terrible prospect because the chief attribute of the true God is that He does not change, a major proposition in Psalm 102.

The past, a fairly remote past to be sure, evokes God as faithfully standing by His people and in contexts that could not have been more calamitous. Of such contexts one, the crossing of the Sea of Reeds, stands out by its gigantic proportion. As the greatest wonder which God worked on behalf of the people, it became especially engraved in their memory. It is that event which now the psalmist recalls in order to strengthen his faith in God's faithfulness. Clearly, a God who worked such an astonishing miracle was not—to give some modernity to the psalmist's train of thought—a mere creation of man's wishful thinking. He had to be a uniquely truthful God who could be counted upon in all calamities forever.

The psalmist then describes that crossing in a way which deserves special attention. Not so much because his account of it illustrates that the Bible can describe the same miracle in different forms, but because he provides one of the very rare texts in the Bible where one finds nature animated. Yet this animation is a very special kind. Not even in its most poetic part, the psalms, does the Bible presents nature as having its own volition in reference to itself and to its parts. The Bible does not betray a trace of the Greek view in which stones fall toward the earth because they have a longing for their "natural" place in it. Rather, if nature has in the Bible an animated reaction it is only in the form of a response to God's voice. Here, too, the Bible is in a class apart from other ancient and modern religious literature where the world is a huge animal, an idea where all pantheism begins and ends.

So different is indeed the God of nature, as given in the Bible, from Nature itself as to remain wholly unnoticeable even when various parts of nature are giving a tumultuous response to Him. In a line, which should seem priceless for any interpreter of miracles, biblical and ecclesial, the psalmist declares that although God's very path led through the mighty waters, "no one saw your footprints." For when God passes through by allowing something incomparable to occur, He does this without forcing man into a blind submission. Still the miracle stares in man's face so that he might recognize God's direct guidance.

And just as God guided Israel through the hands of Moses and Aaron, hands that could work miracles, so does God guide the New Israel through hands (think of saintly popes and bishops) that time and again worked miracles. Those hands can always be raised as if they were the arms of an infallible judge to pronounce on miracles that, as our Lord promised, would always abound in "the flock of God which he redeemed at the price if his own blood" (Acts 20:28).

Psalm 78

This is one of the longest psalms and like most such psalms it needs few explanatory comments, beyond those that can be found in any properly annotated Bible. The plains of Zoan are, of course, the plains around Tanis, the Egyptian name for Zain, a city on the Tanitic branch of the Nile's delta and the residence of Rameses II. There the pharaoh of Exodus time held court and it is from there that the Jews began their escape from servitude. The Bible does not specify either here in verse 9, or elsewhere, the battle in which the sons of Ephraim proved themselves unreliable.

Their failure seems to symbolize a broader failure which is the chief concern for the psalmist here. It is not the failure of nerve, but the failure of memory. The mind lives on memory. Educators who for decades have frowned on the time-proven method of learning by rote, now begin to realize that unless the memory is trained, it will not learn and what it learned it would readily forget. Only furrows (or memory paths) drawn into one's grey matter during one's childhood prove to be of lasting value. The psalmist indeed urges the elders and the parents to drill their children's memory about "hidden lessons of the past," or else they will become like their fathers, a rebellious race.

But what is the cause of that pattern of rebelling? The psalmist finds that cause in a resolve not to remember. Of course, one does not want to remember truths and facts that keep one always on one's toes. Relaxation, the great shibboleth of our times, was also the catchword among the Israelites of old. They loved to sit down to eat and drink so that they might play all the better (Ex 32:6). It is always inviting to sit back and relax if this helps one to forget what is to be remembered above all.

And this is the psalmist's great charge: "They forgot the things he [God] has done." Those who think that if they only saw a miracle with their very eyes, they would forever be fervent servants of the Lord, should pause. They would just as well forget that miracle as did those who witnessed God's great deeds, the "magnalia Dei," on the plains of Zoan, and during the Exodus. In fact, in the very wake of seeing the rock split and turn into a gushing fountain, their faith in God seemed to evaporate: "Can he also give us food?"

God came through, but they had to learn the price of slighting God. A plague that decimated the rank and file of Israel followed in quick order: "They were struck down while the food was still in their mouths." The rest reconsidered but not too long. Their protestations of loyalty were "mere flattery." Their hearts were not truly with God. And if one asks, why?, the psalmist is quick with his answer: Their mind was not focused on God. They made no effort to remind themselves of some crucial events of the past. And once more they put God to the test.

Here we come to the part, perhaps the most dramatic part of the psalm in which the psalmist recites facts as if he were aiming a machine gun at his people or at least at their memory. The ten plagues are recounted in rapid, relentless order, one graphic detail after another. The dynamics can easily carry away the one who wants to pray this psalm. Before he knows, he is beyond that marvelous sequence, without fixing anything of it in his memory. Perhaps it would be useful to amplify each line from verses 42 to 53 as follows: "They did not remember that He worked his miracles in Egypt; they did not remember that He turned their rivers into blood; they did not remember that He sent dog flies against them," and so on and so on.

Today, when so much leeway is given to "creative" approaches to the recitation of the psalms, this innocent innovation, a mere help for one's memory, might perhaps be introduced without incurring the wrath of some self-appointed guardians of the liturgy. If liturgy is truly God's service, let it serve the rule that God must be served in spirit and in truth. But unless the mind is reminded of things so dear to God, one's prayer can hardly become the elevation of the mind to God.

The last part of this psalm tells us something about its origin. Nowadays, when dubious sociological categories are heedlessly projected into exegesis, it has become a fad to see in this psalm a propaganda piece written by the power circles in Judah. Surely, the tribe of Judah was not beyond some political tricks devised against the other tribes. The Bible is all too clear on the point that the secession of the Northern tribes, all ten of them, was triggered by some power hungry individuals in Judah. But the pre-eminence of Judah was not entirely of human make. To forget this is to forget the salient points of Israel's history, so unexplainable by human standards. Perhaps the "children of exegetes," too, would retrain their memories so that "their children's children" would do better than their rebellious fathers, who turned their back in the battle. This they did, although armed with bows, that is, with all the sound weapons to oppose the rationalists for whom it made no difference whether it was Yahweh, or Baal, or Zoroaster, or Gautama, or Confucius.

For we must stay with Judah and its king David to whom was entrusted the Ark of the Covenant and its perennial future. There is nothing more important to remember if one is to pray as a Christian is supposed to pray. For Christ is not Christ unless He is the son of David.

Psalm 79

Most commentators see this psalm as an echo of the destruction of Jerusalem by Nabuchadnessar. The echo sounds like the voice of Jeremiah, who laments what happened, acknowledges the guilt, appeals to Yahweh's compassion, and invokes divine punishment on those who perpetrated the sacrilege. He does all this with an intensity and sweep that sound like the roar of a tidal wave.

Jeremiah's diction derives much of its strength from attention to concrete details. The psalm evokes vultures in the air, pools of blood on the ground, and heaps of corpses all over. Later, he recalls "the groans of prisoners" and makes us see those who are "condemned to die." Had he played to the galleries, he would have included gory details, such as the gouging of the eyes of King Zedekiah after he had to witness the execution of his own sons, including the crown prince.

But being a religious man Jeremiah's attention was riveted above all on Yahweh and His compassion. We can easily guess what was in Jeremiah's mind as he reminded Yahweh of Jacob being devoured. Jacob or Israel was the apple of God's eye, the special object of divine love. Jeremiah feels certain that God cannot fail to come to the people's rescue. In addition to God's love, the cause of His own glory would require it. Jacob was the flock of His pasture, a fact which constitutes Jeremiah's final appeal for divine forgiveness and compassion. The prodigal son comes to mind. Though utterly prodigal and wretched, a son still he was and the son of a true Father in heaven.

In speaking of the guilt of the people Jeremiah speaks both of the sins of his own generation and of the sin of their fore-fathers. Here Jeremiah could have easily passed in review the abomination piled up during Manassah's sixty-year-long reign, during which even the scrolls of the Torah became apparently lost. But just as in reference to the actual physical devastation, in reference to sins that triggered it Jeremiah exercises great re-straint. He seems to have wanted to give a hymn of manageable size for the use of people who were at a loss for words.

Christian nations that saw their sanctuaries and cities destroyed by pagan hordes could find this psalm very germane to voicing their own sorrow and hope. Yet they could not use some of this psalm's verses without some mental reservations. Once more the Christian finds himself up against the idea of vengeance which he cannot and must not invoke.

Psalm 80

The psalm begins with a portrayal of God in a combination of a very terrestrial and a very heavenly scene. Even today, when sheep and shepherds have become a curiosity in lands overtaken by machines, it is easier to imagine God as a shepherd than as one who sits on a "cherubim throne." To picture those celestial beings, flying with six wings that cover them entirely, one should recall either Isaiah's vision of his own calling or the great vision which Ezekiel had at a time when the tribes of Ephraim, Benjamin, and Manasseh—all to the north of Judah—had become a mere memory, tribes that stand out vividly in this psalm. Therefore its composition very likely antedates the end of the entire Northern Kingdom in 721 B. C.

The imagery of the vine remained vivid to the very end of the Jewish kingdom. The huge door of the Second Temple, as rebuilt and redecorated by Herod, had a large vine sculpted on it. As the Eleven accompanied Jesus from the Cenacle to the Mount of Olives after the Last Supper and looked back on the Temple they had occasion to notice that vine. It evoked to them Jesus' words: "I am the vine, you are the branches." As such they would be pruned again and again if they were to bring forth fruit. Some verses of this psalm, dominated by the image of the vine, must have also echoed in their memory. The image of the people as God's own vineyard was a chief symbol of everything connected with the Covenant.

On more than one occasion the vine, as transplanted from Egypt, was subjected to devastation in various degrees. The one referred to in this psalm may have come early after the reign of Solomon which was the high water mark of the Jewish Kingdom, stretching from the great river (Euphrates) to the sea (the Mediterranean). Now parts of the vineyard lay devastated by intruders, described as "the boar of the forest" and "the beasts of the field." Its walls lay in ruin, parts of it were burnt down, and any passerby could pluck its produce. Such was a sharp contrast with the vine's best form, when it cast its shadow over the mountains and its branches rose higher than the "cedars of God," obviously the cedars of Lebanon.

The verse, "O God of hosts, bring us back. Let your face shine on us and we shall be saved," repeated three times in the psalm, may suggest an exclamation on the part of those whom the invaders dragged away into servitude. Or the verse simply voiced the desire for a general restoration of a better past. The psalm raises only once the question why all this happened and only once indicates that God abandoned the people because the people forsook Him.

A brief but pointed expression is given to the awareness that without God's assistance to the leader (identified by the psalmist as "the son of man") whom God had chosen, the hoped for turnaround would not come to pass.

In the Targum this "son of man" is taken for the Messiah and the same interpretation has been offered by most exegetes until some rationalist exegetes took the view, a strange one indeed, that the people are "the son of man." In exegesis as elsewhere rationalism has its moments of an illogicality bordering on irrationality.

The devotional applications of this psalm are inexhaustible. One may think of the devastation which sin, let alone habitual sin, produces in the vineyard which is the soul. One may think of periodically repeated spiritual decline within religious orders. But the most obvious application relates to the great reversals within the Church at large, to the loss of entire Christian nations to the cause of true faith.

Cardinal Wiseman held this psalm to be the prayer for the conversion of England. Children of other "Christian" nations will equally find this psalm expressive of their own predicament. One should only think of the loss of faith all across Europe in recent decades. The magnitude of that devastation was best put in 1984 by the bishop of Fatima, as he told a gathering at the Technical University of Vienna that the loss in question was a greater calamity than the explosion of an atomic bomb.

The few Catholics surviving in North Korea, once a flourishing mission area, may have their own fondest wishes voiced in this psalm. And the same holds true of the Vietnamese. But one should not yield to despair. Next to the somber facts of history there are some brilliant ones, resplendent as if the light of God's very face were shining on them. One may think of the "resurrection" of the Church in France following the havoc wrought on it by the Revolution. All too often those who are the intellectuals of the day, turn blind eyes to changes already under way. In 1830 Victor Cousin, professor of the Sorbonne, took the view that faith was already dying out in Paris and within a few decades it would be largely extinct all over France. Once more reports about the demise of the Church were premature as well as immature.

As to Paris, Catherine Labouré was soon to have her visions immortalized in the Miraculous Medal. Less than three decades later the Virgin appeared to Bernadette in a distant corner of France and made it clear to the enemies of the Church that they were not to win. In Italy Don Bosco served evidence that the Church, God's vineyard, was full of vigor. The raising of a statue for Giordano Bruno in Rome in 1900 was a celebration by militant anticlericals oblivious to their being already rolled back. Half a century earlier Newman preached about the Second Spring of faith in England. In North America heroic priests and nuns carried the faith across stretches of a land much vaster than all the European countries from which they had set out armed only with faith in the Church as the sole ark of salvation.

It is easy to imagine the feeling of those heroic souls were they to see today the well-nigh complete disappearance of the Catholic character of most Catholic colleges and universities, to say nothing of the closing of about half of Catholic high schools. Self-styled Catholic professors roam, like so many "wild beasts of the forest" across Catholic campuses. This happened because of a widespread yielding during the 1960s to the mirage of a human nature good in its own terms.

Still the light from God's face will not fail to shine forth, provided strong and loud will sound the verse: "God of hosts bring us back, let your face shine on us and we shall be saved." But this voice will grow weak and insipid in God's ears whenever we no longer think of ourselves as "the exiled children of Eve" and feel therefore no pressing need to be brought back from the wastelands of mere nature.

Psalm 81

Beginning as it does with a call to "ring out your joy to God our strength," this psalm may have an especially strong appeal at a time such as ours when "joy" has become a magic word.

Undoubtedly, God made a Covenant with man in order to fill his heart with joy. If there is a revealed truth, this is it. Through his servant Moses, God ordered a special feast to be established to celebrate joy. The Feast of the Tabernacles, referred to in this psalm, was that very feast.

A popular feast it was, almost a fair, with shofars resounding. It had its standard paraphernalia, huts made with boughs and branches, certainly a source of fun for the young. Parents who had to build those huts and then had to clear up the mess may have been glad that there was only one such Feast all year along. Think of Christmas.

The psalm itself is a call to very serious reflections as it is a classic reminder that regardless of whether one is in the Old or in the New Covenant one's joy should be tempered with very hard thinking. The branches and boughs were to be so many reminders of a time when Israel lived a hard life in makeshift huts, wandering through the desert. For the good things of life in the Promised Land they had indeed to be most grateful.

No politician would dare to propose a national feast to be spent in shacks as a reminder of depression times. No President would suggest that the people should live every year for a few days in log cabins with no running water in order to appreciate the newly acquired amenities of life. No innovative liturgist would suggest that the faithful spend one Sunday in unheated churches during winter, because the Holy Family had no central heating, indeed no heating at all. Today one can hardly believe that Fr. O'Hara, President of Notre Dame and subsequently Cardinal Archbishop of Philadelphia, put some undergraduates in their place with a reference to the Holy Family as they complained of cold during early morning masses in Advent. Half a century later many find it an imposition to go to "convenient" evening masses which impress one more as a celebration than a participation in the most awesome sacrifice.

Today religion often degenerates into the kind of politicking where everything is promised in return for practically nothing. Time was when a young President could still call on Americans to ask themselves what they can do for their country instead of asking what the country can do for them. At that time appeal still could be made to religious fervor in the youth as they volunteered for the Peace Corps. Today, another young President praises the great contribution of homosexuals to the country and rejoices in the embrace of a Hollywood bent on making a mockery of faith and morals. He sat on his hands, together with his Vice President (once a divinity student), when Mother Teresa spoke at a breakfast prayer meeting about the rights of the unborn. He went as a "healer" to Columbia High school in Littleton and thanked the youngsters there for "keeping faith" but left the "faith" unspecified. Even some of the religiously minded there failed to speak of life beyond the grave as the chief object of Faith writ large. Some ministers buried some of the victims without a word about eternal life and final resurrection.

According to the Bible, the price of joy is to be ready for tests, for hard tests indeed. But the supreme price to be paid for joy, which God alone can deliver, is the resolve not to have foreign gods, that is, false gods. Soon those false gods proliferated in Israel and they have a field day in our post-Christian society. Once called Baal, Nut, and Marduk, they now answer to the names Money, Sex, and Power. They all extort their dues once the investments made in them mature. And whenever not willing to pay the price for true joy, individuals and society find themselves abandoned to "their stubbornness of heart, to their own designs."

A frightening prospect indeed that should give a rude awakening from dreams "about being fed with the finest wheat and honey from the rock." The phrase as applied to the Eucharist, whose reception demands the willingness to die with Christ, should make it clear that those dreams, so materialistic, are entertained despite the conditions set by the God of the Covenant, who, after all, is a jealous God. The Christian "Ode to Joy" should be very different from faddish chants that are now part of a popularized liturgy full of sentimental crooning, done to the accompaniment of instrumental music of ever lower taste.

Psalm 82

This psalm, so truthfully describing a perennial situation, has another feature that should greatly recommend it. It describes the dire consequences which the abuse of judicial power brings on unconscionable judges. Fortunately, no trace here of a curse invoked on them. The psalm should strengthen our awareness of the fact that there is no judicial system that could be independent of God's laws written in man's heart. The chief promoters of the idea of natural law were always those who insisted on God's supernatural dispensation as well. Now that this supernatural perspective is a taboo in society, the basic, purely natural distinction between good and evil is approaching a vanishing point. To make the farce, if not the tragedy, complete, "Solomonic wisdom" is invoked for coping with ethical problems raised by cloning, by genetic engineering, by euthanasia, by sex change, and by in vitro fertilization. Appeal to that wisdom is all too often made by those who do not want to imitate Solomon who, at least in the beginning of his reign, still knew full well that such wisdom is the gift of God. Otherwise, he would not have prayed that more than any other gift, the gift of wisdom be given to him as his royal heritage.

Most importantly, in these times when even children are nudged to take a judgmental stance against their parents, when everyone in society is making a pastime of judging everyone else, when newspapers and TV channels make fortunes by passing judgments on anything and everybody, except on the media itself, let this psalm be recited by keeping in mind the words: "Don't judge, lest you be judged."

Psalm 83

This psalm is a classic in realism in more than one sense. It first portrays something to which only a sense of false security can make one blind. In these post-Holocaust times a fearsome modernity seems to lie in the resolve of ten hostile nations, named in six short lines (verses 7-9), who decided "to have the name of Israel to be forgotten forever." Victory over them, mainly achieved by Gideon, made an indelible mark on Israel's memory. Isaiah twice evoked "the day of Midian" in a markedly messianic context (9:3 and 10:26).

Those six lines may bring to mind as many lines in the Documents of Vatican II. There in the context of the work of the Church in human culture, a pointed warning is served about the unremitting opposition, lasting to the end of time, of the world to the Church. One wonders whether not six lines but six pages should have been filled in those Documents with that warning if such is indeed the basic condition of the Church in the world. The scarcity of those lines reflects the growing silence about the fact that the Church on this earth is a Church militant.

Of course, the Church cannot soldier and wage campaigns in the manner of a nation, in fact in the manner in which the Old Covenant as a nation had to wage wars. In these times of photo reporting it should not be difficult to imagine the cruelty that went with the devastating attack of the Israelites on some of their enemies as described in verses 10-14. But while it is easy to imagine such cruelties, it is not allowed for a Christian to entertain as much as a momentary wish for a divine vengeance that would descend on the enemies of the Church as "a fire that burns away the forest, as the flame that sets mountains ablaze." Such and subsequent lines, that include the wish that "shame and terror be theirs forever," ought to be recited with heads hung in shame for having occasionally entertained such a wish.

Psalm 84

If the appeal of beauty is increased by contrast, the beauty of this psalm is certainly enhanced by the dire specter evoked by the preceding psalm. There all is harshness, here everything is gentle peace, "the loveliness of the dwelling place of God." To illustrate it, the psalmist proves himself a poet of first rank as he points at the sparrow and the swallow that are attracted as if by a magnet to the altar of God, to make their nests in its cornices. Then, as if to outdo himself as a poet, the psalmist presents the attractiveness of God's dwelling place with a reference to pilgrims as they happily march toward that dwelling place, regardless of the toils of the journey. Poetic exaggeration is, of course, the psalmist's claim that the pilgrims' happiness makes springs gush forth in arid valleys, symbolized by one which the psalmist calls "Bitter Valley." They feel as refreshed by their joy as the soil when relieved by the autumn rain.

It is, of course, a psalmist and not an aphoristic poet who states that "happiness is the source of ever growing strength." But no more than other psalms is this one an utterance of mere human wisdom. The happiness it extols is a happiness tied to one's tying himself to the altar of God. And since no altar makes sense unless it is the place of sacrifice, the only sense in which the happiness is proclaimed in this psalm should be all too clear. As to the reference to the "Anointed," it should direct one's mind and heart to those, priests, who alone are "anointed" so that they may perform the liturgical sacrifice. There they function in the person of the One who was at the same time both altar and victim. Let this psalm be also a prayer for such vocations who fully understand the role they are called to.

Psalm 85

The relatively placid tone of this psalm is rather unexpected in view of its topic. Jeremiah would have formulated its message with a vehemence. The starting point, a rather sad condition of the people, is not portrayed in a dramatic way. Yet there is some drama, if not tragedy, implied in the reference that all this had already happened before and that one has to beg God once more for His favors.

Were this pointed out with some force in this psalm, it might not give wrong ideas to the unwary, lost in dreams about an immediate future in which "mercy and faithfulness meet, while justice and peace embrace."

But the truth is that heaven does not come to earth. Only with the onset of a New Heaven and a New Earth will it become true that "faithfulness shall spring from the earth and justice will look down from heaven." Until then the earth shall bring forth many brambles and thorns. Man, even the redeemed man, is forever a fallen man, whose main aptitude is to fall.

Nothing would be more mistaken than to see the promise of a social program embodied in the closing verses of this psalm, as if they assured us of general prosperity and universal peace. In reciting this psalm one cannot think long and often enough of a statement in the great social encyclical *Rerum novarum* of Leo XIII who poured cold water on such expectations. He in fact called a cruel farce the claim that all injustice, all deprivation could be eliminated from this earth. What he said with an eye on Marxists, holds true of neocapitalists as well.

Psalm 86

While some psalms are meditations and some are outright sermons, this psalm is truly a prayer in which the individual does not speak to himself or to others about God, but speaks directly to God. The psalm is a prayer "for all seasons" in spite of the fact that the psalmist specifically refers to his having been rescued from the shadows of death.

We all had one or several such close calls which became deeply engraved on our memory. Think of almost fatal car accidents and similar close bruises with death. The psalmist does not seem to imply that he had just escaped. In that case the psalm's tone would probably be much more agitated than it is. Likewise, we may often have days of ordinary agitation when we can but cry out to the Lord all day long, begging for help, guidance, and recognize God's goodness and mercy. Such are the days when ruthless competitors, indeed outright opponents, put strong pressure on us. We may, of course, be disheartened by the weight of our sins, but the psalmist says what no one can say any better: "But you, God of mercy and compassion, slow to anger, O Lord, abounding in love and truth, turn and take pity on me." Nothing forbids us then from thinking of ourselves as the children of that "handmaid of the Lord," the Virgin Mary, through whom God displayed his greatest mercy, as we continue with the psalmist: "O give your strength to your servant and save your handmaid's son."

Psalm 87

The first Jewish Christians must have thought of this psalm as they gathered in the Council of Jerusalem in 50 A. D. to face up to the question of some Gentiles. Were they to be circumcised, were they to observe the Law? Were the Gentiles to become Jews if they wanted to join those who were the first followers of Christ?

The agreement they reached was very much in favor of the Gentiles. They were to observe only a few Jewish precepts one of which, the abstaining from illicit sexual union, was a basic human precept before it became a specific Jewish law. Converts from the Gentiles could all the more be expected to observe them because "for generations now Moses has been proclaimed in every town" (Acts 15:21)

Judaism enjoyed catholicity to a noteworthy degree insofar as it had gained converts or at least sympathizers in great numbers all over the *oikumene*. Such converts among all the nations were referred to in this psalm, which held out the hope for something much greater. Not only some Babylonians or some Egyptians, or some from Philisthia, Tyre, and Ethiopia were to come to Sion, but Babylon, Egypt and all the other nations were to call Sion their Mother and to "dance and find their home there." The Church Catholic was to become that place.

The Church became known as "Catholic" already in the letters which Saint Ignatius of Antioch wrote in 110 A. D. No group of heretics, and no matter how widely they spread, succeeded in wringing that adjective from the Church of Rome. There were times when Arians greatly outnumbered Catholics, but they did not cease being called Arians. The greatest irony suffered by Protestantism lies in the very name which they themselves invented in 1530. The idea of a "Catholicisme non-Romain" remains a mere wish.

The frustration which some Protestants feel may be gauged from the French Calvinists' decision to replace the word "Catholic" with "universal" in the Creed. They now profess to believe in "one, holy, universal, and apostolic Church." Meanwhile the Mother of all churches in Rome is being visited in ever larger numbers from all over the world. In respect to the great Jubilee of 2000, Rome found the inadequacy of hotels to accommodate the pilgrims to be a greater problem than those known as Y2K.

But even the Church, with a catholicity far surpassing anything which Judaism could claim in that respect, cannot expect all nations to associate with her all the time. In fact the Church loses again and again entire nations. The Church refused to buy the loyalty of some rulers at the price of compromising with truth and principles. Henry VIII comes to mind, or Elizabeth I, or Tsar Ivan IV of Russia, or the Swedish king John III who in 1577 expressed his wish to abandon Lutheranism. It is well to recall such facts in this age of ecumenism some of whose

"Catholic" protagonists often speak and plan as if the lessons of history mattered not at all.

Psalm 88

In speaking of the psalms from the Christian perspective, the "cursing psalms" seem to represent the only major difficulty. There is another, which is the very theme of this psalm. The theme is desolation bordering on utmost hopelessness. It would, of course, be wrong to argue that Jeremiah, who most likely inspired or perhaps even authored this psalm, lost all hope. In that case he would have stopped crying day and night to God about a situation which indeed appeared hopeless, humanly speaking. Thrown into a pit so that he might die there slowly of hunger and thirst, Jeremiah saw no way of escape whatsoever. This psalm evokes the same "Sitz im Leben" which also applies to Psalms 40 and 69, with less drama but with an even greater despondency. Unless God rescues him, Jeremiah sees in front of him but the shadowy existence which is in store for the dead according to the Jewish perception of his times and for some time afterwards. He almost presents God as if a bargain could be struck with Him: God should save him because only the living can praise God. It does not occur to Jeremiah that God in no way needs man's praise and that even the dead live by living to Him.

But this is not all. Jeremiah's latest misfortune seems to him to be the last link in a life story that had only dark moments to it: He sees himself "wretched and close to death" from his youth on. He moans and groans partly because all this happened to him for his having accepted his calling.

It should be enough to recall various pages from the Acts of Apostles, and later countless examples from the lives of saints and martyrs, to find the case of Jeremiah most instructive. After all, Jeremiah was one of the greatest spiritual figures of the Old Testament. Yet he had no solution to the question of suffering, let alone to a life spent in most wretched trials. Stephen's radiant face, and of others' equally radiant countenance in facing death, pose a stark contrast to this psalm. What would Jeremiah have said, one may ask, had he seen Saint Perpetua and her companions smile as they were being tossed on the horns of fierce bulls

in the amphitheater of Carthage in A. D. 203? They looked happy
because they looked at death as the beginning of a life far more
real, far more rewarding than anything conceivable in this life.

All this started when the good thief heard the words:
"Today you will be with me in Paradise." From that moment on
the poor wretched fellow must have looked forward to death.
Those unable to contemplate that scene, so gruesomely comforting, may take momentary refuge in a remark of Newman's. A
Christian, he wrote, should expect death with the eagerness of
schoolboys ready to go home for Christmas vacation. The scene
here is comfortingly fearsome.

In reciting this psalm we should use it as a gauge to
measure the extent to which we have progressed from the Old to
the New Testament, or to which we have slided, with our
groaning and moaning, back to the Old again and again. About
the possibility of that backsliding the Letter to the Hebrews
served an early warning with lasting timeliness. The Christian's
prayers should never be void of real hope and firm assurance.

Psalm 89

In the title of this psalm Ethan the Ezrahite is named as its
author. In its section on the reign of Solomon, the Book of Kings
(3 Kg 5:11) mentions Ethan, who might have indeed lived to see
the sack of Jerusalem by the Pharaoh Shehsenq in the fifth year of
the reign of Roboam, the successor of Solomon.

It must have been shocking to see such a sudden downfall in
the fortunes of David's kingdom after it had achieved so great a
prosperity and international renown during the reign of
Solomon. Thoughtful people must have looked for an answer to
the disturbing question of whether the promises made to David
were trustworthy.

The question is all more disturbing as the promise came
from a truly mighty God. It is that divine might which is
celebrated in the first of the psalm's three sections. God is first
shown in His heavenly court, but the chief evidence of His might
is taken from His power over nature. He is described as victorious over the sea, including Rahab, the mythical sea monster. In
the second section God's might is seen in the rule of His justice

enjoyed by the people. It is a divine favor which exalts the power of the nation. A timely remark, to be sure, in this age of cruise missiles, stealth bombers, Trident submarines, and star wars to boot. The phrase, printed on the almighty dollar bill, should perhaps be printed in the form of the question: Do we place our trust really in God? Do not all too many of us place our hopes in our portfolios, health insurance, and retirement policies?

The second part of the psalm celebrates David's power as conditioned on his having been chosen for the role to initiate an everlasting dynasty. It is a role that hinges on his having God for his Father in an emphatic sense. David is God's first-born and his descendants on the throne would inherit that special status. Were they to prove faithless, God's promise still would remain valid: "I will never take back my love, my truth will never fail." And again: "Once and for all I swore by my holiness, 'I will never lie to David, his dynasty shall last forever'." In order to put across the totally unconditional character of that promise, God goes one better as if His swearing by His holiness would not be good enough. He declares the promise to be as unchangeable as the course of the sun and the moon: "In my sight his throne is like the sun, like the moon it shall endure forever."

This is one of several precious instances in the psalms about the Hebrew mind's ability to do "natural theology." The idea may be an anathema to some Barthians and to their Catholic camp followers, but the passages cannot be struck from the Bible. The biblical view of nature is that of a stable nature, with far-reaching consequences for the eventual rise of natural science.

But if the promise made to David is irrevocable to such an extent, then how to explain the sudden sack of Jerusalem and of the land around it? There is no gainsaying the ravages. The psalmist excels in his graphic portrayal of details, beginning with his seeing David's crown rolling in the dust. The various ravages inflicted on the nation, though they postdate David's death by almost half a century, seem to be so many slaps in his very face.

The psalmist then utters his own complaints as if they were David's himself. He clearly wants a resolution of his agonies before he departs from his life. In a way typical of the children of the Old Covenant, he wants an answer in this life. This is where we, children of the New Covenant, must go far beyond the psalmist's perspectives if we want to pray this psalm with true spiritual profit. And we must do this because the Incarnation itself begins with David. Though eminently the first born of God, Jesus is also the Son of David, born of a virgin from the House of David. "Hosanna to the son of David" were the words that greeted Him as He rode on a donkey into Jerusalem. Therefore "Christians are spiritual semites," to recall a momentous remark which Pius XI made, in March 1938, with an eye on the storm gathering against the children of Abraham. The New Covenant will forever be rooted in the Old and in its promises to come with *the* Son of David. The firmness of the New is a piece with the reality of the Old. In gratitude for this let us ring out the closing doxology of this third "book" of the psalms:

Blessed be the Lord forever. Amen, Amen!

Book IV, Psalms 90-106

Psalm 90

Modern man learned that everything is evolving. In learning this, man has unlearned that evolution, like any process of change, makes sense only if it rests on something that does not evolve. For those who find this statement a bit abstruse, there remains the plain fact that the proposition, "everything is evolving," conveys a non-evolving truth. The equally famous modern insight, according to which everything is relative, is a very absolutist statement.

What all this has to do with this psalm? The answer lies with the statement that everything is evolving. This in fact is true even of literary forms, among them the kinds of poetry. The history of literature of any nation also shows that earlier times abounded in poems simply descriptive, whereas reflective, introspective poems came much later.

On that basis one's first instinct is to assign a rather late date to this psalm, full of profound reflections on the shortness of life. It contains lines that strongly evoke Jeremiah. There are, however, two characteristics of Jeremiah's writings (be they prophecy or poetry) that are not found in this psalm. One such characteristic is the elemental longing for justice to be served on the wicked. The other is his throbbing, almost volcanic diction.

Both, but especially the latter, could be in evidence in view of the topic of this psalm, which is deeper and more moving than the brevity of life, if this were not deep and moving enough. Yet for all its gripping diction, the psalm is marked with an almost sweet resignation into what no one can change. Fatalists, or at least Stoics, could strike such a sweet, melancholy chord, yet not without despairing. But the author of this psalm uses another chord as well, wholly alien to those for whom God is at most an abstract principle. For the author of this psalm God is very much alive, infinitely more than any man can be.

Who is then the author of this psalm, so kind, so sweet in facing the most agonizing reality of life, its fleeting brevity, and yet so fully alive to the presence of a God whose life is not limited by any boundary, past or future? In the Old Testament there is only one man about whom the Bible makes it a point that he was "the meekest man on the face of the earth," indeed "by far the meekest man" (Num 12:3). The man was Moses, a man of God in a preeminent sense, the only man who was given the privilege to see God face to face. His face became so radiant that he had to cover it with a veil.

Indeed, should we take, because of the Hebrew title of this psalm, Moses for its author, all of its parts will appear to form a coherent whole. The psalm is the reflection of an old man on the rapid passing of life. Today he would say that the movie of one's life suddenly seems to be over. One can therefore imagine that, as he wrote this psalm, Moses was thinking about the veil to be soon put on his dead, motionless face. He does not argue in the style of modern man that life has not treated him right. He does not explode, he does not cry out for vengeance on the wicked who deprived him from final success.

In Moses' life the wicked were those Israelites, almost all the adults, whose disbelief lured him into doubting God's word. As a punishment God barred him, too, from entering the Promised Land. He could see it only from a distance. Imagine the feelings, say of General Eisenhower, had he been barred from going with his troops into Normandy and finally into Berlin!

Moses lived to twenty and hundred, though not in the days of Methuselah, when as a centenarian he would still have been looked upon as a mere youngster. In Moses' day even a man with a strong physique had to be glad if at least his mind and eyes still remained sharp, as was the case with Moses in old age.

Precisely because Moses was able to look back into the far past, when he was only seventy or eighty, he now knew all the more keenly the inevitable: He would die. Death alone might not pose him a major problem, as only the unwise would ever think that death somehow makes an exception or two. But the sigh that brings this psalm to a close, a sigh for success, points to Moses. He knows that neither he, nor the Israelites, who rebelled in the desert, would see a successful end to their wandering. They are swept away in God's fury, for having sinned against Him.

Life cannot be started all over again, but at least for its remainder it should be guided by wisdom: "Make us know the shortness of our life, that we may gain wisdom of heart." For the few days or years left for us, may we be filled with joy before the day of Eternity dawns for us and especially on that day.

If one thinks of the wear and tear of forty years of wandering in the desert, one cannot help hearing Moses refer to the younger generation ready to enter the Promised Land as he turns to God: "Show forth your work to your servants, let your glory shine on their children." His prayer, "Give success to the work of our hands," is a prayer for their success, and the prospect of this is his sole comfort. He does not have available to him that great personal consolation which the New Testament holds out in the form of a personal eternal life after death.

If one takes philosophy not for an exercise in recondite propositions of logic, but for the love of wisdom, one is right to expect some profound philosophical insights in a psalm so intent to draw the best form of wisdom from reflecting on life. Philosophy was unable to come up with anything so concise about God's eternity as the opening verse of this psalm: "Before the mountains were born, or the earth and the world were brought forth, you are God, without beginning or end." It behooves man to keep in mind the reality of such a Being, if he is to find a sense of endurance as he longs for success to balance his afflictions, especially those that rapidly multiply as one grows old.

Psalm 91

The typically oriental and ancient imagery that fills this psalm should pose no problem. Only the pedant would take umbrage to being moonstruck at night, or hit by plague that prowls in darkness. Though falconry is no longer a sport even among the rich, one can readily imagine the fowler eager to bag a prey or two. As to the arrows that fly by night, they have their modern counterparts in cruise missiles.

The dynamics or logic that gives a structure to this psalm is spelled out twice. It consists in the words: "You who have said: 'Lord, you are my refuge'." This is stated both at the start and toward the end of the psalm. Almost each line in this psalm somehow assumes those words for its starting point. Let us keep this in mind, if we are to pray this psalm with the intensity which it calls for.

References to dangers threatening during the night turned this psalm into a favorite evening prayer. But the reference in it to sunstroke and the fowler, who needs broad daylight, make this psalm a prayer appropriate for any hour of the day. Since much of our driving is done during the day, we should be all the more ready to cry out, "God is my refuge!" in begging Him for protection from drivers overcome with road-rage.

As to the verses, "For you has he commanded his angels, to keep you in all your ways. They shall bear you upon their hands, lest you strike your feet against a stone," they gave rise to many futile speculations because they entered into the Gospel account of our Lord's temptation by the Devil in the desert. It is more profitable to ponder our Lord's most explicit words about angels guarding each and all of us. The prayer, "Angel of God, my guardian dear, to whom his love commits me here; ever this day be at my side, to light and guard, to rule and guide," may be a fitting antiphon to this psalm.

Psalm 92

This psalm might have been written by Jeremiah in one of his rare moments of triumph. One of these may have been the first celebration of the Passover by his protégé King Josiah after that central rite of Judaism had not been performed for half a century. At that time Jeremiah may have been thirty, with the strength of "a wild ox" and with pure oil shining from his face and arms.

The theme of this psalm may be taken for an elaboration of Psalm 1 which is riveted on a contrast between the righteous and the wicked as symbolized respectively by a healthy plant and by mere chaff. Here the symbolism is applied to the wicked only in a line which states that they spring up like grass but quickly perish. The psalmist's attention is focused from the start on the just man who does not tire if singing God's praises in the morning and even during the "watches of the night" and does so at the accompaniment of "the lyre and the ten-stringed harp."

What, one may ask, can make for a happier atmosphere? Indeed the psalmist's face is radiant. He is not only glad, but feels that strength which joy brings. He describes it as the condition of a man who is in perfect shape, like a "palm tree" or a "cedar of Lebanon." He sees no danger ahead of him. He looks forward to an old age when he would still be full "full of sap, still green."

It would be easy to mistake this psalm, so full of an optimism oblivious to any adverse turn, for a divine seal on the idea of a perennial youth. One wonders whether anyone with osteoporosis or with Hodgkin's disease would have composed this psalm. But in those days, when infant mortality was ten times what it is today, those who survived into adulthood had a sap of vitality in them well into their old days.

When even with no such sap in one's muscles one can still say that "In him, my God, there is no wrong," one shall have lived up to a major test of faith. The dying Oscar Wilde, who longed to see a priest and, by the mercy of God, was looked upon by one, is a case in point. His was a paradoxical case indeed, because a few years earlier he still claimed in his rambling "De profundis" that any narrow street in London contains enough misery to refute the notion of a loving God.

Psalm 93

Now that we know that the earth on which we live is more fragile than an eggshell, that the continents are drifting, that the earth is being bombarded by huge comets and meteors, that our Earth-Moon system, indispensable for the rise of life, biological and intellectual, is the product of a huge collision, that the universe is truly violent, this psalm may give rise to sober thoughts. We must, of course, think above all of the fact that, contrary to our psalm, the earth does not sit fixed firmly on the seas and indeed it has no fixed position at all. The earth moves, regardless of whether Galileo did or did not utter the words: "Eppur si muove!"

With an eye on verse 1b of this psalm and several other verses in the Bible, Luther achieved a dubious first by declaring Copernicus a fool. The Catholic Church, in fear lest Protestants might think that it did not really respect the Bible, condemned Galileo in an act in which papal infallibility escaped only by the skin of its teeth.

There remains, of course, plenty of stability on earth as well in heaven. There would be no science were the laws of nature not stable, that is, fully consistent, mirroring a nature also fully consistent in its operations. Neither any of those laws, nor their full system are necessarily what they are. Their specificity proves them to be one of an inconceivably large number of similar sets, equally specific.

The only rational explanation of this is that one of those sets was chosen by a truly creative power. If not the waves of the ocean, the waves of various types of energy rushing back and forth through cosmic space, still call for our joining them in their praise of the Lord. If we fail to do so we shall enthrone those laws, or more likely ourselves. Scientists, like other human beings, love to play that most dangerous game, which is to play God. May the recitation of this psalm be a much needed antidote to this deadly temptation.

Psalm 94

Every psalm has a line with a special appeal to it. In this age of unremitting concern for mental health, the verse, "when cares increase in my heart, your consolation calms my soul," should strike a deep chord in the mind.

Of course, this psalm would not be a psalm if it touched but the surface of the search for the real source of cares, of nagging doubts, of inner torments, and of excruciating agonies. At a time when all real causes of our troubles are swept under the rug in a frantic effort to satisfy societal consensus, this psalm probes uncomfortable depths. It points at the evil that underlies all ills and woes that beset the mind and the heart.

Nothing is easier than to transpose this psalm's perspective to our times that are indeed chock-full "of arrogant speech," and of judges that legislate immorality. Worse, they do so by doing what causes the psalmist's chief grief: they reason, speak, and decide, and set programs in motion as if everything were relative, as if man were not beholden to God. Their chief target is, of course, the God of Jacob, the God of the Covenant, the God who came with a supernatural revelation, infinitely superior to what any nation's gene pool could have produced. For only about a God who could and did indeed speak to mankind can one also assume that He also hears and takes notice.

Even today there is nothing naive, nothing outdated, in the psalm's apparently anthropomorphic series of questions: "Can he who made the ear not hear? Can he who formed the eye not see?" Even if one ascribes to blind evolution all the biological wonders of the ear and especially of the eye, one merely blinds himself if one refuses to consider the question: why and for what purpose is evolution?

It is the privilege of the human mind to ask this question, and in fact the mind raises this question whenever it asks any question, including questions prompted by cares far more decisive for mental health than science can ever dream of. Those questions were raised long before science arose, and will be asked after man has become surfeited by science.

Against judges, who write senseless interpretations of a Constitution born in belief in the Creator and in the principle, wholly unexplainable by evolution, that all men are created equal, one can have no better refuge, no better stronghold than God, who—let this not be forgotten—can only be reached by prayer. One could find no better antiphon to this psalm than the verse in the Letter to the Hebrews: "It is good to have our hearts strengthened by God's grace" (13:9), which, whatever its mysteries, is always ours for the kind of asking which is prayer.

Psalm 95

Although the new Ordo introduced many changes into the order in which the psalms are recited in the Divine Office, the position there of this psalm has remained unchanged as if it were a rock. And just as every day in the past, now for almost two thousand years, that Office begins with this psalm, a great invitation to praising God, the Rock who saves us.

The invitation, "Come, hail the Rock who saves us," strikes a joyful note, because it is followed by the exhortation, "With songs let us hail the Lord." A saving God is indeed the one in whose hands are "the depths of the earth, the heights of the mountains, the sea and the dry land," that is everything, in sum, the entire universe. He created because He loved.

The mere thought of such a powerful God should temper one's joy with respect and awe. Joy is the characteristic of a being endowed with free will, who can therefore laugh, but also tremble. But free will is no laughing matter. It connotes the most fearsome factor in man, responsibility, which, with respect to God, is a matter for eternity. Before such a God one has to bow deeply, indeed, with this psalm's invitation, one has to get on one's knees. In spite of this some "experts" in Bible and Liturgy claim that it is neither biblical nor liturgical to kneel. For good measure they ripped all kneelers from the pews.

The rest of this psalm shows strong similarities to Psalm 81. There, too, joy in God is balanced with fear of God. For as long as we are humans, we are free to respond or not to respond to a God who keeps inviting us for an ever more truthful union with Him. He does this through testing us as He tested His people at Massah and Meribah, so named because they were the "place of test" and the "place of quarreling." Tests are part and parcel of human life so that our union with God may have a merit to it. May we never quarrel with God and lose thereby the merit for having lived up to some earlier tests. This is the only Order of Merit worth pursuing. May the somber ending of this psalm, so different from the hopeful tone on which Psalm 81 comes to an end, be a reminder of that pursuit's seriousness.

Psalm 96

"O sing a new song to the Lord," such is this psalm's opening call. The psalmist calls for a new song, as if none of the old songs would do. In fact, as long as an experience, a commitment is vivid, it will always come up with something new. As long as man lives in time, he will have to produce something novel.

Novelty ceases only with death. Man lives by acting and any act introduces some novelty in the universe.

I still vividly remember an allocution of Paul VI to a massive general audience to whom he stressed this very theme. The theme was greatly elaborated by John Paul II often under the caption of the "acting man." John XXIII had already stressed the same theme by acting rather than by discoursing. Soon afterwards Karl Barth felt impelled to remark that Rome stole the thunder of the Reformation.

Some conservatives will demur. But they, too, must hold that since nothing is so eminently living as God, our songs to Him and about Him must always have a freshness to them. This is not to suggest that old songs should be discarded and unlearned. As long as one's mind and heart are truly tuned to God's wavelength, any old hymn will reveal something novel, whenever one hits upon it. A good poem, a good hymn never grows stale. The psalms are a case in point. Those who give free rein to any Dick and Harry and Jane to dip in the shallows of their musical creativity and redo liturgical music at the regular intervals of a few years, should pause. Some of what they gather certainly shows their skill in scattering time-proved texts and melodies. Danger looms large when the actual generation wants to teach without readiness to learn from those before them. This is the procedure characteristic of all dilettantes.

All this may sound uncalled for by this psalm, which is so plain as to discourage commentary. One thing should, however, be noted. Toward its end, the psalmist speaks of the trees of the wood that shout for joy. Psalm 98 has even more of this personification or animation of nature. But neither the hills in that psalms, nor the trees in our psalm are said to talk to one another. The earth is said to rejoice but not in order to delight the champions of that pantheistic view of it which nowadays goes by the name Gaia. Pagan Greeks had already worshipped her. New pagans merely reinvent her together with other pagan gods of old. A little noted trouble with this is that such gods do not invite new songs, in fact no songs at all. They are not known to have ever been worshiped by chants. The profundity of this psalm's call for a new song is still to be mined.

Psalm 97

This psalm, a paean of God, may seem noteworthy for the order in which nature and people are reviewed as exploding in praise to the Lord. First, the earth, the coastlands, the clouds, the mountains, and the skies, or the main parts of nature as known by the Hebrews. Only then do the people join in. Once more we are in the presence of a sequence which shows that the people of the Covenant did not slight nature's witness about the Lord, even though the witness of the Covenant was and still is far more overpowering.

Psalm 98

Here is another psalm that begins with "sing a new song" as if old songs would not do. Since once more we have a psalm on hand that speaks for itself, a few incidental comments will not usurp the place of a detailed commentary that would be unnecessary anyhow.

The present author was eleven when he, as a choirboy, sang a composition for four voices, with verses 3b-4 being the text. The composer, the choirmaster of the cathedral of the town, was a talented musician, though not to the extent that his name should be recalled here. The melody chimed with the various musical instruments—trumpets, harps, and horns—as given in those verses. More than once did I sing that composition. Years later I had an improvised choir perform it in Rome and made considerable impression on those present, who, let it be made clear, included no cardinal, no bishop, not even a single monsignore. Three members of the choir were monks from the Abbey of Monserrat, famed for its choir, who had been singing in it from boyhood.

Over so many years now I have kept whistling the tune to myself, though not in order to prove that an old song can always be new. The obvious does not need a conscious demonstration. As to "the rivers clapping their hands and the hills ringing out their joy," remarks made in connection with Psalm 96 should suffice.

Psalm 99

This psalm is an homage to God, the sole king of Israel, and calls twice on everyone to bow down in worship before Him. The idea of God as the sole king, even though the nation has a king, is a logical consequence of the Bible's view of God as the only true sovereign. No wonder that kings of Christian nations ruled only in God's name. Even in times of political absolutism, the kings, not excepting Louis XIV of "L'État c'est moi" fame, were hemmed in by the laws of God, in principle at least.

Was this psalm composed as Samuel agonized over the people's request for a king? If Samuel himself composed the psalm it would show his spiritual greatness in an added light: Even the priests, Aaron and his descendants, and Samuel himself, were not absolute rulers. They were humans and as such apt to fall. But their God, since He was the true God, could forgive them without losing anything. Just as God does not give away anything from His own when He creates, so with His forgiving. This why God's forgiveness knows no limits.

Psalm 100

A thanksgiving psalm for big and small mercies to be sung by those who feel in their bones that God made them and therefore they belong to Him. The text of the psalm would forever inspire composers as long as there are some who have that gut feeling. Their number, just as those of painters and sculptors of religious subjects, seems to peter out and rather rapidly. Otherwise "The Millennium Dome" outside London would not have already been recognized for what it is, "The Pagan Palace."

Psalm 101

In the Grail translation this psalm is given the caption "a pattern for rulers," which not only fails to do justice to this psalm but is bordering on the miscarriage of justice. One should indeed be horrified on being subject to a ruler who is literally hell bent on rooting up all evil in the land. This is not to suggest that one should not pray to God that He give us rulers who are above reproach, whose private lives are not tainted by anything base, who do not associate with liars, who do not profess doubts as to the meaning of the verb "is," who look for the faithful in the land and not for the faithless, who are not in cahoots with those who make an art of practicing deceit, who do not set up the wicked—yes, the wicked—as alternate models of virtue but silence them, who do not strengthen the decibels of misinformation against the just.

Only in heaven shall we know the prayers that earned a Saint Louis for France, an Edward the Confessor for England, a Saint Stephen for Hungary, a Saint Henry for Germany, a saint Wenceslaus for Bohemia, a Saint Leopold for Austria, a Saint Olaf for Norway, and so forth. The list would become endless if we included also some princes and counts, already inscribed in the registry of saints, and even some prime ministers not yet canonized. Although aware of some equivalent of Newman's dictum that "to touch politics is to touch pitch," they engaged in politics without becoming politicians. Think of De Gasperi, of Adenauer, and of Schuman. But it is no less important to recall that all these great rulers tempered justice with mercy. The psalmist seems to have forgotten that after he had given the caption, "mercy and justice," to his song, he sang of no mercy but only of justice.

At crucial junctures, those who ruled from the Chair of Peter, always came down on the side of mercy, even at the risk of incurring the charge of being compromisers with faith and morals. Were they such, their continuity would defy explanation. Compromisers are connivers but, contrary to that famed papal historian, Ranke, connivance can hardly work over several generations, let alone for over almost two thousand years, the span of papal history.

Reformers, think of Calvin, who employed spies to catch the slightest infractions of the faithful within his theocratic Geneva, failed to ponder the injunction of the Gospel against those who intended to pull out all the weeds and on a short notice at that. True reform in the Church always relies on both justice and mercy, a point which so many self-appointed reformers in the

Church cannot ponder long and hard enough. If there is a psalm that ought to be recited with great caution, this is it. Let the silent antiphon to this psalm be the remark of Odilo, the great abbot of Cluny. He preferred, so he said, to be sent to hell for his having been too merciful rather than too just.

Psalm 102

Jeremiah's voice is heard through all the three parts of this psalm. In the first he turns to God as one who feels that he is coming to the end of his strength. His bones, so he tells God, are burning away with fire, his heart is like withered grass, his skin clings to his bones because in his dejection he has no strength even to eat. A pelican in the wilderness, a lonely bird on a roof, such is his self-portrait. Few poets ever said so much in so few words.

Worse, Jeremiah finds himself surrounded by vilifiers. He does not tell who they are, perhaps because there is little point in belaboring the obvious. Like in music a pause, in poetry, too, a well calculated silence is all too effective. Of course, to appreciate that silence we must recall that even after the destruction of Jerusalem there were some who failed to admit the obvious: Jeremiah's dire prophecies and his advice, that went so much against the grain of those who took religion for national aggrandizement, were after all from God.

The second part of the psalm is one of the finest expressions of an unshakable faith in God, which is all the more impressive as it has for its background a Jerusalem shaken to its very foundations. But Jeremiah has no doubt that God will "listen to the helpless," that He will "hear the groan of the prisoners." And if this had not testified to an unshakable faith, Jeremiah conjures up the future: the children of those who groaned as they were carted away to Babylon would one day proclaim God in a Sion rebuilt to its erstwhile splendor and security. Unlike elsewhere, Jeremiah does not thunder. No traces of vindictiveness here even in the guise of thirst for justice.

So far this psalm exuded the highest form of true spirituality. In the third part Jeremiah adds a theology soaring to new

heights where he presents the never-changing God and, therefore, absolutely faithful God.

Theology as a discourse about God, instead of being a
discourse about theologians ruminating about Him, would not
be real if it were not to take its starting point from man's misery.
For all his confidence in God, Jeremiah knows that the trials
practically broke him and his career as a prophet: God has
"broken his strength in mid-course." Jeremiah feels that his days
are shortened, an experience common to all upon whom great
trials are inflicted. Earlier he said that his days were "vanishing
like smoke," using the Bible's classic image for utter transience.
But he does not give up the hope that he would see things turn
for the better. He hopes that in that sense his days "will be
complete."

Well, for that completeness, so ephemeral after all, he turns
to a God whose "days last from age to age." And now there
follow three verses which are among the finest in all the Bible:
"Long ago you founded the earth and the heavens are the work
of your hands. They will perish but you will remain. They will all
wear out like a garment. You will change them like clothes that
are changed. But you neither change nor have an end." The
author of the Letter to the Hebrews (1:10-12) found in these
verses the highest acclaim of the divinity of the Son.

The full bearing of these verses was not exhausted when the
Christians used them against the divine eternity of the heavens,
this fundamental proposition of Hellenistic pantheism. The
relevance of those verses should seem no less vigorous in these
times of process theology whose champions have no strength to
reject out of hand the fundamental tenet of their master, Whitehead, that the ever changing universe is the ultimate entity. It
even generates, according to Whitehead, that factor which less
sophisticated earthlings call God.

But back to Jeremiah and to the Letter to the Hebrews,
which deserves to be recalled here for a reason even more important than those verses being quoted there. The reason should
seem all important if one is to see the manner in which this
psalm should be a prayer for the children of the New Covenant.
The grand conclusion of that Letter is a panegyric of the faith of

some great figures of the Old Testament who endured shocking trials and died without seeing the fulfillment of their hopes. They all prayed, as Jeremiah did, for the completeness of their days, but the author of that Letter holds them high in order to suggest that a new kind of faith, largely indifferent to the number of one's days, can alone cope with an all too often cruel reality.

One can, of course, fully sympathize with Jeremiah, but not to the point of forgetting that, painful as this may be, we must pray above all that God's will be done even if He cuts short our days in life's mid-course.

Psalm 103

If there is a psalm that speaks for itself, this psalm certainly does. In fact it does this so well as to limit the commentator's task to a reflection or two. One should at least point at the moving manner in which the psalmist portrays God's merciful love. One wonders whether ever an expression would be found that would convey that love so powerfully as the line: "He crowns you with love and compassion." And this is just one of several such lines in this psalm. Another, "He renews your youth like an eagle's," should have a special appeal as the percentage of senior citizens, resembling wrinkled bald eagles, grows ever faster. The psalmist describes the extent of God's love as something that can be measured only by the distance that separates the heavens from the earth. He categorically describes God as a being who is "compassion and love." The New Testament phrase, "God is love," is a strict echo of this. The psalmist's declaration that God's compassion for us is that "of a father toward his children," anticipates the prodigal son's father.

The composition of this psalm may have been occasioned by an unexpected return to health from a grave sickness, as the psalmist praises God for having "rescued him from the grave." Lazarus may have found the full meaning of this line after he was called back to life from the grave, although his body had already begun to decompose. However, it is not a literal resurrection of the body which the psalmist has in mind. He simply means, as one finds this repeatedly in the psalms, the unforeseen restoration of health after a close brush with death.

Such superabundance of unforgettable expressions in a single psalm is certainly appropriate to a psalm that wants to celebrate a mercifully divine love, which, so the psalmist declares, is everlasting.

Herein lies the rub, or the only and subtle imperfection of this psalm. For if that love is truly infinite, and there cannot be any doubt that the psalms and the other books of the Old Testament mean "forever and forever" in a strict sense with no limits to it, then one is faced with a problem of whether God can really love man forever.

Although the Old Testament states in general that God loves whatever He had made and He made all things, among them very excellent and majestic things, it never states that God's love for the sky or for the ocean is everlasting. Man alone is the object of such an overflowing love and compassion. But can that human being be such an object? Hardly so if he is but grass that has a short life span, if he is nothing really more than "a flower of the field," that blooms and withers, something to be "blown away by the wind," never to be seen again.

For such a fleeting being is man in the very words of this psalm. But then what remains of God's everlasting love for man? Can it truly be everlasting if man himself is not to last forever? To these questions the plainly affirmative answer came only in the New Testament. In this most important sense, too, the New was bringing to perfection what could be voiced in the Old Testament only between the lines of its most precious, most moving attestations of God's eternal love for man.

Let therefore the chant blare forth from our hearts: Give thanks to the Lord all his angels, all his hosts, all his works, but especially, "My soul (this immortal soul of mine, the pledge of my bodily resurrection), give thanks to the Lord."

Psalm 104

A tornado, a hurricane, a typhoon, a desert storm, a tidal wave, a terrible drought brought by El Nino may at any moment put the bucolic happiness exuding from this psalm in a proper perspective.

This is a point far more important to note insofar as this psalm is a prayer and not an occasion for an exercise in comparative literature. Some of the learned filled reams of paper in order to prove that this psalm is but a copy of Akhenaton's hymn to the sun. In trying to prove this, they remembered everything except the notion of true monotheism. They did no better than that Egyptian guide who in my hearing assured a group of tourists (at a location from which the naked eye could see about twenty pyramids on the horizon), that monotheism originated in Egypt. Surely, but not by the Egyptians of old. The guide was naive, but not malicious, unlike Sigmund Freud, the author of *Moses and Monotheism*, which tells much about his often twisted argumentation.

Surely, it is but natural to expect that if a large family, indeed a tribe, lived for perhaps two hundred years in an area, Zain, near the cultural centers of Lower Egypt, they could but learn a great deal about the literary and religious lore there even if they, as proper to a tribe, kept to themselves. The Jews did not have to learn from the Egyptians that the sun's rays fueled life. Nor had they to learn from them the elementary art of admiring nature, big and small. They were, of course, attracted to the Egyptians' splendid achievements that must have included music as well. The Hebrews listened to the Egyptians' songs and gave them a spin that turned them into something markedly other.

Indeed nothing shows so well the Jews' "otherness" as their attributing to an invisible God, absolutely above any visible creature, be it the sun, the power to give life. In Akhenaton's "Hymn to the Sun," the sun is the "thou" in the lines, "When thou settest they die." In our psalm it is an invisible Lord, immensely superior to the sun who is the "You" in verses 27-30: "All of these look to you to give their food in due season. You give, they gather it up: you open your hand, they have their fill. You hide your face, they are dismayed; you take back your spirit, they die, returning to the dust from which they came. You send forth your spirit, they are created; and you renew the face of the earth." All of these, not excepting the sun or the moon or the stars, or the sacred cows and holy scarabs, to say nothing of gods whose grotesque bodies combined the features of several animals.

To grasp the incredible difference between Akhenaton's hymns and this psalm, it is enough to invoke the enormous distance between nature worship and the worship of the Maker, the sole Maker of nature. One must try to savor that difference with a most vigorous grasp of their respective cultural impacts and with a visceral resolve never to yield an inch to cultural relativism, this most pernicious plague of modern times.

Let us not forget that there was a time of pan-babylonianism in exegesis, before a pan-egyptian phase there, and lately a sort of pan-ugaritism. Champions of such trends shy away from discussing why, say, Akhenaton's hymn never caught on even in Egypt, why the Babylonians wanted to hear Sion's songs from their Jewish captives. As to the Ugarites, they are now mere memories on clay tablets.

We come closer to this psalm as a prayer if we look at it as something closely paralleling what is given us in Genesis 1. Yet since this psalm long antedates that famed, obviously post-exilic chapter, the parallel merely brings out the obvious. The world picture had to be the same both for the psalmist, possibly of Davidic or Solomonic times, and for the author of Genesis 1, who lived after the Exile. Since both lived before the Hebrews learned anything Hellenic or Hellenistic, they viewed the world as a cosmic tent. Therefore they both described it in the same steps. But their respective purposes were very different, though not contrary.

In Genesis 1 God is set up in the role of observing the sabbath rest. Here the psalmist describes God's work as the maker of that cosmic tent (He stretches out the heaven like a tent) to be enjoyed by man and to remind man that life arises and vanishes in total dependence on God.

There is a cheerful atmosphere in this psalm which one, protected by technology from the violence of nature, may certainly cherish. Surely, when volcanoes are seen, with the psalmist, as being operated by the touch of God's finger, they will not look devastating, although they are. But the psalm subtly cautions against yielding to naive optimism vis-à-vis nature, an optimism not only naive but also false as it appears all too often spread out in the pages of *National Geographic* or *The Smithsonian*, to say nothing of TV nature programs, where the colors are more resplendent than anything nature can produce.

Rarely is in those secular, indeed secularist, "bibles" anything intimated of what this psalm so plainly spells out in verses 28-29. There one sees God who both gives life and withdraws it. Yet for the godless, too, the earth is not only the marvelous cradle of life, but, from the purely biological viewpoint, is also life's huge cemetery. Defunct species far outnumber those living at present, in spite of the fact that in no past age were so many species alive as today. The godless may explain death but is hard put to argue that life had to arise. Those who pray this psalm have a distinct advantage over the godless even from the purely logical viewpoint, to say nothing of viewpoints evoking morality.

Our psalm ends on a strictly moral tone, which is anathema to all nature worshipers for whom the only forms of sin are the "crimes" committed against the environment. Quite other, very old fashioned sinners are meant by the psalmist when he exclaims: "Let sinners vanish from the earth, let the wicked exist no more." Clearly it is not without some grave restrictions on one's perspective that the psalm allows us to say: "I will sing to the Lord all my life, make music to the Lord while I live." What worldly wisdom would never teach, this psalm, celebrating the world, firmly enjoins: "Let my thoughts be pleasing to Him" and not to the mermaids of Malibu Beach and their public relation agents.

Psalm 105

This and the next two psalms are among the longest psalms. The comment made in reference to the even longer Psalm 78 may be repeated: They are too clear to call for lengthy observations. In Psalm 78 the psalmist deplored again and again that the Israelites failed to remember the greet deeds of God. Here exactly the opposite is emphasized, namely, that God did not fail to remember His promises that constitute His part of the Covenant with the people. This is why this psalm, unlike Psalm 78, has a very confident tone.

Since prayer is an act of confidence in God, one does justice to this psalm as a prayer by various means that can help bring alive its message. The providential acts of God, whereby He turned a small nomadic tribe into a nation that carried salvation history, should forever be a chief motivation for confidence in God who always remembers what He promised. Those great acts, the "magnalia Dei" recounted in this psalm, are the background against which one can see small acts, small providential interventions of God in one's own life. Such acts can indeed fill in our notebooks as many lines, if not many more, as the ones composing this psalm. Only one should recall and remember.

Time and again this psalm calls for a repetition of what it explicitly states at almost the very start and at the very end. "He remembers his covenant forever, his covenant for a thousand generations" (verse 8) and "for he remembered his holy word, which he gave to Abraham his servant" (verse 42).

To be the servant of God demands a keen memory, a never faltering awareness of the rulings and promises of one's Master. The most faithful of such servants was Joseph, the husband of Mary, prefigured by the biblical Joseph celebrated in this psalm. For just as Joseph, son of Jacob, was the master of the pharaoh's house and ruled all the pharaoh possessed, so is Joseph, Mary's husband, in that household of God which is the Church.

The first session of Vatican II comes to mind, a session that filled many with a sense of frustration. Nothing seemed to have been achieved. Some overactivists held up for ridicule that session as having nothing more to its credit than the insertion of Joseph's name into the Canon of the Mass. In fact this happened not so much because the Council Fathers had postulated this, but because an elderly bishop requested it and did so in a tone close to sobbing. John XXIII, who watched the session on closed circuit TV, picked up the pen and the request was granted. So now we say in what is now the first or Roman Canon: "In union with the whole Church we honor Mary, the ever virgin mother of Jesus Christ our Lord and God, we honor Joseph, her husband, the apostles and martyrs . . ." Regrettably this venerable Canon is being said on fewer and fewer occasions. But well proven texts have a way of reasserting themselves in the long run.

The insertion of Saint Joseph into the Canon was as unpredictable by the wisdom of the "new" theology, as would have been the success of Joseph in Egypt. But the psalms celebrate not man's ways but God's ways that time and again confound men and especially the learned among them.

Psalm 106

"They did not remember," was the suggested refrain to Psalm 78. "God remembered his promise," was to play the same role in Psalm 105. For Psalm 106 the choice of a refrain is again obvious: "They forgot what God has done" and kept forgetting it. This psalm presents the fearsome results of studied oblivion.

To see this psalm in its true light is especially needed at a time, when, partly because of the Holocaust, it has become a theological fad (to say nothing of societal and political fads), to avoid saying anything which is not positive about the Jews. For this the Jews bear a goodly share of responsibility, especially in areas where they wield enormous influence.

A display in the Natural History Museum in New York is a case in point. A long hallway of it on the second floor is filled with large display cases illustrating the history of anthropology, or rather of family life, among ancient peoples. The display (I saw it around 1970) comes to a close with a very pleasing presentation, all in full size figures, of Jewish family life two thousand or so years ago. One wonders. Does that history have Jews for its end point?

This idealization of Jewish family life, as surpassing anything else, may be a sticking point, especially in view of this psalm. For indeed there was a time when the Jews "even offered their own sons and their daughters in sacrifice to demons. They shed the blood of the innocent, the blood of their sons and daughters, whom they offered to the idols of Canaan. The land was polluted with blood" (verses 37-38). This is not to suggest that this was a steady practice and a widespread one. Yet it had to happen often enough to be pointedly recalled in this clearly post-exilic psalm. The memory of atrocious acts is long a-dying. One such act, possibly because it involved the king itself, a descendant of David, is mentioned in 2 Kings. Manasseh sacrificed his own son, another descendant of David, to Moloch, by throwing him into that god's fiery furnace.

Again, one should not idealize the married life of all Christians, although its ideal is far superior to what is offered in the Old Testament. One must not gloss over the abysmally low sexual mores during Renaissance and Rococo times, to say nothing of times such as ours when many "loyal" Catholics side with the "loyal" opposition in matters of birth control, abortion, and free sex.

But whether Jews or Christians are the ones to be reminded of the dangers of a studied oversight of ideals, they alike can cry out with the psalmist: "O Lord our God save us! Gather us from among the nations that we may thank your holy name and make it our glory to praise you." For, immediately before this cry, that on the face of it may bespeak desperation, the psalmist assures us that for our sake "He keeps remembering his Covenant."

As to the Jews being a rebellious race, in the very words of this psalm, let us, Catholics, remember some of our rebellious forebears (think of those swelling the ranks of the Action Française, of the Falange, of the Ustasha and other "perfectionists") who at times acted in open defiance of Rome's directives. Protestants should have the privilege of washing their own dirty linen in public. And all, including Jews and Muslims, who are truly repentant, should be ready to import, if necessary, clotheslines by the boatload.

For only with a deep awareness of the wages of sin, so much emphasized in this psalm, may we all utter worthily the closing doxology of this fourth "book" of the psalms:

> Blessed be the Lord, God of Israel,
> for ever, from age to age.
> Let all the people cry out:
> "Amen! Amen! Alleluia!"

Book V, Psalms 107-150

Psalm 107

Four kinds of punishment for faithlessness are surveyed in this psalm. One is hunger that hits those wandering aimlessly in the desert. Another is hard labor in dark mines. The third is sickness. All three are presented in the same manner: first the description of the desperate predicament, then the crying out to God for help and God's merciful response. This is followed by the exhortation for thanksgiving for having been liberated by God from the particular trouble: "Let them praise the Lord for his goodness."

This structure may lend itself to a dramatic presentation when this psalm is recited in choir. The first strophe would be recited by one with a bass voice, though in a whisper as if to convey the depth of suffering caused by sin. The second strophe by a tenor voice crying out in loud agony for God's help. The third strophe a response shouted by the entire congregation grateful for God's saving intervention. The psalm is so graphic and dramatic as to call for some such recitation.

The fourth case is even more dramatic, though it is hard to say that the peril of sailors on the high seas is the result of some sin on their part. At any rate, it is an old piece of wisdom that those who cannot pray should take to the high seas. That was before the age of luxury liners, although the Titanic was not the last of such liners to go to the bottom of the ocean.

The last two sections are parallel presentations of the respective fate of the pious and the wicked. The pious flourish like a well-irrigated land, the wicked turn into something like lava waste. May it always turn out that way, one may add the pious wish, which is all too often mere wishful thinking. God's ways are not man's ways, which, let us not forget, is a very biblical truth, especially in its reverse: "Neither are your ways my ways," warns the Lord through his prophet, Isaiah (55:8).

Psalm 108

This psalm resounds from the start with joyful confidence in God. Joy is always contagious, but deceptive as well. As we begin this psalm on the note of an overflowing confidence, "My heart is ready, O God," should we not stop for the length of a breath and ask ourselves: "Is our heart really ready?" For unless it is, this psalm will sound on our lips as a mere flattery of God and a deception of our own very selves.

An honest consideration of this question is all the more important because this psalm, unlike Psalm 60, which it reproduces verbatim from verse 7 on, does not have for its background a defeat, which had a sobering effect. In this psalm a rather joyful situation seems to precede the calling to arms. But precisely because joy can easily diminish one's realism, one should stop and reflect on coming to the verse about the fortress, or Edom's capital city Petra. Petra was not only a well-nigh impregnable natural fortress but also a citadel of the cult of some base urges of human nature. On climbing to the highest of its well-preserved high places, H. V. Morton of *In the Steps of the Master* fame, was prompted to think that "if the priests and priestesses of Petra could come back, they would be able to hold an orgy under the moon without the knowledge that the shadow of centuries has ever fallen on their altars."

The well-nigh impregnable status of Petra is a symbol of the resistance of fallen human nature to promptings from above. Whether lust or pride or greed is the nature of that citadel in the individual, it must first be conquered before one can truthfully begin this psalm: "My heart is ready, O God." Then one can safely reach out for the psalter because one's praises of God will do much more than awaken the dawn. They will prompt a hearing in God's very ears.

Psalm 109

This is the chief of all cursing psalms and also a chief thorn in the side of those who hold two propositions: one is that the Bible is the inspired word of God, the other is that a follower of Christ is bound to love his enemies. This at the minimum means that the Christian cannot curse anyone.

From the early times Christian interpreters of this psalm and of the other cursing psalms suggested that the curses should be taken for factual outcome. Very biblical is the principle that crime invites its punishment. The specifications of the punishment are taken up through much of the psalm, constituting its main body (verses 6-19). The graphic concreteness of those verses is searing, to say the least. As curses, they are unbearable.

With Christ's betrayal by Judas, the psalm obviously obtained its "full" meaning, which may have included the fate of other betrayers of Christ as well. Apart from Judas' tragic demise, Arius' pitiful end is also a case in point. Many other cases could be reported about those who repaid Christ "with evil for good, with hatred for love," the concluding expression of the opening part (verses 1-5) of the psalm.

The second and shorter part of this psalm (verses 20-31) resumes the theme of its opening verse, though with some vengeance. This makes it difficult to recite all those verses with Christ in mind, although the reference to one whose "heart is pierced" evokes Him on the cross and the line, "all who see me toss their heads," recalls some present at His crucifixion. Verses in which the psalmist describes himself as one who is "poor and needy," "shaken off like a locust," "fading away like a shadow," and whose "knees are weak from fasting," do not exactly fit our Lord, although evocative of His suffering.

But the really sticking point in this section is the resumption of curses, while God is being praised for having come to the rescue of the psalmist, who may have been Jeremiah himself. In the new breviary, this psalm (together with Psalms 58 and 83) is no longer read. Some Protestants find disingenuous the reason given in the Apostolic Constitution on the Divine Office issued in 1970 by Pope Paul VI, who referred to "the difficulties that were foreseen from their use in vernacular celebration." Before taking issue with that Constitution, those Protestants should ponder the extent to which this psalm is still a text of prayer among Protestants, and if so, who they are and how often they pray it.

The real issue is far deeper than pedagogy about prayer. The issue is a point on which there is no meeting of minds between Protestants and Catholics. Catholic belief in the Bible is predicated on the fact that the Bible was born within the Church and not the other way around. We have a hierarchy, an apostolic succession, they don't. We know that only the authoritative Magisterium can guarantee any book, any verse in the Bible as divinely inspired. Those who don't care about the history of the scriptural Canon, may best ponder a dictum of Augustine's, all whose phrases (and they fill twenty or so folio volumes) are often a paraphrase of biblical verses: "I would not believe the Bible were I not prompted by the authority of the Church."

But it is precisely that authority, and not the mere beauty of the psalms, that turned them into the constant prayer of the Church in the very first place and in a measure the like of which one cannot find even within orthodox Judaism, to say nothing of liberal and mainline Protestant realms. I cannot help remembering the astonished reaction of a Protestant theologian from Tubingen, who could not believe his ears when, quite incidentally, I told him in 1969 that as a Catholic priest I recited all the psalms within one week, each week. He would still be surprised on learning that since the new Ordo priests still recite all of them in four weeks and that the same psalms resound all over the Catholic world each and every day as a global chorus.

Psalm 110

If thirty years count for one generation, then sixty some generations of Christians have already prayed this psalm as a praise to Jesus, the Messiah, the eternally begotten Son of God. Whether all the words they prayed were clear to them all the time is doubtful. Even more doubtful is that they could readily follow the train of thought of a psalm which may seem more mysterious than all other psalms. But pray they did, praise they did, and had their soul filled with the sense of certainty and peace. Wherever the Latin liturgy extended, every Sunday the Vespers began with the hallowed words: "Dixit Dominus Domino meo . . ." This psalm also set the tone of the Christmas liturgy which had for its center the temporal birth of the eternally begotten Son: "From the womb before daylight I begot thee." It attests the pre-eminent status of this psalm that it was retained as the only invariably present in all Sunday Vespers according to the new Ordo.

The soul's total dedication to the Word that became man is greatly helped by reciting this psalm in its Grail rendering, because there a clear distinction is made between two "domini." One is the Lord, the other is David's special Master. Moreover in the translation it is not merely said that the Lord speaks to the Master, but that the Lord gives a revelation to him. The Lord reveals the Master's extraordinarily superior status.

There are other messianic psalms, but this psalm stands apart in a class of its own. All psalms are in a very broad sense messianic, because they present problems, individual and communal, that have their resolution in the future. Some psalms define that future as a very special one, the coming of an end to the ills and woes of Israel, and through it, of all nations. These psalms are specifically messianic psalms. In all or most of these, the figure of a future king of Israel looms large who would achieve the final victory over the wicked. That future king is supposed to be a descendant of David. Psalm 2 states, for instance, that the princes and kings of the earth would try in vain to loosen the hold which that king would have on them. Psalm 45, a royal wedding psalm, presents that future king in the splendor of a spectacular wedding procession. Or rather because the wedding is so splendid, the psalm takes on a messianic character. Ordinary weddings are not the places for such a splendid display of riches and beauty.

Moses already spoke of a future prophet that would have a voice even more authoritative than his. Micah prophesied that Bethlehem would be the birthplace of the Messiah. In Second Isaiah the Messiah is portrayed as the suffering servant of Yahweh. But only in this psalm is something stated about the Messiah which puts Him in relation to David, his forefather, into a position that seems to contradict the fact that He is David's descendant. In this psalm it is not only declared, but declared as a revelation of God to somebody, whom the psalmist, most likely David, identifies as "my Master," that the Master would sit at

God's right hand. It should be enough to recall that the Bible always makes the angels stand in God's presence. Therefore the sitting posture of the Master should seem even more extraordinary than the fact that all his enemies would be put under his footstool, that is, totally subjugated. The author of the Letter to the Hebrews had indeed this in mind when he asked: "To which of the Angels has God ever said, 'Sit at my right hand, till I make your enemies your footstool'?"

Although the word "revelation" need not be taken in a sense which theology much later worked out, the word certainly conveys that a communication from on high takes place, which man can learn only by listening. There is no trace here of a distillation from a communal experience. On the contrary, it was this psalm that in a large part created a community of believers. They listened in awe to the silence of the Master who utters no word in this psalm. The Messiah, the Master, stands by the right hand of God, to receive words uttered from the Highest and receives also the praises of the one whose Master He is. The one is David, of course. No combination of praises can conceivably be higher. God and His special servant David form, so to speak, two sides of a duet of supreme praise.

In Jewish perspective no one could be higher than David if from his loins was to be born the Messiah, here called David's Master. But can the Master be higher than David if he is David's son? Hardly so in the typical Semitic perspective of ancestry. This was the conundrum put by Jesus to the Pharisees, who received a lesson in precisely that respect which they found most offensive to them. The upshot of what Jesus told them was nothing less than that they, the teachers, still had much to learn. This they would have found intolerable, even if that additional matter to be learned had not forced their attention away from a very materialistic notion of the Kingdom to come.

And yet Jesus did not even press the teachers with other, even more incisive verses of this psalm that referred to the priestly status of the Master, a status not inherited from Aaron, but along a line, Melchizedek, a Canaanite priest, who blessed Abraham and therefore was superior to him. Could the superiority of the Master be stated more forcefully than by a reference not only to David but also to Abraham? Again, Jesus did not press the point that the Master was begotten from God before the break of the dawn, although this could strongly suggest a beginning that preceded the uttering of "Let there be Light" in the beginning and therefore was no temporal beginning. The pedagogy used by Jesus did not mean the piling of argument upon argument. He would have thereby distracted from the clarity of the argument He judged to be most telling.

Not to be familiar with all such implications can but diminish the spiritual profit one should derive from praying this psalm. But pray this psalm we must, and more fervently than any other psalm, because Christ hallowed it in a very special sense. If this psalm served Him as a means to convey subtly His transcendental status, then our appreciation of this psalm should surpass our devotion to all other psalms, much more humanely appealing as many of them may be.

There is an added reason for our high esteem for this psalm that should fill our believing hearts with sorrow as well. When after the destruction of Jerusalem in A. D. 70, the survivors of the rabbinate gathered to make sense of what happened, they tried to redefine what makes a Jew a Jew even in the absence of a Temple, indeed of Jerusalem. In their search for the redefinition, they could not help thinking of what their forebears did in A. D. 62 to James, the brother of Jesus. According to Josephus it was a widely held opinion among Jews that the destruction of the City and of the Temple was a divine punishment for their atrocious act. (Josephus fails to note that the same year was also the year when the reconstruction of the Temple, begun by Herod, was completed. Once more, completion was the beginning of the end.) The rabbinate that gathered in Jamne, could not help being aware of that opinion. And they knew full well that James' death was triggered by his refusal to deny Jesus as the Messiah.

As the rabbinate kept gathering intelligence about the deeper convictions of Jewish Christians, they could not help learning of the references they made to this psalm. So the rabbinate decided that this psalm, until then held to be a messianic psalm on all hands, was not really messianic. Some such decision must be assumed to have taken place, if one is to explain that for about two hundred years this psalm was not considered to be messianic by Jewish scribes. Then, after Christians and Jews disappeared from much of the wider Jerusalem area, the psalm once more reappeared as messianic in Jewish eyes. The evidence is still to be translated into English from the learned pages of the vast commentary which Strack and Billerbeck wrote almost a century ago about the light which one can gather about the New Testament from the Talmud and related writings.

But just as facts cannot be changed, words once written down remain forever in the docket, especially when the words are God's revelation to our Master. Jesus emphatically approved our calling Him by that name when at the Last Supper He bowed down to wash our feet so that we may follow His humility. He was humble from the moment when on the first Christmas He, the eternally begotten Son, came to dwell among us. Let the praying of this psalm be a prayer for the Jews that they no longer wait for the coming of a Messiah other than the One who humbled Himself to the point of dying on the cross.

The Messiah has already come. If the experience of sixty generations can teach anything, He is more vigorous than ever. Some Jewish efforts to make Him appear non-existent, are vain indeed. While some crosses may be removed here and there, the Cross looms firm and tall as the globe turns around. Christ keeps drinking from the stream by the wayside and his Sacred Head is rising higher and higher over the whirls of history. This in spite of the fact that His enemies resort to all conceivable means to slight Him, to turn Him into just one of the religious geniuses. Let the praying of this psalm be a proof of a total commitment to the unique grandeur of Christ. He leaves all competitors by the wayside and confounds all arguments aimed at divesting Him of His status of standing at the right hand of the Almighty.

Those not tuned to the great lessons of apologetics about Christ might take a lesson or two about Him from art history. He certainly cannot be eliminated from the history of painting and sculpture. As to architecture, many of its greatest accomplishments are a monument to His divine status. Far more than anyone He inspired the greatest masterpieces, such as the mosaics of Christ the Pantokrator in Romanesque basilicas. Few are fortunate to see the huge image of Christ gazing down from the apse of the Norman cathedral in Cefalu, Sicily, as the Sunday vespers are being chanted. But we all must try to build up in our heart a mosaic of our faith in Christ, a mosaic more resplendent than anything made by man's hands. Having already entered a Temple of no human make, He now stands at the door of each soul and knocks for admittance. "If today you hear his voice, harden not your hearts" is a perennial warning of Psalm 95. Future began with Him and all future belongs to Him. It would be foolish to miss the boat of history which is counted from His birth, both backward and forward. There is no "Common Era" except the one in communion with Him.

Nor is there a cosmos without Him in whom God created everything. The Lord's words to David's Master should resound in our ears as crossing through the entire cosmos, which today looms incomparably larger in its countless galaxies than a cosmic tent covered with a firmament. In a truly cosmic sense, Christ is the Alpha and Omega, compared with whom the gigantic cosmos looks puny indeed, to say nothing of a "fundamental particle" called omega, which, like other such particles, is anything but fundamental.

Psalm 111

Although this psalm is alphabetical, a single theme dominates it throughout. It is the faithfulness of the God of the Covenant whose "justice stands forever," who "keeps his covenant ever in mind," whose works stand "firm forever and ever," who "established his covenant forever," and whose "praise will last forever." Most logically the psalmist concludes that the name of such a God "is to be feared," and that therefore "the fear of the Lord is the beginning of wisdom." It would be preposterous to try to add to this any word of wisdom.

Psalm 112

This psalm celebrates the just man and does so by including some pitfalls, which lurk in the psalmist's holding high the earthly prosperity of the just man. The precariousness of such prosperity should be clear to anyone in his right mind, but especially to those who are justified by God's grace which is obtained by Christ, who became poor so that we may share in riches that no moth, no rust can touch.

Psalm 113

The spiritual pitfalls gaping in the previous psalm seem to be filled in this psalm which celebrates God who "from the dust lifts up the lowly," who "from the dungheap raises the poor," and even provides children for the barren wife and thereby a proper homelife for her. For such reasons alone the first six verses of this psalm are a full-throated praise of God. This psalm has always been part of the old Sunday Vespers. The Vespers even now are crowned with the Magnificat, or Mary's praise of God's mercy to her. It was in her that the words of this psalm about God, who "leans down from on high," found their finest realization, insofar as He considered the lowliness of his most special handmaid and exalted her above all other creatures.

Psalm 114

Though eminently religious songs, the psalms were also the songs of a nation steeped, by God's choice, in true worship. As such a nation the Jews could not have found a more appropriate national anthem than this psalm, which is about the birth of the Jewish nation in the crucible of history. The psalm could be sung by them as Americans sing "Oh, say can you see . . ." or the French, "Allons enfants de la patrie. . ." Both anthems are about the passing of a people from political oppression to liberty.

This psalm echoes the exhilaration felt by Jews as they passed into circumstances where they could freely worship the true God, their God. It was a genuine spiritual redemption for them. This is why the Church used this psalm from early on as part of its celebration, at Easter, of the greatest spiritual transition: from sin to the life of grace.

Provided the word "primitive" is not tagged with a sense of contempt, this psalm can safely be called primitive. It exudes a sense unspoiled by undue reflections. It conveys a refreshing view of reality, both of nature and especially of events of nature that reveal a higher power at work. The psalm communicates above all a sense of marvel and gratitude that make the mind of children and of primitive people so much alike.

The verse about "hills jumping like lambs" may recall an event from 1927 when the high banks of the Jordan caved in about 30 miles north of Jericho, obviously as the result of a minor earthquake in a valley which is a geological fault-line. The flow of the Jordan was blocked and its bed could be crossed at Jericho for hours. The God of Nature could very well use natural events that He could certainly foresee with perfect accuracy, in order to promote His supernatural plan of salvation.

Faith has to be a "reasoned service," as Paul, that great champion of grace, emphasized (Rom 12:1). Still, after it has done its work, reason must not block the spontaneous outburst of admiration in plain view of a miracle. Let the praying of this psalm be a potent means of nurturing that spontaneous reaction, even if some call it primitive or childlike. We all must be like children if we are to enter the Kingdom of God.

Psalm 115

This is not the place to discuss the merits of considering this psalm, which the Septuagint translators joined to the preceding psalm, as a distinct psalm according to the Hebrew tradition. From the viewpoint of contents, arguments can be formulated in both directions. The object of this psalm is certainly different from that of the previous psalm where the latest event is the miraculous crossing of the Jordan.

Once having penetrated the Land of Promise, the Hebrews were confronted everywhere with pagan idols whose worshipers bested them in battle now and then. At one point they even captured the Ark of the Covenant. It was then most natural for them to taunt the Hebrews with the question: "Where is your God?" Their answer, "Our God is in Heaven," was further elaborated with the confidence characteristic of those who were gaining the upper hand. Soon it became a custom with the Jews to pour scorn on pagan idols. They did this not so much with abstract arguments as with graphically scornful remarks: "Their idols have mouths but they do not speak, they have ears but they

do not hear . . . ." Nothing could be so taunting as such a series of
graphic challenges.

This resistance to idols and contempt for them was even
more animated within the New Israel when it became its task to
preach monotheism to all nations. Enemies of Christians soon
took the defense of idols for a chief religious and cultural task.
Those devoted to that task could but be irritated by phrases that
echoed the mocking of idols in this psalm, phrases that often turn
up in the Martyrs' Acts. When confronted with those scornful
remarks about idols, some of those pagans were memorably
incensed. This was the case with Julian the Apostate, as he
passed through Antioch on his way to meet the Persian army.
From one of the houses he heard women's voices singing the
lines: "Their idols have mouths but they cannot speak . . . . Their
makers will become like them and so will all who trust in them."
Julian inquired. He was told that a certain Christian woman
Pablia and her companions were singing. He vowed that upon
his return he would mete out proper punishment. They all
happily survived the one who, unbeknownst to himself, was
heading into his very last battle.

Let us, therefore, celebrate with those devout women and
with all believers the historic triumph of faith over idols. For
believers of all ages were meant by the exhortation: "Sons of
Israel (the entire laity), sons of Aaron (all the clergy) bless the
Lord!" For this is our chief task on earth. One would greatly
misunderstand a later verse in the psalm about the earth given
to man as if we on earth could do anything with impunity.
Nothing secures the earth for man more than man's unstinting
attention to singing the praises of God. In this age of feverish
pastoral activities, let some credit be given to those of us who
opted not for the role of Martha, but of Mary.

Psalm 116

Devout people making vows often occur in the pages of the
Bible. Some of those vows were strange by our modern standards
or rather tastes. Samson vowed never to cut his hair. A thousand
years later Paul's vow consisted in cropping his head. Soon the
monks in the East vowed that no razor would ever touch their

mane and beard, whereas the monks of the West thought that their vows should be made manifest by leaving their heads bald with only a thin crown of hair on it. But there was no question about the spiritual dignity of vows. Contemptuous questions about religious vows came only with some Christians taking a "purely" biblical stance.

In this psalm one reads twice the verse: "My vows to the Lord I will fulfill, before all his people." The thrust of this psalm hinges on that verse. Since vows witness one's deep trust in God, thanksgiving is a normal follow-up to the help which God delivered in reply to the vow.

No thanksgiving was ever more profound than the one which Jesus uttered at the Last Supper. There "He gave thanks, broke the bread and said, this is my body." He did the same with the cup. His life, which was a vow, a commitment, to God's will, came to its culmination at that moment. No wonder that this psalm, in which, in addition to vows, an emphatic reference is made to the cup of salvation, has always been seen in the light of Christ's raising His own cup of salvation. This psalm cannot be better prayed than by first immersing one's mind into the mysterious atmosphere of that Supper. It sacramentally anticipated Christ's death on the cross; it initiated the rite which the apostles and all those whom they commissioned were to re-enact; it was also the great testimony (martyrdom) from which all future martyrdoms were to derive their meaning. Let us also recall that those, the Twelve, slated to be the prime witnesses, ran away when the moment of trial came as if to prove that, on his own, "no man can be trusted."

Psalm 117

This briefest of all psalms seems to discourage any effort to comment on it. Its brevity may remind one of Saint Benedict's rule: "Prayer should be brief and pure" (Rule ch. 20). Saint Aloysius, too, comes to mind, who felt sorry that he could not recite even one Our Father without being distracted. This psalm is even shorter. No excuse for praying it with our minds wandering away from its words. Let us turn this psalm into one of our favorite ejaculatory prayers. No thought can indeed be more comforting than that "God's merciful love endures forever."

Psalm 118

Anyone whose head has been enveloped by wildly buzzing bees
and stung by not a few of them would be well positioned to see
something of what was in the head of David as he composed this
psalm. One would be in a far better disposition if in addition one
had also been in the thick of a wild skirmish, where time and
again one might be on the point of being brought down, though
not finally. For even for David, who lived in circumstances where
wild bees could be encountered everywhere, their threatening
buzz, "they blazed like a fire among thorns," served to convey
something far more serious, than the purely personal misfortune
of being stung to death. The psalm is his exuberant thanksgiving
for having been rescued from an encounter that could easily have
put an end not only to his life but to all he was to be. And that
all was nothing less than to serve as the very concrete cornerstone in a Covenant into which God has transformed the Davidic
Kingdom, with its vast messianic vistas.

Nor would David have been David had he not turned his
triumph, "there are shouts of joy and victory in the tents of the
just," into a religious celebration. The religion of David was
genuine. It began with a call to thanksgiving in which all had to
take part: "Let the sons of Israel, let the sons of Aaron, let those
who fear the Lord say: His love has no end!" If religion is a re-
tying of man to God, nothing reveals so much the best in religion
than the confidence that God is love, which is the strongest tie.

After two thousand years of Christian preaching, it has
become almost trite to think of God as love. De-Christianization
lurks behind the popularity of the design in which the letter O
appears tilted to the right in the word LOVE. Here the really
important thing to note is that Christianity proclaims God as
Love, because it has inherited that notion from the Jews. They
alone among all other ancient people had the daring to think that
God was loving in a way far surpassing sentimentalism, although
even that remained beyond the ken of other peoples. The love of
the God of Israel was a saving Love.

Israel experienced that love on many occasions and saw it
demonstrated in the fate of its God-given leaders. Now it was
David's turn to have that experience. He knew that he was saved

in an encounter that humanly speaking would have been the end of him, and of his broader destiny. He seemed to be "thrust down and falling." Once on the ground he might just as well have thought himself to be in his grave. With the awareness of having been saved practically from death, he, a truly religious man, had no choice but to think that what happened was not wrought by him but by the Lord: "The Lord's right hand has triumphed, his right hand has raised me up." As a truly religious soul, David would not take credit for anything that only the Lord could bring about.

The fact that it was not he but his son, Solomon, who would build the Temple, that central concrete symbol of God's reign in Israel, indicated that it was the Lord who would build it, though with David as its cornerstone. David's enemies wanted to vitiate that very role but in vain: "The stone which the builders rejected has become the cornerstone." For David there remains only one thing to do: to go forward in procession with branches in hand up to God's altar and shout: "His love has no end!"

It is easy to summarize this psalm, so clear in its structure, so sincere in its sentiments, so vivid in its scenes. But the full dimensions of this psalm remained hidden until Jesus entered into Jerusalem in the midst of delirious crowds who cut branches from the trees and shouted: "Hosanna to the Son of David!"

Such an outburst of enthusiasm could not go unnoticed by the pharisees who for some time kept buzzing about Jesus like a swarm of bees, ready to sting Him with questions in order to trap Him. They knew that He was not a run-of-the mill messiah, stirring nationalistic sentiments, but one who posed a threat to any and all messianic hope steeped in nationalistic aggrandizement. Rank nationalism was the centerpiece of their hopes. Jesus therefore had to be disposed of.

Indeed, two days after that triumphal procession of His, they surrounded Him in the Temple where He was once more preaching. And since those hopes of theirs were intimately tied to all the observances of the Mosaic Law, they tried to lure Him into making a statement critical of that Law. They took Him to task at His authoritative tone of preaching: "On what authority are you doing all these things?" But Jesus turned the tables on them with a question about the authority of John's baptism. This question they could not answer without trapping themselves.

Since Jesus knew that His hour was coming, He suggested in unmistakable terms the true nature of His authority, fully aware of the fact that they would reject it, with ominous consequences for them. He told them that God's vineyard would be taken away from them after they had killed the very son of the owner of the vineyard. From the image of the vineyard Jesus went straight to the image of the cornerstone, citing the verses of this psalm. He seems indeed to have even paraphrased those verses in order to leave no doubt whatsoever about the deadly seriousness of what they entailed. Not a few important manuscripts have those verses in this form: "The man who falls upon that stone would be smashed to bits; and he on whom it falls will be crushed" (Mt 21:44).

This psalm is therefore not merely a prayer to celebrate Jesus' triumph as if it were not a fearsome event as well. For already Peter and the rest had to fear for their lives as they had to face a threatening Sanhedrin that was stung to the quick on hearing Peter quote from this psalm the verses in which David spoke about his having been raised by the Lord's right hand.

Many of those present must have heard a few months earlier Jesus quoting that psalm in reference to His being the cornerstone. Now they had to hear from Peter another application of this psalm, an application no less ominous for them. They simply could not comprehend the sense in which it was triumphal for Peter and the rest. For the apostles themselves were still to learn the full meaning of Jesus' words, "Unless the grain falls to the ground and dies . . ." (John 12:24).

These two aspects of Jesus' triumph are inseparable from one another. This is a point to be kept in mind as we turn this psalm into our prayer that has to be a Christian prayer. Of such prayer a mental incorporation into Jesus' deeds and sentiments is the highest form. No psalm can be better used for that purpose than this one. Jesus Himself, the cornerstone, applied it to Himself and subsequently Peter, whom Jesus made the Rock, applied it to that supreme triumph of Jesus, His resurrection. With that a new day dawned on mankind, a day that never sets.

Let it therefore be our cry day in and day out: "This day was made by the Lord, let us rejoice and be glad!" This psalm is not an invitation to merry-making with Easter bunnies and egg hunting.

Psalm 119

In his little book *Reflections on the Psalms* C. S. Lewis was eager to note that he wrote it as "an amateur to amateurs." For all his expertise in English letters, he never presented his skill with phrases as a proof of theological accomplishment. But in writing on the psalms one cannot avoid coming clean with one's theology, whether amateurish or not, or at least making some intimations of it. Unless one restricts oneself to the task of giving a translation as close to the Hebrew original as possible (which itself remains problematic in not a few places), one cannot help doing theology while interpreting the psalms. Theology becomes heavily involved in respect to this psalm, a series of prayerful reflections by a child of the Old Testament on the crucial role of the observance of the Law.

Paul of Tarsus was one such child and he must have known this psalm by heart and all the more so as he had for the Law the same burning love which comes through this psalm at every turn. For the author of this psalm the Law, or God's specific series of commands, is life, safety, support, and delight—all taken in a superlative sense. There is no trace in this psalm of the hairsplitting concern for "perfect" observance for which Jesus excoriated the Pharisees. But then why did C. S. Lewis write that during his focusing on psalms, that came rather late in his life, he found nothing more disturbing in the psalms than precisely that concern for the Law. He wrote this as introductory to the chapter "Connivance." Did he overlook something, something rather obvious? Was he himself conniving?

In writing that book C. S. Lewis, who rather easily earned the reputation of being a foremost apologist, did something worse than theologically very amateurish. For it was not the mistaken trust in the observance of mere externals that seemed to bother really the distinguished Oxford don to whom Cambridge gave a chair. It was rather the absolute certainty of

Fundamentalists and Roman Catholics which the author of *Reflections on the Psalms* saw lurking in this longest of all psalms.

Certainty is not certainty if it is not absolute, a point which C. S. Lewis might have learned from Newman's *Grammar of Assent*, had he cared for the greatest Oxonian of modern times. Whatever the certainty of a Fundamentalist, the certainty of a Roman Catholic is both an intellectual stance and also the status of good conscience. Such a conscience is an awareness that one has performed that basic duty of a follower of Christ which is the keeping of the commandments. Jesus said so. "If you love me," He told the apostles, "keep my commandments." He also said that His burden was light and His yoke was easy.

The temptations of ordinary life, say, those of an Oxford don or of a baker in Kalamazoo, or of a retired colonel in Tunbridge Wells, may be at times grave but never such that many Christians would not have succeeded in coping with them. Many a lay Catholic could maintain himself or herself in the state of grace over long stretches of time if he or she diligently made use of the chief channels of grace known as sacraments.

Something of this transpires in Tolkien's biography by H. Carpenter, in connection with the three years that preceded Tolkien's marriage. Tolkien, also a prominent Oxford literary man, and C. S. Lewis had friendly relations before contact between the two began to peter out. A reason has much to do with C. S. Lewis' idea of the Church. He pictured it as a large hall from which many apartments opened where Christians lived according to their particular choice of apartments, each standing for a Church and all on equal footing. In the big hall one merely wandered around until one settled on one or another apartment.

The "Mere Christianity" which Lewis advocated and which he could readily accommodate into the broad expanses of the Church of England, had a distinct touch of vagueness to it. No wonder that Lewis' rapport with Tolkien, a no-nonsense Roman Catholic, grew weaker and weaker. Lewis' predilection for vagueness found itself exposed whenever something really specific arose on the theological horizon. This explains his attitude toward this psalm and toward the praises of the Law there. A law is not law unless it is specific, and the same remains the case even if the law is called "ordinance," a term that tolerates more vagueness than the former. In order to take the edge out of this psalm, Lewis read something into it which is not there at all. It contains not a whit of the certainty of pharisaism.

It would be a great mistake to take this psalm for an exaggerated praise of minute observances of which there is no hint at all, a remarkable feature to be sure. A Christian, who is liberated from the yoke of the Mosaic Law can feast on this psalm by using a simple device: Having in mind the two great commandments, the love of God and the love of neighbor, superior to all the Mosaic Law even in the latter's very perspective, the Christian knows that he does full justice to this psalm when on reading there the word "Law," he thinks of the Law of Love as broken down into specifics in chapter 13 of Paul's First Letter to the Corinthians. Beyond that the Christian must not exert his mind too much as he prays this psalm, the strangest among all alphabetical psalms. It is close to being a verbal acrobatics that forestalls the development of a train of thought. Proposals about a system in this psalm may safely be left aside. Since all verses in each stanza begin with the same letter of the Hebrew alphabet, the thought had to be fitted to a limited number of words. This could but constrain the thought itself.

Still the psalm abounds in lines that are not only gems of religious insight, but statements above all about the primacy of God's grace. Verses 33-37 are especially a case in point. Does not awareness of that primacy blare forth in the requests that God may train one to keep His statutes to the end, to observe them with love and with delight? Is not God's grace extolled in the request that one's heart be bent to His will and not to love of gain? If man can, on his own, turn his eyes from what is false, why should he beg God for help to do so? Karl Barth, who took the Rule of Saint Benedict for a noble tool to underplay God's grace, should have pondered the fact that the Saint took from this psalm the verse (116), which the monk, as he makes his profession, should recite so that he may implement it with God's grace.

The last stanza, called Tau by the last word in the Hebrew alphabet, bursts with those gemlike verses. Through them the psalmist cries out for God's help; he begs God that His hands be ready to help him; he states that he longs for God's saving help; and finally admits that he is a mere lost sheep who needs to be sought out by God. This could hardly be the prayer of a pharisee as portrayed by none other than Christ, the Good Shepherd, who went out of His way to find the lost sheep among whom no pharisee, old or new, would ever count himself or herself.

Psalm 120

This psalm is the first of fourteen psalms, consecutively placed in the Psalter, all of which, with the exception of Psalm 130, the famed *De profundis*, have the charming label, "pilgrimage song" (or song of ascent), affixed to them. No theme gives them a common bond, but possibly because with the exception of one they were brief, they had a special appeal to pilgrims. These short songs, that could easily relieve their fatigue, are the best folkloric expression of Israel's piety. They are the best also in the sense that the same piety did not care to preserve other popular songs, of which there must have been a plenty in ancient Israel. To anyone animated by that piety its uniqueness was all too clear. Israel alone was instructed in the Law, Israel alone was chosen by God, Israel alone carried salvation history. The Messiah, who fulfills history, was to come from Israel. Keen awareness of all this was the reason why, unlike the folklore of other nations, the folklore of Israel was an eminently religious folklore. This is why only the religious songs and only the best of them were deemed to be preserved.

Insofar as pilgrimages were occasions of folkloric creativity, the annual gathering in Jerusalem to celebrate the Passover was in that sense, too, the chief of pilgrimages. Undoubtedly many more than a dozen such songs were on the lips of Israel of old. Pilgrimages are particularly conducive to the composing of ever new songs. Within a few decades the pilgrimages to Fatima inspired more than a hundred hymns, some of them tediously repetitious. A commentator on the psalms may for that reason, too, be pleased that he has to consider only a dozen or so pilgrimage songs. They all carry on them not only a distinct touch of individuality, but also the mark of an unmistakable timeliness.

It would indeed be difficult to think of a more timely theme than the one registered in the very first of the pilgrimage psalms, Psalm 120. It reverberates with a sense of frustration that seizes anyone who lives in close quarters with those who not only hate peace but promote their craving for conflicts with deceitful lips. If diplomacy is "war waged by other means," to recall the remark of a famed modern theoretician of war, then one should recognize the whisper of treacherous tongues for what it is. In this age of TV broadcast from satellites, of an Internet that has invaded most households, it would be vain to dream of media-free places, that is, places of peace. No more places with blackout from propaganda served up as mere news. No more Meshech, no more tents of Kedar, mentioned wistfully in this psalm. Peaceful living exists more and more only on paper. Travel agencies, to say nothing of anthropologists, keep destroying even the last oases of peace, with the full connivance of the public that wants peaceful places, while polluting them with warlike noise.

On the political scene all lands are full of those who thrive on denouncing real and imaginary abuses, often by lying about them in a way that should pass for rank abuse of the normal intellect. Even within the Church, fewer and fewer are the areas that could be likened to the distant tents of Kedar. Now even the cloistered religious are supposed to rise to the highest ridges of the seven-storey-mountain of contemplation by "engaging" in inner city apostolate. No wonder that all too often monasteries and convents have become places where chatter is a daily marathon, with plenty of infighting as its spillover. In the world at large lying is written off as "economizing with truth" and liars as "spin doctors." Endless are, indeed, the reasons for exclaiming with the psalmist: "O Lord, save my soul from lying lips, from the tongue of the deceitful!"

The art of advertising is often a skill in deception. More and more lawyers openly boast that their chief aim is not to serve the cause of justice but to have their clients off the hook, whatever hook or crook this may take. Newspapers extended their editorials to every bit of their reporting to serve not the truth but special interest groups, and the chief among these, a major political party.

Psalm 121

In olden times as well as today when it is so easy to fly even over the Himalayas, mountains are still the best means given by nature for self-protection. The Swiss may be especially brave but their mountains come very handy to their bravery. Whenever possible, man built his cities on mountaintops, or at least on the top of hills. And whenever such a hilltop was surrounded by a mountain range, it seemed doubly protected.

Such appeared to be the case with Jerusalem. And those mountains stood by unfailingly. They were so many guardposts on which one could rely with full confidence. All this symbolizes in the psalmist's eyes the manner in which the Lord guards his own. The manner is total as seen from the side of God who is the maker of "heaven and earth," that is, of all totality in the strict sense. Later the same idea of totality is restated with respect to time and action. God always guards us regardless of whether the sun or the moon rules the sky, regardless of whatever man does, whether he goes or comes. It seems that God, our guardian, never sleeps nor slumbers. Such anthropomorphisms should serve to awaken us to the actual concreteness and immediacy of God's presence in our lives.

It remains for us to prove ourselves worthy of such protection. We shall go a long way in that respect if we often invoke our guardian angels, through whom God chose to protect us. Christ's words about children whose angels constantly see the face of God (Mt 18:10) should be of great moment indeed.

Psalm 122

The setting of this psalm is easy to imagine if one has seen reconstructions of what Jerusalem and its immediate surroundings looked like in Jesus' time. Huge walls loomed large in front of the pilgrims after they turned the last bend of the road hugging the last hill. The psalm presents the pilgrims as they have just arrived within a stone's throw of Jerusalem and now march toward one of its gates. They are full of the joy of having accomplished a noble undertaking. It began when word spread in their village that a pilgrimage would form. Those who joined it felt a wave of happiness run through them: "I rejoiced when I heard them say, let us go to the house of the Lord."

For not so much Jerusalem as its House of the Lord pulled the Jews from far afield, whatever the dubious attraction of a huge city, of a capital, and of its diversions. To be sure, the House of the Lord and Jerusalem were inseparable. Still it was the House of the Lord that made Jerusalem what it came to be in Jewish eyes. And herein lies the gist of this psalm which is clearly stated in the psalm itself: "For the love of the House of the Lord I ask for your good, for your peace, O Jerusalem."

The fact that Jerusalem is the capital, that it is by far the most strongly built among Israel's towns, that one is supposed to praise the Lord there, that all the thrones of David, that is, the administrative offices of the nation, are there—all this gave a very special importance to Jerusalem. As such it could function only if peace reigned there.

But the psalm makes it clear that this peace is not asked for the sake of Jerusalem, but for the sake of the House of the Lord there. That House was the concretization of the spiritual reality which Yahwism represented. It could function only if peace was implored for it. Peace is a gift to be obtained by prayer.

One wonders what was in the mind of some spiritual Jews (and quite a few of them were trapped in the City during its final tragic siege) as they saw a horrid bloody clash unfold between two anarchist Jewish factions, one of whom dominated the larger Temple precincts, the other the Temple itself. By then the Jews had for centuries been torn by the strife between the Pharisees and the Sadducees, or the "conservative" externalists and the "progressive" pseudo-believers. Disunity in thought once more presaged the destruction of spiritual riches as well.

All this is very applicable to the New Jerusalem, the Church and the incomparable spiritual riches deposited in her. If this psalm teaches anything, it teaches the enormous measure in which the Church needs peace. Father Congar's book, *The Peace of My Church,* comes to mind, a book published twenty years after Vatican II. The book is a sigh for earlier times when peace within the Church was far greater than after Vatican II, although the Council put the word Peace on its banner. Such was the observation of one who already in the late 1930s was in the forefront of working out the theological rationale of reform movements. The worthy Dominican (eventually a Cardinal) must have come to see that the rationale would have been well served if this psalm had often been on the lips of the Council's *periti.*

Saint Irenaeus, the martyr bishop of Lyons in whom so many see the invisible theologian of Vatican II, would have no doubt as to why peace has become in short supply within the Church after Vatican II. To all real and self-styled *periti* who loved to invoke his name, he would refer not so much to his name, "peace loving," as to an essential aspect of his theology of restoration, or reform. The aspect is condensed in his nowadays often forgotten statement about the manner of finding the truth. The phrase, "Ad hanc enim ecclesiam . . ., " in full English rendering states: "With this Church, because of its superior origin, all Churches must agree, that is, all the faithful in the whole world; and it is in her that the faithful everywhere have maintained the Apostolic tradition." Already in Irenaeus' time Rome was the great spiritual point of attraction for Christians. In going there today in the spirit of pilgrims, one cannot find a better pilgrimage song than this psalm to be prayed for the peace of the Church, the New Jerusalem.

Rome deserves to be protected. Its churches, its monuments, its palaces have an incomparable cultural value of their own. But that value pales in comparison with the spiritual riches which Jesus tied to the point where the Rock or Peter, established by Him, was to be laid to his eternal rest. For the sake of remaining tied to the point that alone conserves integrally the riches of redemption in Christ, pray for the peace of Rome, for the peace of its palaces, of its administrative offices. Not yet a Cardinal, but already living in post-Vatican I times, Newman, who did not think that the definition of papal infallibility was opportune, insisted that one owed filial obedience even to orders issued by the administrative offices of the Vatican.

This was not suggested by an ecclesiastical careerist, but by a prophetically spiritual soul. Newman knew that peace is the work of justice, or of truth commonly held and obeyed. Jesus Himself specified peace among his followers as the chief witness on behalf of His message. Such is the only way to bring about something of Zechariah's prophecy which echoes this psalm as it states that the nations "shall come to seek the Lord of hosts in Jerusalem and to implore the favor of the Lord" (Zech 8:22).

Psalm 123

This psalm can hardly appeal to the modern mind that sets so great a store by asserting independence in every respect and therefore issues all too often in abject dependence on one's miserable self. In an age when it has become *passé* to bend one's knees before one's bishop, let alone to kiss his pastoral ring, this psalm may seem to prescribe an outrageous attitude. It is that of a slave, or at least of a servant, who fixes his eyes on his master's each and every move to fathom in advance all his intentions. Add to this, in this feminist age, that the psalm holds high the maidservant who would not lose a single detail of the motions of her mistress' hands. If one finds one's soul filled with disillusion, it may be wise to reconsider the direction of one's eyes. These can become furtively self-centered, especially when one thinks that one is looking for an "interiorized" religion, floating on a higher level than its "institutionalized" kind. Nothing brings on so much self-contempt and self-deception.

Psalm 124

The Holy Land is full of ravines that a sudden cloudburst turns into beds of torrents against which there is no defense. Such a scene loomed large in the eyes of exegetes when one of them, Jean Steinmann, was swept to his death near Petra in 1963. In this age that abhors cruelty to animals we shall hardly see the revival of falconry, a favorite theme in Renaissance paintings. They invariably show the subtly cruel faces of gentlemen hunters, proud of their "gaming" skills, but never the happiness of a bird that now and then makes good its escape from the clutches of a hawk. Only those will be unattracted by this psalm who delude themselves into dreaming about a threat-free existence. The psalm was one of "Israel's songs," reproduced in verses 2-5, and a song of the New Israel, too, for its miraculous escapes.

Psalm 125

This psalm harks back to the celebration, in Psalm 121, of a mountain, surrounded by a ring of mountains. So does the Lord surround His own people. The confidence is voiced that He would not let the wicked rule for too long a time over his own people. Too long an endurance of the rule of the wicked would undermine the perseverance of too many. In countries where institutionalized, atheistic Communism lasted for three generations, the spiritual, cultural, and intellectual damages were far more extensive than in countries that had to endure the Red Paradise only for two generations. Europe would not still be Europe if the French Revolution had kept it in its terrorizing grip for forty years instead of a mere decade. And what about the Nazis? Has not Pius XII told J. F. Murphy, a roving American ambassador (who could hardly believe his ears), that the Nazis posed a greater threat to the Church than the lackeys of Stalin? Still, it is always in God's own good time that the wicked will be driven away. Once away, other groups of the wicked will move in. Make no mistake about that. Worse, the wicked man is hiding in every pious soul, and is ever ready to raise an ugly head. This will be overlooked only at one's greatest spiritual peril.

Psalm 126

One must have endured long years in captivity, in exile, in the underground, to appreciate this psalm in the measure it deserves. Otherwise one can hardly sense the laughter, the incredulously joyful cries of those who had the good fortune (and trustful resolve and courage) to return from the Babylonian captivity to Jerusalem. The world today is less willing to admit its marveling as it witnesses the often miraculous resurgence of Christians in this or that part of the globe. The world rather prefers to hear announcements about the imminent burial of Christianity, which somehow is always postponed. For Christians there should be much food for thought in the sequence set in the second part of the psalm: The seeds for a joyful harvest are always sown in hardships, and watered with one's tears or at least perspiration.

Conversely, when there is too much merrymaking in sowing the seeds, the harvest may be very tearful indeed.

Psalm 127

The typical building constructed by an Israelite was a house, a home. He further built it for a purpose, which more obviously commended itself at a time when the family was the basic economic unit and even the unit of defense. The family as the essential complement of the house is celebrated here. Can a psalm be more timely than this at a time, ours, when one-parent families are held to be of as much worth as "traditional" families? Young people are less and less willing to marry and raise a family. Instead, they shack up. The percentage of American women 15 years and older who live in marriage dropped from 87.5 in 1960 to 49.7 in 1996. It would be no real risk to say that since then that ominous drop has continued unabated. Further, the average American family lives in one place no longer than three years. Even nomads of long gone times showed a better appreciation of wife and children and of a steady hearth. Society may have to taste to the full the bitterness of pseudo-marital arrangements in order to appreciate anew the wisdom proclaimed in this psalm: families are the greatest blessing for man to have. In praying this psalm I cannot help thinking of a stately mansion on which his architect-owner placed a granite block with the words engraved on it: "Nisi Dominus frustra." Vain is indeed any effort that wants to possess steadily anything in disregard to God. People who defied God or at least ignored Him could come up with monumental constructions, but nothing truly constructive could be achieved unless one was willing to serve as a mere subcontractor to the Lord.

Psalm 128

In ancient Israel men made up most of the pilgrims. For a while man may enjoy the company of other men, but soon his thoughts will be carried back to his home, to the dinner table where he is surrounded by his wife, "a growing olive tree," and his children, so many "shoots" on it. This psalm suggests that unlike in later

Rabbinic tradition, one's wife was sitting at the table and not merely serving at table her man and the sons she bore to him. This psalm calls even more strongly than the preceding one for reflections centered on the vast positive goods which God connected with family life. The marriage ceremony is a proof that although the fall of Adam and Eve deprived man of many blessings, God left man with the blessing that family life should bring along.

Psalm 129

"This is Israel's song," is the explanatory note given by the psalm to its first line, "They had pressed me hard from my youth." The song seems to be verbally reproduced in verses 2-4. With a little modernity, the psalmist might rather have said, "This is Israel's national anthem," a hymn composed with a reference to the transformation of the Hebrews from a tribe into a people, after having been scourged by the whips of Egyptian slave masters.

To recall long past trials is proper if only to remind one about the uncertainties of a prosperous present. Quite different is the case when one dwells on the past in order to foment the flames of revenge under the pretext that certain crimes ought not to be forgotten ever. One has to recite with great apprehension the second part of this psalm, the only cursing psalm among psalms sung as one ascended to the Temple with one's gift. Frightening is the image of grass that withers before it flowers, the fate invoked on one's torturers. But more frightening should sound the warning that in bringing one's gift to the Temple one should first seek sincere reconciliation with others (Mt 5:23).

The Jews always found it difficult to accept that being God's chosen people, also meant being specially subject to God's often strange ways. They could not understand what the Letter to the Hebrews—yes to Hebrews—meant in saying that God's love toward His children often manifests itself in harsh disciplining. An incredibly harsh truth, although as old as the hills. Indeed to a hill Abraham had to go and be ready to sacrifice Isaac. To the Golgotha God's own Son had to go, after having been scourged. Hence the Christian custom of praying this psalm on Good Fridays so that one should really forget as one truly forgives.

Psalm 130

This psalm, best known as the *De profundis*, does not carry the label pilgrimage psalm, sandwiched though it is between psalms sung during pilgrimages. On a cursory look this psalm may not seem to fit in with the happy mood which often animates pilgrims. Pilgrimage songs usually convey the note "sursum corda" instead of "de profundis."

Awareness of one's sins can easily weigh down the soul to abysmal depths. There the sinner can only bewail his wretchedness and become hopelessly lost in his predicament. Then he would not remember from this psalm anything except its reference to those depths opened up by one's iniquity, depths filled with decaying "flowers of evil," to recall a set of Beaudelaire's poems that contains one with the title "De profundis."

Apart from the first line of that poem in which Baudelaire turns to the One whom alone he adores (presumably God), all the other lines center on his sense of wretchedness and misery. Another famed literary piece, a very long letter written by Oscar Wilde from the Reading Jail to a gay friend of his, does not contain even that much in the way of spirituality, negative as it may be. The letter, to which the editor of Wilde's works gave the title "De profundis" is full of self justification carried to the kind of extreme where Wilde disclosed that "while Metaphysics had but little real interest for me, and Morality absolutely none, there was nothing that either Plato or Christ had said that could not be transferred immediately into the sphere of Art, and there find its complete fulfillment."

Wilde called this word of wisdom of his "a generalisation as profound as novel." He merely paddled on the stale old waters of *l'art pour l'art*. To crown the comedy, all this occurred to Wilde while sipping coffee with André Gide, hardly a stalwart of moral philosophy, whose *L'Immoraliste*, a self portrait, should have been called "L'Amoraliste." One should now know what to think about the impropriety of giving "De Profundis" as title to that booklength letter. When the abysmal depths of amorality are taken for moral profundity, discernment between virtue and vice is abandoned and so is the perspective within which sin appears in its deepest sense, an offense of a most holy God.

One need not be a theologian to sense that enormous difference which both those literary pieces represent in relation to our psalm. The reason for that difference is easy to spot. Unlike in those pieces, where God is hardly visible or appears in a farcical form, in our psalm He dominates almost every line. This is why our psalm could just as well have been remembered not so much as "de profundis" but as "sursum corda." For the God of the Bible is a merciful God. Otherwise He would not have spoken to mankind. With that God, plentiful is the value called redemption. Only such a God can be looked for with the kind of longing expectation that fills the soul as he waits as does a nightguard for the daybreak.

In a broader sense the "daybreak" is the end of one's pilgrimage on earth, a journey that may be marked with many mishaps, with many precipitous falls. This is not to suggest that special satisfaction should be taken with the state of affairs as described in Chaucer's *Canterbury Tales*, written at a time when morals were indeed at a very low ebb. But even on a pilgrimage that took the fifteen-year-old Thérèse Martin, later known as the Little Flower, to Rome, her sensitive eyes could notice scenes that exuded little spirituality. That pilgrimages to Fatima had from the start the seal of penance on them is one more vote on behalf of the genuineness of the role of Lucia, Francisco, and Jacinta, three incomparable glories of a truly Pilgrim Church, of whom the last two are now among the Blessed.

Psalm 131

This psalm, so movingly brief, may remind one of perfect creations of art that are such precisely because of their stunning brevity. Chopin's "Prelude in A major" may come to mind, or Goethe's eight-line poem, "Uber allen Gipfeln ist Ruh' . . ." What can call for a shorter comment than the contemplation of a child's peaceful resting on its mother's breast after it has been fed? Nothing worse could be done to Mary Cassatt's painting "The Mother and the Child" than explaining it with a learned analysis of her palette and brushstrokes. Paintings that have for their title, "Madonna with Child," should be admired in worshipful silence. Such is the attitude which this psalm calls for. It is not for aesthetics to teach the kind of trust which true believers must have in God. With that trust in place, gigantic projects will not overwhelm the soul, so apt to get lost in "great and astonishing things." True humility alone can find meaning in chores that appear utterly trivial.

Psalm 132

Of all the pilgrimage psalms this is the only one which is tied to an event and indeed to a very momentous one. As the pilgrims approached Jerusalem from the west, they passed through Kirjat-jearim of Ephratha. They could not help thinking of the procession that carried the Ark of the Covenant from there to its final resting place, the City of David, Mount Zion.

The event, described in chapter 6 of the Second Book of Samuel, prompted David's vow that he would not rest until he built a proper dwelling place for the Lord. A gigantic enterprise it was, which David could only prepare but not execute. Yet, once more a sincere good intention counted for work done. In return David received the promise that his son would succeed him on the throne and that the line of succession would never end. No nation could ever expect more than a solemn divine promise that it would endure forever. It was, however, to be a most special endurance, that of a divine Covenant.

One day, a twelve-year-old Jewish lad was singing this psalm with other pilgrims and with thoughts, which we may guess as we reflect on the miraculous endurance of the Covenant sealed in His blood, the only means of a Rest with no end. That Rest, as the Letter to the Hebrews (Heb 4:9) emphasized, was left to the People of the New Covenant.

Recitation of this psalm may precede any great undertaking, however inconspicuous outwardly. More than one saint found the verse "This is my resting place forever," a seal put on his or her life's undertaking. Such was the way in which Bernadette Soubirous recited this verse, after she moved from Lourdes to a convent in Nevers. Let us not forget the Queen of all Saints, who literally served as the Ark of the Covenant. Her assumption into heaven may be implied in the declaration of the Apocalypse: "God's temple in heaven opened and in the temple could be seen the ark of the covenant" (11:19), the container of supreme Rest.

Psalm 133

In respect of brevity this psalm vies for first place with Psalm 131 that takes its cue from the child's resting in full contentment on its mother's breast. The compact beauty of sincere brotherhood should dissuade one from lengthy, let alone from long-winded comments on it. Augustine, who wrote thousands of pages on the psalms, might have here risen to the occasion but he did not. Instead of a mere page, he wrote ten as can easily be seen in the full English translation of his *Enarrationes in psalmos,* published in the halcyon days of the Oxford Movement.

The reason for Augustine's apparent prolixity is worth recalling. He had to face the Donatists whom a modern biographer of Augustine set up as the polished religionists in contradistinction to the impoliteness he tried to find everywhere in Augustine. Only the saint fails to appear in *Augustine of Hippo. A Biography* as if striving for holiness had not been the very essence of much of Augustine's adult life. The Donatists, like other "refined" enemies of Catholics were ready to make alliance even with the disreputable, provided these hated Catholics. The disreputable in question were a wild group of monks, called *circumcelliones.* They were so named because they were never inside but always outside their cells. They contended that the monastic institution (community living under rule) was not Christian because the word "monk" (monachus) was not in the Bible. Augustine himself was the founder of one such monastic community, formed of his own priests in Hippo, for whom he wrote a Rule, subsequently used by the Augustinian canons. Augustine therefore had to explain a thing or two about monks living under rule and about this psalm's relevance. The result was a public discourse for which he used this psalm as a text.

Clearly, Augustine had to offer more than his celebrated praise of the monastic institution, which began as follows: "This is a short psalm, but one well known and quoted, *Behold, how good and how pleasant it is, that brethren should dwell together in unity.* So sweet is that sound, that even those who know not the Psalter, sing that verse. . . . For these same words of the Psalter, this sweet sound, that honeyed melody, as well of the mind as of the hymn, did even beget the Monasteries. By this sound were

stirred up the brethren who longed to dwell together. This verse
was their trumpet. It sounded through the whole earth, and they
who had been divided, were gathered together. The summons of
God, the summons of the Holy Spirit, the summons of the
Prophets, were not heard in Judah, yet were heard through the
world. They were deaf to the sound, amid whom it was sung;
they were found with their ears open, of whom it was said, *They
shall see him, who were not told of him; they shall understand who
heard not.*"

Augustine then pointed out that our psalm can be given a
monastic dimension only because the monastic or religious life
has its *raison d'être* in Christian brotherhood. Christian religion is
a communal religion. The first Christians had everything in
common out of a spontaneous zeal. No one can love God whom
one does not see, if one does not love the brethren one sees—so
argued John the Apostle.

As to the psalmist's graphic encomiums of brotherly love,
they were all too natural in a hot and arid land such as Palestine.
There one readily thought of the oil needed to sooth one's face
under the blazing sun, and of the dew that brought relief not
only to desiccated humans but also to the parched soil. The use
of oil had to be generous in the rite whereby Aaron was ointed
the first High Priest (Lev 8:12), whereas dew came especially in
great abundance from the snow capped Hermon.

There can be no dispute about the psalm's applicability to
our Lord's statement that whenever two or three gather in his
name He is in their midst. But can people gather in His name if
they don't also pray together? Then and only then will they
experience the full truth of the psalm's opening line that is very
pleasant and very sweet for brethren to dwell together. Such is in
brief Augustine's celebrated commentary on this psalm.

About ten years ago the bishop of Waga Waga in Australia
(the name means "many blackbirds" in the tongue of the local
aborigines) kindly showed me around in his new seminary. It
included also the bishop's residence. The bishop, he said, must
live with his priests or at least with his seminarians and he
quoted an Apostolic Letter by John Paul II. I cannot help thinking
that this psalm was especially dear to that inspiring bishop

whom, so he told me, some of his fellow bishops considered to be off his rocker. Perhaps they should have worried about the empty halls of the huge National Seminary at the mouth of Sydney Bay and about the Church going to the rocks in some places "down under." Twice I had the sad privilege of seeing something of this at first hand. Different were the heroic days of the Church in Australia when priest-monks worked from their priories to the great benefit of the souls confided to them.

Psalm 134

This psalm takes one to the Temple court where the pilgrims gather for prayer at the first nightfall following their arrival in Jerusalem. The psalm is a plain call for prayer, for blessing the Lord, blessing Him with arms raised high, with faces turned toward the huge door of the Sanctuary itself, the Holy of Holies. For the rest of their stay in Jerusalem, the pilgrims heard the same call each evening, responded in the same way, and received the same blessing as the priests cried out: "May the Lord bless you from Sion . . . "

This was the blessing they all longed for. Jews time and again risked their lives to get inside the walls of Jerusalem for the Passover. Part of their reward was to hear this blessing when after a scorching day the cool evening came. They were ready to stay through the night with arms raised again and again as if to carry their heart and soul to the One who lives on high, though very specially in the Sanctuary in front of them.

When as a twelve-year-old Jesus first went up to Jerusalem, he certainly was exposed to a communal experience of a night-long prayer. Given the oriental temperament, the experience had to be much more emotive than our modern candlelight vigil services. Even then it was still very different from the experience of entire nights spent alone in prayer where one's mind is more free to think God's thoughts alone. It was after having spent alone an entire night in prayer that Jesus chose twelve from among His disciples so that the blessings He brought from heaven might rest on them and be channelled through them to all men for the rest of the night of history.

Psalm 135

As it stands, this psalm may be best pictured as an exhortation to the people gathered in the Temple court. The people are reminded first of the fact that they were chosen by Yahweh for Himself, a point of crucial importance for grasping the way in which Jews were supposed to look upon themselves. To nurture this perspective of self-appraisal, they were, so the exhortation goes, to keep in mind the great facts of Exodus and of the conquests of the Promised Land, both exceeding human calculations. They were also to keep alive the mocking contempt of idols, already voiced in Psalm 115, which is found here in a somewhat abbreviated form. The psalm ends with a triple call on the people to join in blessing the Lord. The actual way of carrying this out may be seen in the next psalm.

Psalm 136

This psalm, whose content is almost identical with the preceding one, is clearly structured to be a communal song. The psalm alternates in double lines, of which the first, standing for an act of the Lord evidencing His love for the people, may have been shouted by one or two priests, whereas the people voiced their consent with the rousing acclamation: "for his great love is without end!" Unlike in the preceding psalm, here considerable space is given to God's creative acts as manifesting His love.

Recitation of this psalm rightly appears as an implementation of the rule stated in patristic time, namely, that the rules about what is to be prayed set the rules for what is to be believed ("lex orandi statuat legem credendi"). And just as *the* prayer of Christians begins with the Father in heaven, the Creed of Christians begins with the *all*mighty Father.

The *all* is, of course, the totality of creatures or the universe. For common perception, the universe still looks today as it did for the Hebrews of old. There is no need to exert one's mental powers and think of galaxies and supernovae as the psalm refers to the sky and the two great lights fixed on it. Whatever its twofold motions, the earth feels firmly established under our feet. One needs, however, to recall what has already been said in connection with Psalm 8 about the universe as manifesting God's special love for man.

It is, of course, not easy to think of the anthropic principle of modern scientific cosmology as one repeats lines that reflect a very primitive view of the world. It is far easier to make a transposition into post-biblical history and think of Nero, Decius, Diocletian, Julian, Stalin, Hitler, and Mao as one recites the names of Sihon, king of the Amorites, and of Og, king of Bashan, who first tried to exterminate God's chosen people and put thereby an end to salvation history.

The Church cannot praise highly enough God's everlasting love for her wholly improbable escapes from a "final solution." The latter was advocated in Voltaire's call to arms: "Ecrasez l'infâme," which then became the battle cry of those who made it their dogma that "religion was the opiate of the people."

An inscription, "Ci-gît le ci-devant clergé français" (Here lies the late French clergy), engraved in stone and still above the entrance of a former Carmelite convent in Paris, comes to mind. It dates back to the Terror whose protagonists executed many priests in that house. But the French clergy saw a spectacular rebirth, reminding one of the phoenix rising from its ashes.

Those priests knew that the love which is meant in this psalm has nothing to do with sentimentalism. It is rather a happy combination of God's infinite good will and mercy that can generate heroic love in man.

Psalm 137

Exile, even if it is not a concentration camp, is a hardship in many ways. For the Jews exiled to Babylon their oppressors' request that they entertain them by singing the "songs of Sion" was a last straw. It prompted the composition of this psalm, which eventually became the classic song on the lips of Jews in the Diaspora, old and new.

The curses on the Edomites echo the worst in pre-Gospel times. The times when true worshipers of God had to pray for their enemies were still to come, although the urge for vengeance remains as vivid as ever. As to the dashing of heads against a hard wall or a rock, it was a widely practiced way of taking revenge on one's enemies. Forms of murder far more cruel than the one recalled in this psalm were to be devised by man, one of them being the crucifixion, still another the impaling. One ought not to forget perhaps the most inhumane of them all, used against the first Christians in Japan, and known as *ana-tsurushi*. It consisted in suspending the victim by his feet in a narrow pit. To prolong the agony a slight incision was made on the victim's face to prevent the growing pressure of blood in his head from doing its lethal trick too soon.

Still to come was the worst, the use of drugs against the human mind, a technique perfected in the prisons of Stalin and of his satellites. Only little behind them are Western gurus who sang the praises of "new" experiences through the use of "mild" hallucinogens, although in the long run they spark an uncontrollable urge for heroin and cocaine. So much about the most cruel forms of alienation whereby man is exiled from himself.

The Babylonian exile is very much with us. Passages of the Book of Revelation about the "great whore" which is Babylon, or the enticements of the World, writ large, should come to mind. They bespeak of the true status of mankind, a status of Exile, away from God. Those who know this, will know the World for what it is, though they will also know that they are not supposed to condemn and curse the World.

Psalm 138

This psalm may easily pass for the most timely of all psalms. In this age, whose boasted progress has produced so many broken, stunted souls, nothing may appear more appealing than that God is ready to increase the strength of one's soul, provided one asks for that great favor. Although in this psalm gratitude is voiced to God for favors obtained, it is not forgotten that man's predicament will continue to be full of hazards, threats, and opposition. The psalmist betrays a distinct awareness of the fact that man, though the work of God's very hands, may be discarded. Hence the need to ask fervently God's favor and to do this with the awareness of being in the presence of angels. One's guardian angel should be spotted in the front rank of that angelic choir ready to carry our prayers to God's very throne.

Psalm 139

Those who sensed keenly, and almost all saints are an instance of this, the futility of escaping God's pursuit of the soul, must have found in this psalm a mirror for their experience. A memorable expression of this is Francis Thomson's poem, "The Hound of Heaven." Still, it should be noted, that resistance to God's appeal is not portrayed in this psalm on that psychological level which modern man, caught in his own psychic labyrinths, would expect. There is no indication that the psalmist was tempted interiorly to join up with some "blood of men." On the contrary, he is not afraid to ask God to test his utter sincerity and loyalty. He does this in lines which one may repeat only while keeping in mind Paul's warning: "work on your salvation with fear and trembling" (Phil 2:12).

This psalm contains for modern man more valuable material for reflection than a psychological, introspective plumbing of one's motivations. The material, once properly grasped, exposes one to that mental sanity which is sound philosophy of which there is aplenty in this psalm. This is indeed the most philosophical of all psalms. Its main theme is God's omnipresence and omniscience. Most of the times the point is put across in distinctly poetic terms, such as the fastness of the wings of the dawn and the brightness of even the darkest night. But at other times the diction is worthy of the finest metaphysical poets. Only those would be taken aback by this who let themselves be blinded by the cliché that there is a radical difference between Greek metaphysical rationality and biblical existentialism. Once one admits that good philosophy begins with wonderment and keeps exuding it, it will be easy to see metaphysics blare forth from this psalm, which in fact contains utterances about infinity that no mathematician can improve upon.

And if one sees that the difference between wonderment and assent is not an opposition but a complement, one's conversion to metaphysics, as recommended by this very "biblical" psalm, may be complete. It is a metaphysics vibrant with vitality, including its spiritual kind. True enough, the Bible stands for assent, but never for a blind one. Faith, as Paul insisted (Rom

12:1), ought to be a *logike latreia*, a truly reasonable and well-reasoned service, a point that cannot be recalled often enough.

Those desirous of a truly perennial philosophy may find it articulated in a capsule form in this psalm. By praying this psalm devoutly we may go a long way toward obtaining the grace which is the true love of true wisdom. The word "philosophy" means precisely this insofar as it aims at truth and not merely at opinions about it.

Psalm 140

A divine rescue operation is invoked in this psalm in reference to a situation which is agonizing to say the least. One finds himself trapped by the wicked who are rudely such. Traps are of more than one kind. Here in this psalm a physical trap seems to be the case. Other traps are called temptations, some made by others, some triggered by ourselves, still others by mere circumstances. The wicked, too, are of more than one kind. Some rude, some highly polished, some obvious, some artfully covert. Hiding behind them all is the Wicked One, who is ready to assail us at any moment. This psalm should be prayed with the mental disposition demanded by the phrase, "Guard me should the foe assail me," recited after Holy Communion, which is the great shield against spiritual catastrophes, big and small. Their possibility is never remote. The apostle's warning, "Let anyone who is standing upright watch out lest he fall!" (1 Cor 10:12) is a perfect complement to this psalm, which should remind us that man is to be rescued forever.

Psalm 141

Whether one likes it or not, spiritual life, or the determination to live the life of the spirit, which is ultimately to live in the Spirit of God, remains a struggle and indeed a battle. Perhaps the most trying aspect of this battle is that one may be battled by precisely those whom one would expect to be one's allies. In Old Testament times few felt so much tortured on that account as Jeremiah who may indeed have been the author of this psalm. His hands, raised as if in an act of evening oblation, are expressive of a heartfelt prayer which he hopes to lift as a fragrant incense into God's presence. Jeremiah is in full view in the elemental strength with which the psalmist wants full justice to be meted out to his enemies, some of them the princes of the people. May their bones be "broken to pieces as millstone is shattered on the ground," the psalmist cries out. Whereas in this wish he cannot be followed, it would be wrong to forget the millstone which our Lord saw tied around the neck of those who scandalized innocent children. The latter include not only those under age but all of God's children, that is, all those who are rightly scandalized by what they see on occasion perpetrated as the Eucharist, this most sacred evening oblation, being offered as if its main purpose were to promote "inculturation."

Psalm 142

Once more the psalmist is Jeremiah, who is easily the most straightforward of all the prophets. This psalm is a classic in lucid diction as well as deeply felt torments. The prophet is trapped in his path, which may simply mean the performance of his God-given duty. A volcanic soul Jeremiah was, which can be felt in the opening verses of this psalm, where he cries out "with all his voice to the Lord" and entreats him "with all his voice." Such is a perfect libretto for an oratorio. Only a composer is needed who is also a deeply prayerful man. But just as religious themes are fewer and fewer in the works of great painters, so is the case in music. Perhaps another World War has to come to have the din of arms drown out an increasingly pagan, indeed outright animalistic rock music, which answers to the name Heavy Metal. In one way or another we must learn again that God is our sole refuge and that He "alone is left for us in the land of the living." Then, as we find our soul rescued "from this prison" into which we have turned life, we may see proper music composed for our praises of God. Let more and more of us experience the psalm's closing phrase: "Around me the just will assemble, because of your goodness to me." The experience may come in most incongruous contexts. One of these were the walls of a prison cell in Paris on which a Communist, captured by the

Nazis, wrote in his own blood: "Vous seul, Jésus, ne m'avez pas déçu." He was just one of the many who found out that once with Jesus, one is not alone even in utter desolation.

Psalm 143

This seventh of the so-called penitential psalms is similar to Psalm 6, the first of such psalms, in that it contains no reference to sin. But, like that psalm, it is full of references to a lethal situation which, together with other kinds of suffering, is taken in the Old Testament as being brought on man by his sins.

Its concluding verse, "in your love make an end of my foes, destroy all who oppress me," should sound all the more inappropriate as the request is made by the psalmist on the ground that he is God's servant. On the contrary, the more one thinks of oneself as God's servant, the more one should recall Jesus' command that we must love our enemies and pray for any and all of them. No Christian is at liberty to dilute that command ever so slightly.

Apart from that concluding verse, this psalm, echoing Jeremiah's phrases and sentiments, can be prayed with no mental reservations. It may very well happen that the Christian is so tried by God that time and again he may feel he has no strength for anything else except to present his desolation to God. Since God understands infinitely better than we do that we are but dust, we must rely all the more on His loving mercy.

Psalm 144

David sings in this psalm. The warrior and victorious king is a typical son of the Covenant for whom there is nothing beyond the grave except a shadowy condition into which all human life, passing away like fleeting shadows, will be absorbed. Finding himself in a desperate military situation, which he compares to the onrush of a mighty torrent, David therefore cries out for divine help. In a far more concise manner than in Psalm 18, he begs God to appear in the form of a violent storm. And as if this were not enough, he invokes God to produce a convenient volcanic explosion, which he may have known only from hearsay.

In these very times when the specter of a President of the United
States perjuring himself made countless honest hearts sink low, a
special relevance may be found in David's repeated references to
the perjury of those who had already sworn loyalty to him.

As to the second part of the psalm, where a future of plenty
is conjured up, there is a reference to the daughters of the land
as so many graceful columns. The caryatids on the Acropolis
were not an idea exclusive to the Greeks.

Psalm 145

As an alphabetical psalm, this psalm may appear repetitious,
indeed void of a structure marked with progressive line of
thought. But its straightforward logic will readily emerge if one
puts verses 17-18 after verses 19-21. Verses 1-2 and 21 frame the
entire psalm by stating the psalmist's readiness to bless God day
after day. This readiness is then amplified with a threefold
perception or proclamation to each of which are attached the
outbursts of a choir or community about God's infinite compassion (verses 8-9, 13b-14, and 17-18). The second and third of those
outbursts are clearly an echo of the first: "The Lord is kind and
full of compassion, slow to anger abounding in love. How good
is the Lord to all, compassionate to all his creatures."

The first proclamation voices the readiness of all past ages
to bless God (verses 4-7). The second (verses 10-13) lets all
creatures exclaim in blessing God. The third (verses 15-16 and 19-
20) present those creatures as if they were blessing God with
food, this most precious sustainer of life, in their mouths.

Surely, this psalm, so overflowing with the praises of an
infinitely beneficent God, put us at an infinite distance from the
horrendous faces of Meso-American gods who were feeding on
human hearts. Still there are some, Christians by cultural
inheritance, who blame the missionaries in Mexico for having
destroyed all the native books on idolatry. Anthropology, when
turned into a *l'art pour l'art*, is a cultural curse in which there is no
room for the cult of the true God and for true human culture.

It would not occur to coryphei and acolytes of that art that
one could at most bribe those horror-gods, but not turn to them
with prayers similar to the one in verses 15-16 of this psalm that

are its most often prayed part. Christians from early on began their meals with the verse: "The eyes of all creatures look to you and you give them their food in due time. You open wide your hand and grant the desires of all who live." I still remember the voice of my father as he lead us in prayer before meals with those very words.

Now when it has become the custom of improvising prayers before meal, and when most of the time the diction bogs down in platitudes about "fellowship" and "concern," it may be a good idea to recall that there is no point in trying to emulate inimitable phrases, and certainly not with no skill in phrase-making.

Psalm 146

This psalm provides an instance of the truth that beauty, or rather an intense longing for the perfectly beautiful, can easily obstruct one's vision. Nothing can indeed be more perfectly beautiful than that state where all the oppressed receive justice, all the hungry receive bread, all prisoners are freed, all the blind are given back their sight, all those who are bowed down are raised, all the strangers protected, all the orphans and widows are upheld, all the just feel loved by God, and the paths of all the wicked are thwarted. How beautiful, how perfect, how inspiring indeed! Unfortunately no one shall ever see this realized on this earth, which more realistically looks like a valley of tears.

If a psalm is messianic whenever it presents an ideal state of affairs, then this psalm is perhaps the most messianic of them all. This psalm is still to be labeled as messianic. But one cannot make sense of it unless by looking at it in that light.

Lourdes should come to mind. It may not be an exaggeration to say that perhaps one out of ten thousand pilgrims found some relief to his or her ailing, and much lower is the proportion of those who were miraculously cured there. But, countless pilgrims, who went there "bowed down" mentally by their physical pain, returned home heads raised high, filled with trust in God's holy will.

Once more it is the New Covenant that squares the holy songs of the Old with the plain evidence. But the New cannot do without that elemental exultation that bursts at almost every point the linguistic frame of this psalm. The soul which is urged at the outset of this psalm to make music to God as long as life lasts, can certainly take comfort from the fact that the plans of mortal men appear "to come to nothing on that day," which on occasion is a day plainly visible on this earth as well.

Sober realism should never stifle an exuberant appreciation of the many good things that God grants us even in this valley of tears.

Psalm 147

This is an obviously post-exilic psalm which begins with a reference to God's healing all the wounds of the exiled. The healing of many major wounds could readily appear as the healing of all wounds. Those who returned soon found out that many more wounds were in store for them, a point important to recall, lest these consoling verses evoke some Utopistic dreams. The hardships of the Exile were to be dwarfed in comparison with those in store for the Jewish people within a generation after the death of Christ. This happened because of a violent resurgence of Utopistic expectations in the name of a false messianism.

Modern man will be less ready to ponder religious utopias, than to find fault with some verses of this psalm that present both a very primitive world picture but also a much too anthropomorphic involvement on God's part as that picture unfolds. If the bright blue sky disappears from one's view this is only so because, according to this psalm, God himself covers it with clouds, and so on.

Two points are worth recalling. One is that around 500 B. C. or so, when this psalm may have been written, the Greeks began to grope for a rationally more elevated level. Still several of the Greek "scientists" flourishing at that time voiced sentiments that contradicted their mechanistic views which seemed to banish any divine power from the scene. "Everything is full of gods," so Thales wrote after he had also said that "all is water." The way out of this contradiction came with monotheism and was spelled out by Paul in his speech on the Areopagus (Acts 17:22-31).

The other point is to note that once God created the world, He cannot create it again. But for creation to stay in existence it needs God's ever present concurrence. Such a concurrence, an anathema to deists, old and new, is full of an infinite vitality which is strictly metaphysical. It has nothing to do with vitalism, or with the *élan vital*, or with a mysterious *nisus*, or with Process writ large, or with an upward drive towards an Omega point. Those who dreamed up these terms did not fail to invest them with spuriously physical connotations. They thereby turned everything into the kind of confusion where dreams proliferate.

Still those terms may be useful as they activate one's poetic ability to see that not only impersonal physical forces, created by God, are at work in nature, but He himself is at work in all natural processes. Our Lord appealed to His listeners' poetic ability to perceive the enormously graphic concreteness of God's ubiquitous sustaining power. He did so as He stated that not even a sparrow falls to the ground without our Heavenly Father's full knowledge of it and that He himself decks out all the lilies of the field in a splendor inconceivable even by Solomon. Our Lord knew that to His listeners Solomon not only built the Temple but also decorated it in a sumptuous manner.

The perspective of seeing God at work everywhere is even more needed if one is to absorb and savor the message of the second half of this psalm (Psalm 147 in the numeration of the Septuagint and the Vulgate). There snow, hoarfrost, and hailstone are said to fall as if each bit of them were moved by God's fingers, and that only when touched by those fingers do waters freeze. The mood in this second part is even happier than in the first. The Rev. William Paley must have loved this psalm.

Statements about Providence in nature are in both parts of this psalm intertwined with references to God's providence for His people. In praying this psalm in times of peace and abundance, one does well not to forget that the Lord takes no delight in man's display of his own machines of power. Security, national and international, lies not so much with supranational as with truly supernatural factors. Among these supreme are God's two chief commandments, which either the people of the Old or of the New Covenant forget only at their greatest peril.

Psalm 148

If there is a psalm which embodies a structure within which there are similar substructures, this is that psalm. Having in mind those structures one might indeed be tempted to compress this psalm into a single statement: In the heaven everybody and everything, on the earth everything and everybody praise the Lord! For whenever a Hebrew text lists the main particulars of a unit it wants to convey the meaning of totality, of the all. Such is a time-honored rhetorical device. It might be called *totum per partes*, to distinguish it from *pars pro toto*, which predicates the whole in terms of one of its main or characteristic parts. Teachers of rhetoric, now an almost defunct species in academe, might take this psalm for their club-song.

All the angels, all the heavenly hosts mentioned in this psalm, stand for everybody in heaven. The list of all the major physical items in heaven stand for everything there. The list of all major physical features on earth conveys their totality. The list of all major types of animals similarly stands for a totality. And so does the list of all major classes of humans as listed here: kings and subjects, old and young, and so forth.

Since practically nothing was known by the Hebrews of old about the lawfulness of the working of terrestrial bodies, these are said to obey directly God's commands. They are to join all classes of people in praising God who "exalts the strength of his people,. . . of the people to whom He comes close." Once God came so close to man as to become Man, all people have become His people. To all of them are directed Augustine's words from his commentary on this psalm: "Our reflection on this life should be centered on praising God. Precisely because God's praise will constitute the happiness of our future eternal life, we must keep in mind that no one will be prepared for that life unless he practiced its functions already in this life."

Augustine later adds something which should act as a much needed corrective to some dreamy-eyed thinking about praising God: "The delights of future life will not be properly appreciated unless one groans for them in this present life. Anyone who does not groan as a pilgrim, does not rejoice as a citizen because there is no true desire in him." Nothing more can be said about anyone who cherishes the idea of a Pilgrim Church as a pretext for cultivating haziness about clear propositions of the Creed.

Psalm 149

This psalm opens with a call for a new song. This is not the only place in the psalms where one encounters this call. Of course, the singing of the psalms was never meant to stifle creative talents to compose ever new songs. Unfortunately, this can be overdone. It seems to be carried to the extreme when all of a sudden one finds a plethora of older hymns, hallowed by centuries-long usage, fall into studied oblivion. The new which becomes the enemy of the old betrays a sickly pursuit of novelty.

In our eagerness to comply with the call of this psalm for coming up with new songs, let us search for ever new insights into the canonical set of psalms. The history of commentaries shows that even mediocre talents could not fail to uncover novel insights in connection with this or that psalm. A more general insight is the docile acceptance of the wisdom that prompted the Church to leave out certain psalms and certain passages in them in the canonical recitation of the psalms and in their use in the Eucharistic liturgy. The last verses of this psalm, calling for bloody vengeance, are such that may unduly offend some sensitive souls. Unfortunately for them, cruelty shall never be eliminated from man's mannerisms. A pointed reminder of this are these verses in this psalm which therefore may be recited with great profit, provided one knows how to handle two-edged swords which the psalmist wants us to use. It is best to recall that even knives are not to be put in children's hands.

Adults indeed may remain mere children in respect to the use of the Bible which, let it not be forgotten, is a tool sharper than any two-edged sword (Hebr 4:12). It therefore will not fail to invite misuse, at least by neglect, by some of its thirty thousand or so verses. So many instances of this are in the psalms that speak not only of God's praises but also of His judgments. While His praises should never cease to be on man's lips, His judgments are not to be overlooked. Much less should those judgments be taken by the individual in his fumbling and proverbially partial hands.

Psalm 150

This psalm is meant to sound as a symphony orchestra does when the conductor motions the whole choir and all the instrumentalists to perform the final bars of a great composition. The verses of this psalm prompt us to do what the psalms urged from the start: to sing the praises of God who is in His holy place and, of course, in His place in the highest heaven. The Book of Psalms is a book of praises even when the psalmists groan.

The fact that every line of this psalm begins with the word "praise" justifies our seeing it as a great doxology, that is, a "praise to God," appended to the entire collection of psalms. To praise God is, of course, the primary duty of man as a creature. This psalm alone, to say nothing of the entire Book of Psalms, gives a lie to the promoters of a "social Gospel" who contend that religion consists in serving one's fellowmen and not in serving God in that special sense which is to praise Him.

To be sure, no one can add an extra shine to God's glory which remains forever invisible. Nor does the Bible ever speak of man's duty to praise God as if God would need that praise in any sense, as if God's own riches were not infinite in the strictest sense of that often hackneyed word. It is man who needs to praise God, because otherwise he will not comprehend the full meaning of his creaturely status.

There was a time, not too long ago (two hundred years are but a minute or perhaps just a few seconds in the now three-million-year-long human history), when the word "infinite" still appeared even to some champions of the Enlightenment as an adjective to be applied only to God. Today even the word "creation" is boldly applied to mere human actions. The claim is becoming a fad among scientists that they can create universes literally out of nothing. This claim will reduce them eventually to the same level of ridicule to which those prominent Graduate Schools have fallen where, in addition to courses in creative English, a course in remedial creative English had to be introduced. Some scientists poked fun at creation by God as if it were a case of creation of new fashions by masters of *haute couture*.

In such an atmosphere, where in the name of creative cooking all sorts of indigestibles are dished out, there should be no prospect of restoring broad respectability to man's fundamental need to praise God. This need will not be felt until there is a wide resurgence of the true meaning of what creation means. It was early Christianity that combined the word "creation" with the words "out of nothing" to call attention to the nothingness of everything apart from God.

This nothingness will be beyond the ken of cultural gurus who are busy in dismissing the expression, "creation out of nothing." No wonder they see themselves as creators. They certainly create fads and foment sickly attention to trivialities which they present with all the parade of "creative" scholarship.

Surely we are learning an awful lot about ancient forms of lutes, harps, trumpets, cymbals, citharas, drums, and trimbles. We have learned that none of the musical instruments in the Book of Daniel are of Hebrew origin. We shall not learn about ancient Hebrew patterns of dancing which by the nature of things could not survive. Inquiries about them may seem especially dubious as infatuation with ever more decadent forms of dancing has grown in recent times in the measure in which God has been ushered off the stage of arts and letters.

It remains a historical and historic truth that the development of all forms of art owes a great deal to the ineradicable human urge to praise God. Let therefore the voice of mankind sound as a global chorus. To join in that voice is each man's basic duty and the assurance of his sanity, provided he prays with words inspired from above, very human as they may all too often be.

Such is the ultimate reason for man that he should never stop praying the psalms. They are songs given by God to man, and therefore he does his best when he sings them as the farmers, mentioned by Saint Jerome, sang them as they worked in the fields. The fields of labor have become much more varied and far-reaching, but the psalms, too, have revealed more and more about their God-given richness. For this and countless other blessings

Let everything that lives and that breathes
give praise to the Lord. Alleluia!

(continued from p. ii)

Miracles and Physics

God and the Cosmologists
(Farmington Institute Lectures, Oxford, 1988)

The Only Chaos and Other Essays

The Purpose of It All

(Farmington Institute Lectures, Oxford, 1989)

Catholic Essays

Cosmos in Transition: Studies in the History of Cosmology

Olbers Studies

Scientist and Catholic: Pierre Duhem

Reluctant Heroine: The Life and Work of Hélène Duhem

Universe and Creed

Genesis 1 through the Ages

Is There a Universe?

Patterns or Principles and Other Essays

Bible and Science

Theology of Priestly Celibacy

Means to Message: A Treatise on Truth

God and the Sun at Fatima

Newman's Challenge

The Limits of a Limitless Science and Other Essays

* * *

Translations with introduction and notes:

The Ash Wednesday Supper (Giordano Bruno)

*Cosmological Letters on the Arrangement .
of the World Edifice* (J.-H. Lambert)

Universal Natural History and Theory of the Heavens (I. Kant)

[p. 238]

Note on the Author

Stanley L. Jaki, a Hungarian-born Catholic priest of the Benedictine Order, is Distinguished University Professor at Seton Hall University, South Orange, New Jersey. With doctorates in theology and physics, he has for the past forty years specialized in the history and philosophy of science. The author of almost forty books and over a hundred articles, he served as Gifford Lecturer at the University of Edinburgh and as Fremantle Lecturer at Balliol College, Oxford. He has lectured at major universities in the United States, Europe, and Australia. He is honorary member of the Pontifical Academy of Sciences, *membre correspondant* of the Académie Nationale des Sciences, Belles-Lettres et Arts of Bordeaux, and the recipient of the Lecomte du Nouy Prize for 1970 and of the Templeton Prize for 1987.